Landmark Cases in Canadian Law

Since Confederation, Canada's highest court – first the Judicial Committee of the Privy Council in England and then the Supreme Court of Canada – has issued a series of often contentious decisions that have fundamentally shaped the nation. Both cheered and jeered, these judgments have impacted every aspect of Canadian society, setting legal precedents and provoking social change. The issues in the judgments range from Aboriginal title, gender equality, and freedom of expression to Quebec secession and intellectual property. This series offers comprehensive, book-length examinations of high court cases that have had a major impact on Canadian law, politics, and society.

Other books in the series are:

Flawed Precedent: The St. Catherine's *Case and Aboriginal Title* by Kent McNeil

Privacy in Peril: Hunter v Southam *and the Drift from Reasonable Search Protections* by Richard Jochelson and David Ireland

The Tenth Justice: Judicial Appointments, Marc Nadon, and the Supreme Court Act *Reference* by Carissima Mathen and Michael Plaxton

From Wardship to Rights: The Guerin *Case and Aboriginal Law* by Jim Reynolds

Constitutional Pariah: Reference re Senate Reform *and the Future of Parliament* by Emmett Macfarlane

No Legal Way Out: R v Ryan, *Domestic Abuse, and the Defence of Duress* by Nadia Verelli and Lori Chambers

Debt and Federalism: Landmark Cases in Canadian Bankruptcy and Insolvency Law, 1894–1937 by Thomas G.W. Telfer and Virginia Torrie

Reckoning with Racism: Police, Judges, and the RDS Case by Constance Backhouse

For a list of other titles,
see www.ubcpress.ca/landmark-cases-in-canadian-law.

**LANDMARK CASES
IN CANADIAN LAW**

A CULTURE
OF
JUSTIFICATION

Vavilov
and the Future of Administrative Law

Paul Daly

UBCPress · Vancouver · Toronto

32 31 30 29 28 27 26 25 24 23   5 4 3 2 1

Printed in Canada on FSC-certified ancient-forest-free paper (100% post-consumer recycled) that is processed chlorine- and acid-free.

Library and Archives Canada Cataloguing in Publication

Title: A culture of justification : Vavilov and the future of administrative law / Paul Daly.
Names: Daly, Paul, author.
Description: Includes index.
Identifiers: Canadiana (print) 20230440010 | Canadiana (ebook) 20230440096 | ISBN 9780774869089 (hardcover) | ISBN 9780774869119 (EPUB) | ISBN 9780774869102 (PDF)
Subjects: LCSH: Vavilov, Alexander – Trials, litigation, etc. | LCSH: Administrative law – Canada – Cases.
Classification: LCC KE5015 .D35 2023 | LCC KF5402 .D35 2023 kfmod | DDC 342.71/06 – dc23

Canada Council   Conseil des arts
for the Arts   du Canada

Canadä

BRITISH COLUMBIA
ARTS COUNCIL

BRITISH
COLUMBIA

UBC Press gratefully acknowledges the financial support for our publishing program of the Government of Canada, the Canada Council for the Arts, and the British Columbia Arts Council.

This book has been published with the help of a grant from the Canadian Federation for the Humanities and Social Sciences, through the Awards to Scholarly Publications Program, using funds provided by the Social Sciences and Humanities Research Council of Canada.

UBC Press
The University of British Columbia
2029 West Mall
Vancouver, BC V6T 1Z2
www.ubcpress.ca

Contents

Acknowledgments   vii

Introduction   3

1 Why Is Administrative Law So Complicated?   16

2 A Deep Dive into Judicial Review   42

3 The *Dunsmuir* Decade   63

4 The Big Bang   93

5 *Vavilov* Hits the Road   122

6 Unresolved Issues after *Vavilov*   154

Conclusion   173

Notes   181

Selected Bibliography   228

Index of Cases   243

Index   251

Acknowledgments

In the summer of 2019, I returned to Canada after three years in the United Kingdom, at the Faculty of Law, University of Cambridge. The timing was fortuitous. Just a few months after I settled into my new office at the University of Ottawa, the Supreme Court of Canada handed down the *Vavilov* decision. In the whirlwind weeks of December 2019 and January 2020, I spoke about the decision to students, journalists, lawyers, judges, and even friends and neighbours who would not ordinarily take any interest at all in administrative law. I had been interested in the subject for much longer, of course, and indeed had been a consistent critic of the Supreme Court's approach over the preceding decade. In deciding *Vavilov*, the court listened to my complaints – and those of many others – and attempted to fashion a framework that responded to academic, judicial, and practitioner critiques.

Then, in March 2020, the COVID-19 pandemic hit Canada and life was turned upside down. With three young children at home (two, five, and six years old when we were first locked down) for long stretches over the next two years, many research projects had to be placed on hold. As things slowly – oh, so slowly – returned to normal, Canadian courts continued to apply *Vavilov*, with the volume of decisions growing steadily. I watched as the body of case law built up – often from the basement sofa with the sounds of Disney+ or Netflix ringing in my ears – and, via Zoom and Teams, often spoke with lawyers, judges, and academic colleagues about developments in Canadian administrative law.

Around that time, it occurred to me that I might have a book on *Vavilov* in me. On my blog, *Administrative Law Matters,* and in multiple academic articles and presentations, I had criticized the Supreme Court's prior case law, analyzed the *Vavilov* decision, and teased out the implications of *Vavilov* for the future of Canadian administrative law. I was then fortunate enough to hire an exceptional research assistant, Kseniya Kudischeva, who helped me bring all of my thoughts together in a coherent framework. And at UBC Press I found both a wonderful editor in Randy Schmidt and a series of *Landmark Cases in Canadian Law* perfectly suited to a short book on the makings and consequences of the *Vavilov* decision. Another research assistant, Rachel Freeland, provided invaluable support in finalizing the manuscript. I should also acknowledge the helpful comments of the anonymous reviewers, who perused the entire manuscript, and the UBC Press Publications Board.

Most of all, I should acknowledge Liam, Lorna, Luke, and Marie-France. For working parents with young children, the pandemic era was miserable in many ways, with online schooling a particular low point; that we had only just gotten our feet under the table in Ottawa hardly helped. Many others, of course, had it much worse, as they lost loved ones or their dignity or autonomy, or succumbed themselves to COVID-19. In our family unit, we at least had the benefit of human contact every day. Had life gone on as normal in 2020, 2021, and 2022, I am not sure I would have spent as much time on *Vavilov* and its progeny. *Vavilov* was a welcome distraction from the pressures of the pandemic and, frankly, working on it rather than other projects allowed me to spend more time with my family than I would otherwise have done. It might seem like a strange thing to be grateful for, but grateful I am nonetheless. So thanks Liam, Lorna, Luke, and Marie-France for your presence and patience as this book came together.

– Ottawa

A CULTURE
OF JUSTIFICATION

INTRODUCTION

A LEXANDER VAVILOV LIVED A normal suburban life in the United States until, one morning, his family home was stormed by armed FBI agents. Unknown to Vavilov, who had been born sixteen years earlier in Canada, his parents were Russian spies. Hollywood writers would later use his story as inspiration for the popular television series *The Americans*. Later still, Vavilov found himself in the Supreme Court of Canada, his lawyers arguing for his Canadian citizenship and for the wholesale reform of Canadian administrative law.

The Supreme Court is the body that sits at the top of the hierarchy in the Canadian legal system. Its nine judges and their support staff occupy an elegant art deco structure perched above the Ottawa River a few hundred yards upstream of Parliament and looking over the water to the city of Gatineau in the province of Quebec. The grand location befits its status as the final court of appeal for Canadians. In a small number of cases (mostly criminal matters), the Supreme Court automatically hears appeals from lower courts. Most of the time, though, litigants who lost in the lower court need to persuade the Supreme Court that their case involves a question of national importance that would merit a visit to both enjoy the architecture at 301 Wellington Street and fight their battle there. Litigants do this by preparing a detailed application that is then considered in secret by the nine judges, often over a period of many weeks or even months. Then, on a random Thursday at 9:45 a.m. Eastern Time, the Supreme Court tells the litigants whether their case will be heard. The message is published on the Supreme Court's website, and it is a simple thumbs-up or thumbs-down – "leave to appeal" is granted or refused, without explanation.

So, on one of those random Thursdays in May 2018, there was something unusual on the Supreme Court's website. In exercising its discretionary power to grant leave to appeal, the court gave reasons explaining why it had decided to grant leave in three cases:

> The Court is of the view that these appeals provide an opportunity to consider the nature and scope of judicial review of administrative action, as addressed in *Dunsmuir v. New Brunswick,* [2008] 1 S.C.R. 190, 2008 SCC 9, and subsequent cases. To that end, the appellants and respondent are invited to devote a substantial part of their written and oral submissions on the appeal to the question of standard of review, and shall be allowed to file and serve a factum on appeal of at most 45 pages.

The three cases were decided, after a long period of deliberation, in December 2019. The most important of the cases was Vavilov's: *Canada (Citizenship and Immigration) v Vavilov,* where the Supreme Court laid out an entirely new framework for administrative law (and effectively concluded that Vavilov was indeed a Canadian citizen after all).[1] *Vavilov* was the "big bang," a legal landmark that is set to have an enduring legacy.

In this book, I will explain and place in historical context the Supreme Court's decades-long struggle to bring coherence to Canadian administrative law, describe the new framework elaborated in *Vavilov,* and discuss the likely legacy of the *Vavilov* decision.

What made *The Americans* such a great TV program was that its themes transcended the details of the Vavilovs' lives as undercover spies. Their story spoke to all viewers about the challenges of family life, especially preserving a sane balance between professional responsibilities and personal relationships. *Vavilov* deals with less titillating subject matter but is just as transcendent. The case and this book are all about "judicial review."

Judicial review is how the courts control government, ensuring that "administrative decision makers" stay within the boundaries of the law.

An administrative decision maker is someone who works for or on behalf of the government and whose job involves exercising powers accorded to him or her by legislation passed by Parliament or a legislative assembly. The Canada Border Services Agency (CBSA) officer at the border, or a municipal bylaw officer, or even the staff at a driver licensing centre are the most obvious front-line examples. There are more behind-the-scenes ones too, such as commissioners of the Canadian Radio-television and Telecommunications Commission (CRTC), who decide how much Canadian content should be available on TV, for example; and even the federal Cabinet, which hears appeals on technical matters such as railway rates and adopts regulations concerning everything from freezing the assets of supporters of foreign regimes to the types of guns and knives that can be imported into Canada. Each and every one of these people is an administrative decision maker. And, in principle, anyone affected by one of their decisions can seek judicial review to make sure the decision was lawful. The question for the court – which lawyers sometimes call the "reviewing court" – is not whether the decision was the right one but rather whether the decision was made in a procedurally fair way and whether it bore the hallmarks of reasonableness. "Reasonableness" is a very technical term that, as it happens, was at the heart of the *Vavilov* case.

The best place to start Vavilov's story is probably with that of another immigrant to Canada, Thanh Tam Tran, whose travails were considered in *Canada (Public Safety and Emergency Preparedness) v Tran*.[2] At issue in this case was the decision of a ministerial delegate, which was based in large part on a report from a front-line CBSA official (neither of whom was a lawyer), to refer Tran to an admissibility hearing. Tran's ability to stay in Canada hinged on this hearing. Should he have been referred to it in the first place?

Tran's troubles arose due to his role in a marijuana cultivation operation, for which he received a twelve-month conditional sentence. Although this was hardly the gravest of criminal infractions, the *Immigration and Refugee Protection Act* provides that individuals are inadmissible to Canada upon conviction for either 1) committing an offence punishable by a maximum term of imprisonment of at least ten years, or 2) committing an offence for which a term of imprisonment of more than six months is imposed.

Between Tran's commission of the offence and his conviction, the maximum term of imprisonment had been increased from seven years to fourteen years. Tran had a constitutional protection under the *Canadian Charter of Rights and Freedoms* against a higher sentence being imposed retrospectively: before a criminal court, he could be sentenced to a maximum of only seven years. But was the ministerial delegate constrained by this, or could he look to the maximum term of imprisonment at the time he had to decide whether to refer Tran for an admissibility hearing? Alternatively, the delegate had to ask whether Tran's conditional sentence was a "term of imprisonment" in excess of six months. The decision did not go Tran's way, and so he went to the courts.

At the Federal Court of Appeal, Justice Johanne Gauthier upheld the decision as reasonable, but she did so with evident distaste. The first problem was that the delegate had not developed "a purposive and contextual analysis" of paragraph 36(1)(a) of the Act.[3] Given the issues at stake, the absence of a detailed interpretation in the delegate's decision was a significant shortcoming. For one, the rule of lenity – that penal provisions be construed in favour of the accused – was at least arguably in play. For another, the potential retrospective application of an increase in a sentencing provision calls attention to the values underpinning the Charter.

In addition, Tran observed that the delegate's approach could give rise to absurd situations, such as where the maximum sentence for an offence committed long ago is later increased, rendering the individual suddenly liable to removal from Canada. Yet Gauthier felt compelled, in light of the Supreme Court of Canada's instruction to Canadian courts to pay attention in administrative law cases to reasons that *could have been offered* – but were not *actually* offered – in support of a decision, to accept *any* reasonable interpretation that was implicit in the delegate's decision: "Deference due to a tribunal does not disappear because its decision on a certain issue is implicit."[4] This judgment was reflexive deference to a decision maker (in this case, the ministerial delegate), *even where the decision maker evidently had not even considered the principles* at stake. Yet, as Gauthier observed, this deference was what the Supreme Court's administrative law jurisprudence at the time seemed to require.

There was a further twist in the tale. Gauthier explained (this time with exasperation as much as distaste) that it would also have been reasonable for the ministerial delegate to construe the provisions *in favour* of Tran.[5] Indeed, she wrote, it is "obviously open" to other decision makers "to adopt another interpretation should they believe that it is warranted."[6] Another decision maker could adopt a different interpretation in the future. Concretely, this meant that the rights and obligations of permanent residents and foreign nationals convicted of crimes in circumstances similar to Tran's could well depend on whether they appeared before decision maker A or decision maker B. The decision maker had the authority to decide – one way or another, and back again – and that was that. Again, this conclusion was compelled by the Supreme Court's guidance on administrative law.

Tran successfully appealed to the Supreme Court, but the judges did not address the problems that had so vexed Justice Gauthier. Criticism in the legal community grew progressively louder, with *Tran* and other decisions brandished as evidence of severe weaknesses in Canadian administrative law. But it was not until 2018 that the Supreme Court finally turned to address these problems in *Vavilov, Bell Canada v Canada (Attorney General)*, and *National Football League v Canada (Attorney General)*,[7] the latter two being consolidated appeals from a single order of the CRTC. It was not especially surprising that leave was granted for both *Vavilov* and *Bell Canada/National Football League*, as these cases could be considered to deal with very interesting, high-profile matters.[8]

Vavilov was born in Canada to Russian parents who were spies. Normally, individuals born in Canada are Canadian citizens,[9] but there is an exception for children born to "a diplomatic or consular officer *or other representative or employee in Canada of a foreign government*."[10] When Vavilov was sixteen, the family home in the United States was stormed by armed FBI agents, who arrested his parents. A "spy swap" was arranged, which saw the family leave the United States for Russia. From Russia, Vavilov sought the renewal of his Canadian passport. After much procedural wrangling,[11] the Registrar of Canadian Citizenship refused to accede to his request. Indeed, relying on a report prepared by an analyst, the Registrar concluded that Vavilov's parents had been "employees of a foreign government" at the time of his birth, and thus revoked his certificate of Canadian citizenship. Vavilov sought judicial review: he was unsuccessful at first instance before convincing a majority of the Federal Court of Appeal to quash the Registrar's decision.

Bell Canada/National Football League was the latest instalment of the long-running saga that is the CRTC's "simultaneous substitution" regime. For some time, the starting point has been that Canadian broadcasters who are retransmitting feeds from foreign broadcasters are not allowed to alter those feeds in any way *unless* the Canadian broadcasters have permission to do so under the simultaneous substitution regime. If so, a Canadian television station can require a foreign broadcaster to substitute a Canadian feed for the foreign feed, which has been the case during the Super Bowl. From a consumer perspective, the most obvious result has been that for many years, during the Super Bowl halftime show, Canadian viewers have had access only to Canadian advertisements, not the high-profile American versions. From a commercial perspective, the result is that there is a larger advertising pie for the NFL (the copyright holder) and other actors to distribute, because of the national platform provided to Canadian advertisers. After a series of consultations stretching over several years, the CRTC proposed to maintain the simultaneous substitution regime in general but to exclude the Super Bowl specifically. This order was the subject of an unsuccessful appeal to the Federal Court of Appeal by Bell Canada and the National Football League.

Thus, it was no surprise that the Supreme Court decided to invite the lawyers in these cases to Ottawa to discuss spies and the Super Bowl, respectively. What was surprising was that the Supreme Court decided to signal openly its willingness to revisit its judicial review framework. The giving of reasons accompanying a leave to appeal decision was unprecedented. Certainly, when the Supreme Court had previously attempted to reformulate its administrative law doctrine in *Dunsmuir v New Brunswick,* it gave no warning to the parties or the wider world.[12] The giving of reasons this time was almost certainly prompted by the widespread discontent in the Canadian legal community about the unsatisfactory way in which the law of judicial review of administrative action had evolved since *Dunsmuir.* In 2016, a respected appellate judge described Canadian administrative law as "a never-ending construction site,"[13] and at a 2018 symposium, sitting and retired judges, practitioners, and academics voiced a host of criticisms of the Supreme Court's recent jurisprudence.[14] Even the media took notice: on the eve of the release of the decisions in the trio of cases, the Supreme Court's administrative law meanderings were the subject of a detailed analysis piece in the national paper of record, the *Globe and Mail.*[15]

Indeed, the Supreme Court's administrative law construction project dates back to 1979. In the landmark case of *Canadian Union of Public Employees, Local 963 v New Brunswick Liquor Corporation,*[16] Justice Brian Dickson stated that on some questions of law a court should intervene on judicial review only where the interpretation at issue was patently unreasonable. Deciding *when* the deferential standard of reasonableness should apply and outlining *how* the reasonableness standard should be applied have proven to be very difficult, however. This area of Canadian administrative law is known as "substantive review." Other important areas, such as procedural fairness (the procedures administrative decision makers must follow in making decisions) and remedies (the redress available from the courts when administrative decision makers have acted unlawfully), have not presented such difficulties. But substantive review, which courts have to engage in any time an individual or a company argues that administrative decision makers have misused their powers, accounts for the vast majority of Canadian administrative law cases. And, unfortunately, it is the area in which the courts have had the greatest difficulty.

Four points in particular are worthy of emphasis. First, the Supreme Court's approach has been to apply the same framework to *all* administrative decisions, whether issued by front-line officials, ministers, economic regulatory agencies, or administrative tribunals,[17] with interpretations of law *and* exercises of discretion subject to the same doctrinal rules.[18] Nonlawyer ministerial delegates like those who made key decisions in the lives of Vavilov and Tran are subject to the same framework as legally trained adjudicators with decades of experience serving in well-resourced administrative tribunals.

Second, the proverbial reasonable person might assume that where a statute provides for an "appeal" to a court of law, the judges would come to their own conclusion on the questions at issue. But had there been an appeal in Tran's case, the outcome would not have been any different. The Supreme Court had observed that even where a statutory appeal had been provided for, it might nonetheless be appropriate to defer to an administrative decision maker on matters within its specialized expertise.[19] This sensible observation was, in recent years, pushed to extremes, so that even the most carefully tailored appeal clauses – such as those providing for a right of appeal on questions of law or jurisdiction, with leave of the appellate court – did not overcome the presumption that judges should defer to administrative decision makers.[20]

Third, the Supreme Court's position on the role of reasons in administrative decision-making was ambiguous. Although it was made clear in *Dunsmuir* that the sufficiency or adequacy of reasons was not a stand-alone basis for judicial intervention,[21] *Dunsmuir* and its progeny also invited courts (and creative counsel) to supplement sparse or defective reasons with additional *ex post facto* rationalizations, such that the Supreme Court latterly veered incoherently between a "restorative" and a "restrictive" approach to the application of the reasonableness standard.[22] This incoherent veering was, unfortunately, emblematic of the Supreme Court's approach to administrative law as, in the years after *Dunsmuir*, it frequently issued contradictory decisions.[23]

And fundamentally, the very idea of deference to administrative interpretations of law remains controversial. Should a ministerial delegate in cases such as Tran's or Vavilov's ever be granted deference? Heck, even if decision makers are well-respected experts on a particular area of law, why should their views override those of judges, who are independent from government and uphold the rule of law at the instance of citizens? Some members of the Supreme Court, such as Justices Suzanne Côté and Malcolm Rowe, have been hostile toward the notion and have sought to expand the areas covered by correctness review (where judges can substitute judgment on questions of law), whereas others, such as Chief Justice Richard Wagner, Justice Andromache Karakatsanis, and now-retired Justices Rosalie Abella and Clément Gascon, have embraced it fulsomely.[24] Dotted around the country are lawyers who are members of the "deference" camp and the "no-deference" camp. Those who believe in deference fly the flag of "reasonableness review" (i.e., the judge can intervene on judicial review only if the decision is unreasonable), while those in the no-deference camp march under the banner of "correctness review" (i.e., the judge can get involved if the decision was incorrect on a particular issue).

The Supreme Court therefore faced a daunting challenge with the trilogy. It appointed *amici curiae* to assist it, granted leave to twenty-seven interveners, and, of course, invited expansive submissions on the general principles of administrative law from the parties to the appeals. The *amici* were Professor Daniel Jutras and Audrey Boctor. Jutras was formerly the dean of the Faculty of Law at McGill University and, before that, served from 2002 to 2004 as the Supreme Court's executive legal officer. Boctor is a practitioner who previously clerked for the former chief justice of Canada, Beverley McLachlin. The Supreme Court's product, released a little more than a year after the three-day hearing, was contained in the decision in *Vavilov*. By a 7-2 majority (with Justices Abella and Karakatsanis writing vigorous concurring reasons that read as dissenting reasons), the Supreme Court adopted a new framework for judicial review of administrative action. Notably, the majority included a broad coalition of judges, bringing together skeptics (notably Justices Côté and Rowe) and proponents (notably Chief Justice Wagner and Justice Gascon) of deference on questions of law.

The majority reasons sought to achieve two goals: "To bring greater coherence and predictability" to the choice between correctness review and reasonableness review,[25] and to provide "better guidance ... on the proper application of the reasonableness standard."[26] Whether the majority succeeded in this will be the subject of later chapters. For now, let us focus on the concrete outcome of the so-called trilogy, for Vavilov and for football fans.

In their appeals, Vavilov and Bell Canada/National Football League were successful.

Regarding the Super Bowl, the Supreme Court concluded that the authority under the statutory provision that the CRTC invoked "is limited to issuing orders that require television service providers to carry specific channels as part of their service offerings, and attaching [general] terms and conditions."[27] Accordingly, the CRTC's order in relation to the Super Bowl was unlawful, and so the 2020 Super Bowl once again featured Canadian advertisements during the halftime show.

For his part, Vavilov convinced the Supreme Court that the Registrar of Canadian Citizenship's decision was unreasonable. Considering the text, purpose, and context of the *Citizenship Act,* as well as Canada's international law obligations, the court determined that it was unreasonable to conclude that the Canadian-born "children of individuals who have not been granted diplomatic privileges and immunities" are excluded from Canadian citizenship.[28] Since it was clear that Vavilov's undercover-agent parents did not benefit from diplomatic privileges and immunities (quite the opposite!), the court found no basis for the Registrar to revoke his citizenship. Justices Abella and Karakatsanis agreed with this conclusion for substantially similar reasons. The most concrete outcome of the *Vavilov* case, therefore, was that Vavilov's Canadian citizenship was secure. Whether the future of Canadian administrative law is secure is a different question.

In Chapter 1, I discuss why administrative law has been such a complicated subject for generations of Canadian law students, practising lawyers, judges, and citizens by reference to the history of judicial review; the vast array of decision makers and decisions made in the contemporary administrative state; the complexity of concepts such as "jurisdiction," "deference," and "legislative intent"; and the variety of judicial attitudes toward the administrative state. These factors in part explain the difficulties Canadian judges had that ultimately led to the reformulation of administrative law in *Vavilov*.

In Chapter 2, I take a deeper dive into Canadian judicial review. Since the late 1970s, the courts have struggled to develop a set of legal principles to regulate how judges conduct substantive review. From 1988 to 2008, the Supreme Court advocated a contextual approach, where the selection of correctness or reasonableness depended on the interplay of a variety of factors. From 2008 onward, the Supreme Court preferred to rely on a series of categories and then on an outright presumption that in most situations the reasonableness standard would apply. But the relationship between categories, context, and presumptions was never clarified, and the circumstances in which contextual factors would push a decision out of a category or rebut a presumption were somewhat nebulous. And the reasonableness standard was never comprehensively explained by the Supreme Court. That 2008 decision – *Dunsmuir v New Brunswick* – set the scene for a tumultuous decade.

In Chapter 3, I describe that tumultuous decade. I lay out the tensions in *Dunsmuir:* the imperfections in the categories, the lack of soundness of its categories, and the problems created by the adoption of a presumption of reasonableness review. I then explain how the Supreme Court's approach to reasonableness review layered confusion upon confusion, before turning to some of the contradictions in the court's case law, which created a distinction between the "law on the books" and the "law in action." Lastly, I discuss the impetus for revolution created by the changing composition of the Supreme Court.

In Chapter 4, I describe the long-awaited reformulation of administrative law. The Supreme Court's analysis in *Vavilov* has essentially four parts; two are the primary components and two are subsidiary. The two most important components of the new framework for administrative law are a set of simplified rules for selecting the standard of review and a detailed formulation of the standard of reasonableness. I explain the concepts of "institutional design," "rule of law," and "responsive justification" that underpinned these two components. The subsidiary parts related to remedial discretion and how to retrofit the Supreme Court's previous decisions into the new framework. The changes wrought by *Vavilov* were intended to be radical, making deference much less likely in situations where there is a statutory appeal from an expert decision maker (such as the CRTC) to a court, and insisting on the need for administrative decisions to be justified by reasons that are responsive to the arguments, the evidence, and the stakes. Indeed, the new framework attracted strong opposition from two of the nine judges, who wrote lengthy reasons attacking the very premises on which the majority based its analysis. In this chapter, I analyze the majority reasons setting out the new framework and discuss spirited opposition it immediately provoked.

In Chapter 5, I address the reception and application of the new framework by Canadian courts. The area of statutory appeals has been considerably changed, with very significant decisions demonstrating that courts are much less likely to defer to expert regulators on matters relating to the interpretation of the statutes they administer, occasioning a significant transfer of power from regulators to the courts. Reasonableness review, meanwhile, has become a culture of justification in action. Decision makers, such as ministers and labour relations arbitrators, who historically had benefitted from significant judicial deference, are having to adjust their practices to take into account the new normal ushered in by the big bang.

In Chapter 6, I turn to unresolved issues. For the most part, the Supreme Court's analysis in *Vavilov* was comprehensible and comprehensive. On a number of key issues, however, the implications of *Vavilov* are obscure. In order of importance, these unresolved issues raise the following questions: What framework governs procedural fairness in administrative law? Are administrative decisions touching on the Charter still to be reviewed deferentially? And what are the constitutional foundations of *Vavilovian* judicial review? In this chapter, I will explain the importance of these issues and lay out answers and solutions that are faithful to the *Vavilov* framework. Chapters 5 and 6 address issues that are still in a state of flux. To keep abreast of developments in

Canadian administrative law, do read my blog, *Administrative Law Matters*, which also highlights other useful resources.

As Alexander Vavilov discovered, administrative law is hugely relevant to modern life, regulating the relationship between the state and the citizen. The tentacles of the administrative state reach into every corner of our lives and engage matters that are fundamental to individual dignity and humanity. Before *Vavilov*, Canadian administrative law had been in disarray, an unacceptable state of affairs given the high stakes for citizens and state alike. In the chapters to come, I will describe the reasons for such disarray, what the Supreme Court sought to achieve in *Vavilov*, and how the decision may bring "a culture of justification" to Canada's vast array of administrative decision makers.[29]

1

Why Is Administrative Law So Complicated?

IN THIS CHAPTER, I discuss why administrative law has been such a complicated subject for generations of Canadian law students, practising lawyers, judges, and citizens.[1] The discussion covers several topics: 1) the history of judicial review; 2) the vast array of decision makers in the contemporary administrative state, and the decisions they make; 3) concepts central to the development of administrative law; and 4) attitudes toward the administrative state.

Judicial review developed in an incremental fashion from humble historical origins. Over a period of many centuries, judges retrofitted ancient legal remedies to new forms of public administration. This was a difficult operation: administrative law in Canada is not bespoke, or even made to measure, but a centuries-old off-the-rack suit made from outdated fabric. Many of the features of today's law are the result of historical happenstance rather than careful planning: accordingly, it is important to consider the history of judicial review.

In the contemporary administrative state, the variety of decision makers spans a spectrum running from court-like administrative tribunals at one end to government ministers at the other, and they make decisions that can be either general or highly targeted in nature. Some of these decisions have life-changing consequences, whereas others are entirely mundane and have very low stakes.

Concepts such as "jurisdiction," "deference," and "legislative intent" have been central to the development of administrative law. Giving these concepts meaning is inevitably a difficult task, as the contours of each are uncertain (in part because of the haphazard way in which administrative law developed over the centuries); nonetheless, the concepts remain important to understanding present-day administrative law, again because many features of our contemporary legal system are attributable to historical happenstance.

Judges have a variety of attitudes toward the administrative state. Some judges are comfortable with the idea that on questions of law arising in the interpretation of complex regulatory schemes, courts should defer to expert decision makers; others are much less comfortable. If pushed, some judges will concede that a legislative instruction to defer is enough, but others will insist on a reasoned basis for doing so. Judges also diverge in their relative preference for rules as opposed to standards, or, put another way, in their preference for clear categorical distinctions versus a more nuanced, contextual approach. Given the diversity of administrative decision makers and administrative decisions, it is easy to understand why these traditional preferences make a significant difference to the shape of administrative law. Just to complicate things still further, sometimes judges will decide a case based on what they think is the best outcome, all things considered, even if this is not strictly driven by legal considerations.

HISTORY OF JUDICIAL REVIEW

What we now call "administrative law" or "judicial review of administrative action" began to develop across the Atlantic, many centuries ago, in the form of the writs of *certiorari*, prohibition, *mandamus, quo warranto,* and *habeas corpus,* the so-called prerogative writs. These writs were originally designed, by judges sitting in the King's common law courts in London, England, to control the actions of so-called inferior courts around the country. If those bodies erred, the writs could be issued against them, to quash their decisions (making it as though the decisions had never been made in the first place) or to order them to act in a particular way.

Today's centralized court system was then in the earliest stages of its development; most justice was administered locally or in ecclesiastical courts. Of course, overseas in what became British colonies, the common law had not yet arrived – the Indigenous peoples in Canada and other countries developed and applied their own legal traditions. Later, however, when British settlers arrived on the shores of North America, they brought with them the common law. It is therefore impossible to understand Canadian administrative law without appreciating its historical origins in England.

A practical example of these historical origins may help. Consider the operation of the writ of *certiorari*. A common law court could issue a writ of *certiorari* against an inferior tribunal. The effect of this was to transfer the entire record of the proceeding in the inferior tribunal to the common law court: "The theory is that the Sovereign has been appealed to by some one of his subjects who complains of an injustice done him by an inferior court; whereupon the Sovereign, saying that he wishes to be informed – *certiorari* – of the matter, orders that the record, etc., be transmitted into a Court where he is sitting."[2] Once received in the common law court, the record could be scrutinized for error.[3] In this way, the common law courts were able to develop a body of centralized jurisprudence regulating the proceedings of inferior courts.

The writ of prohibition, meanwhile, functioned to stave off encroachments on the jurisdiction of the common law courts; ecclesiastical courts, for instance, could be prohibited from adjudicating on certain matters. *Quo warranto* enabled the common law courts to assess whether a particular decision maker was qualified to act. *Mandamus* and *habeas corpus* were available to correct a wide variety of wrongs, not just those committed by inferior courts.[4]

When deciding whether to grant a prerogative writ in a particular case, the common law courts did not conduct a trial. Judicial review was – and still is today – a paper proceeding, based entirely on the record of the proceedings before the inferior court. Sometimes the record would literally be carted from the other end of the country to be scrutinized in the halls of Westminster. Lawyers would, of course, argue in court about whether the record revealed a basis for the intervention of the common law courts. But there were no witnesses, no jurors, and no dramatic Perry Mason–like moments where a brilliant cross-examination revealed fundamental flaws in a party's case.

Over the centuries, the common law courts extended the scope of the prerogative writs to cover a wider and wider range of bodies, generally reasoning by analogy to justify issuing writs against decision makers that were not, strictly speaking, inferior courts. An early example is *Groenvelt v Burwell*.[5] Here, a physician had been fined and imprisoned by the College of Physicians. Formally speaking, *certiorari* would not extend to the College, which was not an inferior court; indeed, the College was not a so-called Court of Record, nor was it acting judicially. Looking rather to the substance of the matter, Lord Chief Justice Holt held that *certiorari* could be issued against the College: any body with a power to examine, hear, and punish was a judicial body, and any jurisdiction with the power to fine and imprison was a Court of Record. Reasoning *Groenvelt*-style, the courts gradually and incrementally extended the prerogative writs to cover a vast range of nonjudicial decision-making.[6] As one of Holt's successors, Lord Chief Justice Parker, explained several centuries later, "the exact limits" of the prerogative writs "have never been and ought not to be specifically defined," but rather "have varied from time to time being extended to meet changing conditions."[7]

This basic structure was implanted in Canada by the Europeans who landed on the shores of North America. The King's common law courts in London were the "superior courts," with a superintending power to oversee the affairs of every inferior body beneath them. Canada, too, had superior courts, and their continuing existence is recognized by section 96 of the *Constitution Act, 1867*. The judges are appointed by the governor general on the advice of the federal government. Part of their core jurisdiction, historically, is to ensure that inferior courts and analogous bodies (basically, every administrative decision maker in Canada) act within the boundaries of the law.[8] This structure also extends to the civil law province of Quebec.[9] Most legal relations in *La belle province* are governed by the *Civil Code of Quebec,* but the province's public law is (with some modifications) the same as the public law of the other provinces: the operation of the courts, criminal law, and oversight of public administration are done according to common law principles.

* * *

We have seen that administrative law evolved slowly and incrementally. For the most part, the slow and incremental growth of the oversight role of the superior courts was in lockstep with the slow and incremental growth of government institutions. Just as England developed bodies such as Commissioners of Sewers to implement national policy, so too did Upper and Lower Canada create entities like the Court of Escheat and arbitrators to determine and allocate customs duties payable on seabound traffic,[10] as and when such bodies were needed to respond to specific social or political problems. With the Industrial Revolution, however, and mass movement from the countryside to the towns, the need for regulation expanded dramatically. This need was supercharged by the expansion of the franchise: with more voters came more demand for legislation to remedy social problems, such as the absence of a robust system of workplace insurance. As the twentieth century wore on – with two world wars and a major economic crisis in the 1930s – the state in Western democracies played an increasing role, directly managing sectors of the economy, regulating others, and distributing resources to those in need.

This explosion of state activity posed significant challenges for administrative law. There is a reason that the word "Jesuitical" – which evokes casuistic, case-by-case analysis – is not always employed as a term of endearment. Yet the evolution of administrative law has been just this. While the prerogative writs were used to control the actions of an array of administrative decision makers, there was no "administrative law" as such. There were no general principles but various, discrete bodies of law relating to the individual writs: there was a "law" relating to *certiorari,* a "law" of prohibition, and so on, but there was no coherent body of principles that, as a whole, could be described as "administrative law." And, as one can readily imagine, with decisions about the application of the writs rapidly accumulating the case law was difficult to interpret. For example, for purely historical reasons, *certiorari* was available to quash decisions tainted by "jurisdictional errors" but did not extend to errors, even serious ones, "within jurisdiction." Moreover, decisions relating to mere privileges, or decisions that were "administrative" or "legislative" in nature, were excluded from judicial oversight, as only those decisions affecting "rights" and made after a "judicial" or "quasi-judicial" process could be reached by the prerogative writs.

Given the state's increased role in distributing resources in the twentieth century, and making general policy decisions about how to manage national economies, these were severe restrictions. Much of public administration escaped any judicial oversight at all. And this was not a morally optimal position either – slumlords whose decrepit properties had to be razed to the ground in the public interest had "rights" the courts would protect, but indigent people reliant on state benefits had no recourse to the judiciary if ever their benefits were cut off.

Therefore, to observe the mid-twentieth-century literature on administrative law is to look at a world very different from ours. Indeed, this was the time of the "long sleep" of administrative law,[11] a prolonged period of judicial somnolence that gave rise to fears that we had witnessed the "twilight" of judicial review[12] or, at the very least, stern warnings that a "crossroads" had been reached.[13] Standing in the way of progress, clanking their medieval chains,[14] were the tripartite classification of functions into "administrative," "legislative," and "judicial" (only the last attracting much in the way of judicial control); a stark distinction between reviewable "rights" and unreviewable "privileges"; a deep divide between "jurisdictional" error, which attracted *de novo* judicial review, and "nonjurisdictional" error, which attracted none at all; and, of course, the procedural and technical restrictions encrusted like barnacles on the hull of the prerogative writs, which had evolved to be the primary means of judicial control of public administration. In that period, despite the creation of an enormous administrative state, with welfare, regulatory, and managerial functions, vast swaths of public administration were immune from judicial oversight.[15] Even judicial imposition of *procedural* controls on how public officials could make decisions – putting no fetters on the *substance* of those decisions – could not be taken for granted.

* * *

This was soon to change.[16] The origin story of contemporary administrative law involves academics, judges, and politicians working in consort to transform judicial review of administrative action.[17] In his classic text, *Judicial Review of Administrative Action,* Professor Stanley de Smith "provided the academic systematization of the principles of judicial review";[18] in landmark decisions such as *Ridge v Baldwin,*[19] *Anisminic v Foreign Compensation Commission,*[20] and *Padfield v Minister of Agriculture,*[21] the House of Lords cast aside the tripartite classification, the rights/privileges distinction, and the jurisdictional/nonjurisdictional error divide; and politicians effected or permitted, through legislation and delegated legislation, procedural reforms that replaced the barnacled prerogative writs with a unified application for judicial review.[22] This means that individuals whose interests have been affected by governmental action may make an application for judicial review in the superior court. Whereas Lord Reid could safely say in the 1960s that England knew no developed system of administrative law, just twenty years later – the blink of an eye in common law terms – Lord Diplock confidently stated; "[T]he English law relating to judicial control of administrative action has been developed upon a case to case basis which has virtually transformed it over the last three decades."[23]

Similar transformations occurred in Canada: for Professor de Smith, read Professors Harry Arthurs,[24] Peter Hogg,[25] David Mullan,[26] and Paul Weiler;[27] procedural reforms were effected at the federal and provincial level;[28] and over the years the Canadian judiciary invigorated the law of judicial review of administrative action.

The Supreme Court of Canada decision in *Nicholson v Haldimand-Norfolk Regional Police Commissioners*[29] heralded a similar change to *Ridge v Baldwin,* such that where once procedural protections attached only to decisions made "judicially," having an impact on "rights,"[30] they could by the early 1980s be imposed by judges with respect to any decision affecting "the rights, interests, property, privileges, or liberties of any person."[31] The old law of "natural justice," closely modelled on the trial-type procedures employed by courts, was replaced by a context-sensitive "duty of fairness," where the question a court must ask is: "What procedural protections, if any, are necessary for this particular decision-making process?"[32] In particular, individuals are entitled to fair warning of potentially adverse decisions and an opportunity to respond. Indeed, there is an increasing trend toward "active adjudication," where an administrative decision maker becomes more actively involved *within* a hearing process,[33] and, arguably, toward "responsive legality."[34] Moreover, the impact of a decision on an individual has come to play an important role in determining the extent of the procedural protections required in a given case: "The more important the decision is to the lives of those affected and the greater its impact on that person or those persons, the more stringent the procedural protections that will be mandated."[35]

A wider variety of grounds of review became available of governmental action, a trend visible across the common law world.[36] In Canada, the Supreme Court developed a "pragmatic and functional" approach to judicial review (considered in more detail in the next chapter). Rather than relying on a stark distinction between jurisdictional and nonjurisdictional errors, Canadian courts employed a variety of contextual factors to calibrate the appropriate intensity of review – correctness, reasonableness *simpliciter,* and patent unreasonableness – for any given case.[37] On the application of any of these standards, courts were able to probe the reasons and the record to identify any flaws in an impugned administrative decision. Even where the legislature had enacted a privative clause – a statutory provision preventing the courts from judicially reviewing a decision – the courts could nonetheless consider the lawfulness of administrative action – that is, an individual affected by a decision made by an administrative decision maker could bring judicial review proceedings to determine whether the decision maker acted in a procedurally fair manner and whether the decision maker's analysis of the legal and factual issues was reasonable.

No-go areas were eliminated, as the boundaries of nonjusticiability were pushed back. In *Operation Dismantle v The Queen,* the Supreme

Court held that a state actor could not shelter from a claim of a Charter violation by invoking nonjusticiability.[38] All governmental action was, in principle, open to review for Charter compliance. Governmental action was, moreover, subject to judicial review in the superior courts,[39] a constitutional control that the Supreme Court held, could not be ousted by ordinary legislation.[40] Prerogative power has also come under judicial scrutiny, haltingly at times[41] but more confidently in recent years, with more attention to the particular context in which prerogative action is sought to be challenged.[42] Judicial review has also been extended to private bodies exercising public power,[43] and the law of standing has been significantly liberalized, allowing public-spirited citizens and non-governmental organizations to challenge administrative action.[44] It bears mentioning, finally, that governmental bodies have a duty to consult with and potentially accommodate Indigenous peoples when their rights protected by section 35 of the Charter might be affected by regulatory decisions.[45] Administrative decision makers, too, may fall under the consultation obligation,[46] meaning they will have to draw Indigenous peoples into their decision-making processes and "show that [they have] considered and addressed the rights claimed by Indigenous peoples in a meaningful way."[47]

Today, therefore, most administrative decisions can be reviewed in the courts for their reasonableness and procedural fairness: they must comply with the law and be made in a procedurally fair manner; and the reviewing process can be triggered by making an application for judicial review – writs don't come into it. When contemporary lawyers say that decision makers must act within their "jurisdiction," they mean simply that the decision maker must act within the boundaries of reasonableness and procedural fairness. This involves some deference by the courts to the decision makers: in determining whether the boundaries have been respected, the courts will give weight (sometimes significant weight) to the views of the decision makers in question. Again, the idea that a privative clause can exclude an entire area from judicial oversight has long since been rejected: reasonableness and procedural fairness permeate all areas of public administration.

(Jurisdiction, deference, and privative clauses are discussed further below.)

* * *

The upshot of all this is that administrative law is in a constant state of evolution. Textbooks and judicial decisions provide snapshots of what the law is at different points in time, but there is no certainty that things will stay the same. Indeed, the key contemporary concepts of reasonableness and procedural fairness are context-sensitive and so will shift shapes in different contexts.

THE VARIETY OF DECISION MAKERS AND DECISIONS

All Canadians are affected by the administrative state in all sorts of ways: when they return from abroad, apply for a driver's licence, pay municipal taxes, listen to music on the radio, choose a cable TV package, or turn on the gas stove. Officials all over the country make decisions about who can enter Canada, who gets to drive on the roads, how much tax is due, what mix of music, talk, and advertisements is acceptable on the airwaves, whether cable companies have to offer certain channels, and how energy companies can recover investments in infrastructure from users of their services. Hundreds of administrative agencies across Canada churn out thousands upon thousands of decisions every day, about everything from social welfare claims to the amount of French-language content on cable television. These officials are administrative decision makers. Their decisions are subject to the principles of administrative law.

A further complicating factor in grasping administrative law is therefore the sheer variety of decision makers in the contemporary administrative state.[48] The general principles of administrative law are applied in as diverse a range of settings as can be imagined: everything from the life-or-death context of immigration law to regulatory decisions about energy and transport that shape the economic future of the country, to matters of culture in the arts and telecommunications sectors. Environmental law, municipal law, tax law: you name it, there is – somewhere – an administrative decision maker applying it, and therefore making decisions to which the general principles of administrative law can be applied. In a sense, then, administrative law is shaped by the specific substantive areas of law it is applied to. As these change, however, administrative law might well change with it.

Furthermore, the constraints of administrative law are tighter or looser in different contexts. One useful way to conceptualize the administrative state is to perceive it as a spectrum,[49] along which, as Justice Louis LeBel put it in *Imperial Oil Ltd v Quebec (Minister of the Environment)*, the requirements of the law "may vary in order to reflect the context of a decision maker's activities and the nature of its functions":[50]

> The categories of administrative bodies involved range from administrative tribunals whose adjudicative functions are very similar to those of the courts, such as grievance arbitrators in labour law, to bodies that perform multiple tasks and whose adjudicative functions are merely one aspect of broad duties and powers that sometimes include regulation-making power. The notion of administrative decision maker also includes administrative managers such as ministers or officials who perform policy-making discretionary functions within the apparatus of government.[51]

This well-known idea of a spectrum[52] can be roughly mapped as follows: Ministers[53] → Crown corporations[54] → Social and economic regulation[55] → Quasi-judicial[56] → Judicial.

On the purely political end of the spectrum lies ministerial decision-making, where political control through conventions of accountability to the legislature predominates. Here, procedural protections are diminished – indeed, in *Imperial Oil*, an argument that the minister was biased because his department would have won a budgetary windfall from penalizing an oil company failed for precisely this reason. In addition, the range of considerations that a minister might take into account in making a decision is often very broad indeed.

On the purely legal end of the spectrum lies judicial decision-making. By "judicial" in this context, I do not mean decision-making by courts of law. Rather, I am concerned with the application by administrative bodies of objective legal norms to the facts as found. The French term *juridictionnelle*, which does not have a ready English equivalent, captures the idea. Here, political interference is – or at least should be[57] – frowned on, for the distribution of costs and benefits set out by the legislature should not be interfered with by executive fiat.[58] Legal control is heightened, in the sense that the range of considerations that a judicial decision maker may legitimately take into account is tightly constrained: if the question is whether an applicant has accumulated enough days of work to claim an entitlement, the decision maker cannot peer into the applicant's conduct or utility to society. Procedural protections are at their strongest here, where the decision-making process – the application of objective legal norms to facts after hearing from the parties – closely resembles that of a court of law.

Between the two extremes, the extent of political and legal control varies as one moves back and forth along the spectrum, more strongly legal toward the judicial end, more strongly political toward the ministerial end. Thus, not only are the general principles of administrative law a function to some extent of the specific, substantive areas to which they are applied but the weight of those general principles will vary from area to area depending on the nature of the decision maker.

To this must be added the huge divergences between the different types of decisions that are made. At the most basic level, some decisions are general in nature – the promulgation of regulations or guidelines, for example – while some are specific to identifiable individuals or groups – determinations of refugee status or of minimum carrying requirements for cable providers, for example. These general or specific decisions, furthermore, can be made by all types of decision maker, from politicians who give no reasons all the way to adjudicators who give very detailed reasons. And the effects of the decisions can be quite different. The stakes in an immigration case are extremely high, whereas a decision not to fund an application for government support for an academic research project is of a different nature entirely. Even the same type of decision can have different stakes depending on the identity of the parties concerned: if my driver's licence were revoked, I could still get around using taxis or Uber, but if a taxi driver's licence were revoked, the driver's family would face economic ruin. Administrative law's general principles, applied by these different decision makers in such diverse specific areas of substantive law, have to account also for the particularities of the type of decision.

Take three different areas: railways, refugees, and regulations.

- As common carriers, *railways* have long been subject – under the common law and statute – to a variety of duties to those who seek to use their services. In *Patchett & Sons Ltd v Pacific Great Eastern Railway Co,*[59] the Supreme Court explained that railway companies have a duty to accept goods for travel, as long as the requests are reasonable. Those obligations of reasonableness are now set out in the *Canada Transportation Act,* but have to be understood against the backdrop of *Patchett* and several decades' worth of decisions by the Canadian Transportation Agency. Complaints can be made under the Act by shippers of goods whose requests were not accepted: they can argue that the railway was not reasonable, the railway can defend itself vigorously, and the agency adjudicates. Or the agency can initiate a complaint on its own motion, engaging in a much more flexible and open-ended inquiry.[60] Common law, statute, adjudication, investigation – all meshed into the same statutory scheme. There is a limited right of appeal from decisions of the agency to the Federal Court of Appeal, with the permission of a judge, only on a question of law or jurisdiction, and a broader right to seek review from the federal Cabinet (supported by civil servants in the Privy Council Office).
- Someone who arrives in Canada fleeing persecution can apply for *refugee* status. At first, an officer of the Immigration and Refugee Board of Canada's Refugee Protection Division will determine whether the person is a refugee. This is not an adversarial proceeding; rather, the officer asks questions, explains doubts he or she may

have about the claimant's story, reviews documentary evidence, and makes a decision. If the application is rejected, the claimant can appeal to the Refugee Appeal Division in most instances. This appellate body reviews the record from the Refugee Protection Division and comes to its own conclusion about whether the claimant really is a refugee. An unsuccessful appeal is not necessarily the end of the road: a failed refugee claimant can later resist deportation on the basis of a Pre-Removal Risk Assessment, performed by still another type of official. And at most points in this tale, the claimant can apply to the courts to judicially review unfavourable decisions (and have them issue a stay – putting the proceedings on ice – while the review is conducted).

- Railways and refugees involve corporations and individuals. *Regulations,* by contrast, typically involve rules made for the world at large. I say typically because sometimes regulations will target individuals or groups – like regulations freezing assets because of economic sanctions against a foreign country. Regardless, the making of regulations does not involve any sort of adjudicative or inquisitorial proceeding. Rather, they are drafted by civil servants to implement statutes. They can have drastic consequences for individuals and industries, yet for the most part, the only formal requirement is that regulations be laid before the legislature (Parliament for federal regulations, a provincial legislature for provincial regulations) without a member of the legislature objecting – and objections *never* happen. Sometimes, general rules that do not qualify as regulations – the definition is a "confused microcosm"[61] – are not subject to any procedural requirements at all.

This is just an aperçu to illustrate the variety of forms administrative action can take, the range of decision makers involved (sometimes performing different functions), and the differing stakes of the decisions for the individuals concerned. Sometimes the decision maker will be a sophisticated multi-member tribunal (or even the federal Cabinet), but often it will be a lower-level official, such as a civil servant acting for a minister.

There is one last strand to consider. There is a reflexive relationship between the principles of administrative law and administrative decisions. The reasons and records of administrative decisions reviewed by judges are now much more extensive than in the past. Modern records are voluminous, and modern reasons extensive. Administrative proceedings are increasingly subject to the open-court principle;[62] access-to-information legislation imposes high standards of transparency on administrative decision makers; there are many statutory obligations to give reasons for decisions; considerations of fairness between individual and institutional litigants drive the publication of scores of decisions on decision makers' websites; and technological advances facilitate the production of reasons even in the face of large numbers of applications "by employing information technology, using decision templates, drop-down menus and other software."[63]

The upshot is that judges conducting judicial review hearings will have a large volume of material on their desks, reasons potentially running into hundreds of pages, supported quite possibly by an even more extensive record. It is only natural for courts reviewing reasoned decisions to focus on the internal coherence of the reasons given, interrogating whether they do indeed justify the decision given.[64] Judicial review judges are likely to consider that they have the capacity to test whether decision makers' conclusions follow from their premises: there is no special expertise required to assess whether a decision is logical and rational, or whether it is justifiable in view of the relevant legal and factual constraints. Where there were no reasons to scrutinize, as in previous eras, it was much more difficult for judges to conclude that an administrative decision should be quashed.

Where reasons were never given for administrative decisions, the flaws in those decisions or in public administration generally were concealed from the judicial eye. Once reasons came to be given more or less as a matter of course, public administration was on display, warts and all. As soon as judges became aware of shortcomings in public administration (or even just the potential for shortcomings), it was perhaps inevitable that they would develop more exacting standards of reasonableness and fairness to hold administrative decision makers to account.

COMPLEX CONCEPTS

Three concepts have been of central importance to Canadian administrative law in recent decades. One of them, jurisdiction, is found in every textbook in every common law country, often taking up many pages that are often not (sometimes by the author's own admission) especially illuminating. The two others, deference and legislative intent, can be found in other countries from time to time but rarely play the important roles they have played and continue to play in Canada. All three concepts are complex and difficult to grasp.

Jurisdiction
You will often find lawyers – be they advocates, judges, or professors – saying things like "The tribunal exceeded its jurisdiction," "The minister had no jurisdiction to take that decision," or "The regulator made a jurisdictional error." What are they trying to convey?

There are two basic ideas. First, the variety of decision makers described above get their powers from statutes made by a legislature (there are some nuances here about prerogative powers and entering into contracts, but they can be safely ignored). This is their "jurisdiction," which they cannot exceed.[65] Second, the statute grants powers – but it also limits them. If a statute provides that a decision maker can do Y only if X is present, then the presence of X is a precondition to the doing of Y.[66] So, for example, if a tribunal is granted the power to make findings of discrimination with respect to the letting of self-contained dwelling units, then the fact that a given dwelling is a self-contained dwelling unit (X) is a precondition to making a finding of discrimination (Y).[67] X has been laid down in a statute by the legislature. If a decision maker does Y when X is not present, then it is acting in excess of its powers: "Any grant of jurisdiction will necessarily include limits to the jurisdiction granted, and any grant of a power remains subject to conditions."[68]

The primary problem with the concept of jurisdiction is that no formula has ever been devised for distinguishing X from Y: "No satisfactory test has ever been formulated for distinguishing findings which go to jurisdiction from findings which go to the merits."[69] All statutory provisions can be cast in the basic form: if X is present, then the decision maker shall or may Y. The problem then becomes acute, as the boundaries of jurisdiction are "impossible to draw precisely because the two matters [X and Y] [are] inextricably interwoven."[70] Because an X component may be identified in all statutory provisions, a court could invoke the doctrine to justify intervening whenever it so pleases, a risk borne out by the historical record: "There was no predictability as to how a case would be categorised before the court pronounced on the matter. There was also no *ex post facto* rationality that could be achieved by juxtaposing a series of cases and asking why one case went one way and another was decided differently."[71] To say things like "The tribunal exceeded its jurisdiction," "The minister had no jurisdiction to take that decision," or "The regulator made a jurisdictional error" announces a conclusion (in impressive-sounding language) without explaining it. What matters are the reasons for coming to the conclusion – and these are often obscured by the language of "jurisdiction."

Although there is much more to say about the concept, it is unnecessary to wade any further into the morass here, for, as we shall see, especially in Chapter 2, the concept of jurisdiction has been marginalized in Canadian administrative law. Nonetheless, it is difficult to understand the process by which it was marginalized without understanding why the concept is complex. And it is difficult to appreciate why administrative law is so complicated without spending some time discussing jurisdiction – hence the infliction of these paragraphs on the reader.

Deference

The concept of jurisdiction has been marginalized and, in large part, replaced in Canada by the concept of deference. This concept is helpfully discussed by Gary Lawson and Guy Seidman in a recent book, *Deference: The Legal Concept and the Legal Practice*.[72] They note that the use of deference in judicial decisions is in contrast to the conventional use of the term "deference," which tends to involve complete obeisance, say, in "deferring" to another's choice of restaurant. When lawyers use the term, it is typically "to describe a sliding scale of weight rather than the kind of yield likely to be meant in ordinary conversation."[73] In deciding to uphold an administrative decision (or not), a judge will give weight to the views of an administrative decision maker explaining the decision maker's preferred interpretation of a statutory provision or justifying a policy choice. Deference is therefore a way "of representing an allocation of decision-making responsibility among multiple actors."[74]

This allocation can be made in a variety of ways. Giving weight is one possibility; making space is another. Consider an everyday example. Patients visit doctors to receive advice about their ailments and possible cures. Ultimately, patients will decide what to do, but in making the decision, will allocate responsibility between themselves and their doctor. Some patients might simply give weight to the views of the doctor, which go into the mix with what they learned on Google or what they have learned from past experience. Indeed, patients who are trained doctors might give much less weight to the views of their doctor (hence the expression that doctors make the worst patients). Other patients might accept the advice of their doctor, subject to the general quality of the doctor's explanations: as long as these seem reasonable and grounded in the evidence, a patient will accept them; if they are not, the patient might reject them or seek a second opinion.

Deference in administrative law can function the same way. Let's stay in the doctor's office: assume that the patient complains to a disciplinary body about the treatment received from the doctor, the disciplinary body finds that the doctor mistreated the patient, and the doctor challenges this finding in court. The court can give weight to the disciplinary body's findings on what the professional standard of conduct is but keep the final word for itself, or the court can say something like, "a judge can intervene only if the findings were unreasonable or unsupported by evidence," carving out a space for the disciplinary body to develop its interpretation of the standard of conduct. Unsurprisingly, in this area, courts much more often create space than give weight.

The qualifier "in this area" is important. Determining the professional standard of conduct typically involves a value judgment, which is heavily dependent on the context of the patient-doctor relationship and the general approach to such relationships in the community of doctors. It is a question of fact, or perhaps of applying standards to fact (a "mixed" question) – but it is certainly not a question of law. Relatedly, if a government minister determines that it is not in the "national interest" to fund a particular project or allows a particular permanent resident to remain in Canada despite serious criminal offences, this is best characterized as an exercise of discretion. When questions of fact, mixed questions, or exercises of discretion come up before the courts in judicial review proceedings, the courts will generally be very respectful of the decision maker. They will not simply give weight to the decision maker's views; rather, they will accept those views as conclusive, unless there is something seriously wrong with the reasons for those views and/or the underlying evidence.

Where matters become trickier, as you might imagine, is on questions of law. When it comes to interpreting statutes, or case law, judges find themselves doing something they were trained to do since their very first days as law students. Why would they give any weight at all to the views of others, let alone carve out a space for nonlawyers? Over the years, the response to this question has occupied many pages of Canadian law journals and judicial decisions. For the moment, let us simply acknowledge that in some areas of regulation answering questions of law might require technical knowledge beyond the ken of judges – for example, where a body of economists has to determine whether a merger would lessen competition "substantially." Here, space might even be appropriate, notwithstanding that the word "substantially" appears in a statute, and weight surely would be. Of course, expertise is a slippery concept: if you prefer, the rationale for carving out a space or giving weight could be efficiency, inasmuch as the optimal way for judges to spend their time is not second-guessing economists about the meaning of "substantially" in a statute about competition law.

Legislative Intent

This leads us to the third complex concept – legislative intent. It provides another potential justification for deference, alongside expertise and efficiency: the legislature might require the courts to either give weight to the views of a decision maker or simply accept them as long as they are reasonable and based on the evidence.

Here, great care is needed. To begin with, "legislative intent" does not require us to look into the hearts and minds of legislators. We are concerned with the words they used in their statutes, not the message they intended to communicate. "Legislative intent" does not have a free-standing meaning floating in the ether above the words used in the statute. Those words sometimes include so-called privative clauses, designed to *deprive* the courts of the authority to review particular decisions. These clauses can take a variety of forms: they have targeted particular prerogative writs (a "no *certiorari* clause," for example) when this was appropriate, or provided that "no decision shall be called into question in a court of law." Canadian courts (and their counterparts elsewhere in the common law world) have regularly had to grapple with such clauses. Beyond privative clauses, however, one can say that the choice to create a decision maker and give it significant powers – be it a competition authority, a minister, or a disciplinary body – also evidences a legislative intent that the decision maker should not be routinely second-guessed by the courts. Whether this is true and, if it is, whether it requires the giving of weight or the carving out of space has also occupied much of the time of Canada's administrative lawyers.

Evidently, a legislature need not intend, through its language, for deference to be given. It might give decision-making powers to the courts, or provide for appeals from decision makers to the courts. Here again a wide variety of provisions can be found in Canada's law libraries: giving power to courts directly; allowing decision makers to ask courts to give a binding ruling on a question of law; creating a right of appeal on questions of law only (sometimes only with the court's permission); providing for an entirely new proceeding before a court; or simply giving individuals the option of an appeal. Legislative intent and the relationship between clear expressions of intent, such as privative clauses and rights of appeal, and not-so-clear expressions of intent, such as delegating significant decision-making authority, have been a central concept in Canadian administrative law.

The purpose of this discussion has been, on the one hand, to assist in answering this chapter's main question – why is administrative law so complicated? – and, on the other hand, to introduce some concepts that will be central to the story told in subsequent chapters. Jurisdiction, deference, and legislative intent will all rear their heads at various points. There be dragons, but at least the reader will know what to fear from them.

ATTITUDES TOWARD
THE ADMINISTRATIVE STATE

It should be clear from the foregoing discussion that there is no constitution or general codification of administrative law. Quebec has its *Civil Code* and Canada has its *Criminal Code,* but administrative law is not confined to one self-contained handbook that explains the relationship between public administration and the courts. Canada does not have anything like the specialized administrative courts of civil code countries such as France. There, the *Conseil d'État,* peopled by experienced civil servants rather than judges, oversees the actions of public administration, applying a set of rules that are distinct from those that apply between private parties. Public contracts, public liability, and public unlawfulness are governed by special rules, applied by specialized courts. In common law countries like Canada, however, the same superior courts that make decisions about contracts, property, and torts apply the principles of administrative law. They are staffed by generalist judges, not specialists in public administration.

One consequence is that judges do not have anything like a uniform view of public administration. They are not *Énarques* in whom the same principles have been inculcated, generation after generation. Moreover, there is a venerable tradition of lawyers being skeptical of the administrative state. The rise of the state in the twentieth century brought with it an enormous increase in the scope of discretion of government officials. Lawyers, trained to identify and apply rules, have a natural antipathy to discretion. In formulating the general principles of administrative law, they have often sought to tame administrative discretion. In fact, the influential Victorian-era jurist Albert Venn Dicey at one point denied that there was any such thing as administrative law: there was, in the King's courts (just as much in the Dominions as in London), only one law for all, individuals and government officials alike. By the end of his life, Dicey had recanted, but his skepticism of administrative discretion casts a long shadow over the subject.[75]

Judicial attitudes toward the administrative state run along three fault lines: deference and nondeference, form and substance, and reason and authority.[76]

Deference and Nondeference

Some judges are hostile to administrative discretion, and others are much more open to it. Some seek to cut discretion down to the bare minimum, while others are comfortable with deferring to the views of administrative decision makers, especially those who can plausibly claim to be expert in their field of regulation.

Dicey's hugely influential account of English public law identified judges as the "guardians of the rule of law," on whom it was incumbent "to ensure that any person or body relying on power delegated by the legislature abide by the terms and conditions on which that power was granted."[77] A deferential approach to judicial review, however, requires judges to be satisfied by an answer that is merely reasonable, even on questions of law.[78] It does not need to be the answer the judge would have given after due consideration of the question. Intervention is possible only where an interpretation "cannot be rationally supported by the relevant legislation."[79] Deferring to administrative decision makers' interpretations of law requires judges to pull against the current of tradition.[80] Intervention is justifiable only in extreme cases, not in ordinary ones. Administrative autonomy must be respected, tradition put to one side. Whether or not judges accord weight – reserving for themselves the final decision but according significant heft to the conclusions of the front-line decision maker – or space – carving out a zone into which courts will not intrude as long as the impugned decision is reasonable[81] – a deferential approach requires them to no longer think as lawyers traditionally have thought.

If you know any lawyers, you can imagine how much difficulty this has caused over the years![82]

Form and Substance

Some lawyers prefer form, and others prefer substance.[83] By form, I mean the development of conceptual categories, into which decisions must be placed without regard to whether the achievement of the substantive ends intended by the development of the categories is actually furthered by placing a particular decision in a category. By substance, I mean paying attention to the eccentricities of the individual decision and the statutory provisions pursuant to which it was made.[84]

An example might help the reader to grasp the importance of the form/substance fault line. The traditional distinction between jurisdictional and nonjurisdictional error was commonly seen as formal in character. It is formal because it sorts decisions into different categories based on the abstract features of the concept of jurisdiction. It does not operate by reference to the contextual considerations presented by individual decisions. This formalism marked the law prior to *New Brunswick Liquor*.[85] In the 1980s, the Canadian law of judicial review continued to have a relatively formal structure: jurisdiction retained a tenacious hold on Canada's legal imagination, and deference depended in part on a formal feature of decision-making structures, namely, the presence of a privative clause. If there was a privative clause, decisions were sorted into the deference category, as they were "within the jurisdiction" of the decision maker.

But this formal distinction was challenged by substantive opponents, such as the pragmatic and functional approach considered in the next chapter. Applying it forced courts to confront the nature of the statutory scheme, the nature of the relationship between the particular decision and the relative expertise of the decision maker, and the nature of the particular question presented for review. Instead of mechanically sorting decisions into different categories based on their formal characteristics, it was necessary to grapple with the contextual particularities of the decision in question.

In general, some lawyers prefer bright-line rules and categories, whereas others are more comfortable with open texture and contextual considerations. Over the years, administrative law has yo-yoed between form and substance, depending on whether the formalists or substantivists have the upper hand.

Reason and Authority

The last fault line is between reason and authority.[86] Professor David Dyzenhaus has described this as the distinction between "deference as submission" and "deference as respect."[87] Some judges accord deference and apply deferential standards because there is some authoritative basis to do so. Others, though, require a reasoned basis to defer in the first place, and to uphold a decision.

This fault line overlaps the form/substance fault line to some extent. An authoritative basis for deference is a privative clause (or, perhaps, a broad delegation of authority). A reasoned basis for deference is the expertise of a decision maker. For a judge who seeks an authoritative basis for deference, deference is appropriate where a decision maker can claim authority based on a privative clause. By contrast, a judge seeking a reasoned basis for deference will look to contextual indicators such as expertise to justify according deference to a decision maker. Put another way, a judge deferring because there is a privative clause will defer "because the legislature told me to," whereas a judge looking for a reasoned basis will defer only "because doing so is justified by the decision maker's demonstrated competence." And, on the authority side of the line, a judge might happily uphold a decision as long as the conclusion is within the broad bands of acceptability, whereas across the divide, a judge who seeks reason will be satisfied only if the decision maker has provided a sound justification for its conclusions.

CONCLUSION

The goal of this chapter has been to introduce the complexity of administrative law by reference to history, the variety of decision makers, important concepts, and attitudes toward the administrative state.

Historically, today's administrative law is the result of a continual process of slow evolution, retrofitting devices designed for very different purposes to the realities of the contemporary administrative state.

This state has a vast array of decision makers: the general principles of administrative law that have been developed in recent decades are applied in specific situations that differ radically in terms of technical complexity, political sensitivity, and morality.

The general principles contain and are sometimes mediated through concepts – jurisdiction, deference, and legislative intent – that are themselves inherently complex.

Lastly, the general principles and concepts are applied by judges who often have radically different attitudes toward the administrative state and the role of courts in policing the boundaries of jurisdiction, giving deference, respecting legislative intent, and developing the general principles of administrative law. Complexity is layered upon complexity is layered upon complexity is layered upon complexity. In the next chapter, we will plunge into that complexity by taking a deep dive into the Canadian law of judicial review.

Before doing so, though, it is worth making an observation about how the politics of judicial review have evolved in recent decades. When the Canadian courts first built their doctrine of deference, it was in aid of progressive causes. There was a general view that judges were hostile to, for example, labour relations boards seeking to redress imbalances between employers and unions, and would conjure up any old reason to intervene and quash pro-union decisions. In that era, these labour relations boards were peopled by practitioners and academics of unimpeachable credentials, experts in every sense of the word.

But the expansion of judicial review has changed things significantly. The fault line between reason and authority became especially volatile. Opening policy-making, prisons, and immigration to judicial oversight led the courts into areas where the stakes were much higher. Deference was nonetheless expanded, and benefitted decision makers who did not have expertise comparable with that of labour relations boards. With higher stakes but less expertise, those who would have cheered on labour relations boards became more muted – and sometimes openly hostile – to deference. Progressives in the 1970s would not necessarily make common cause with their fellow political travellers of the 2020s and sometimes find themselves in alliances with more conservative thinkers who are skeptical of the contemporary administrative state.[88] I say "sometimes" advisedly, because even within progressive circles one can find differing views on deference: those who advocate for clients who have suffered discrimination before well-funded human rights tribunals might be more pro-deference than those whose practice is primarily representing refugees and those with precarious status in Canada. Where someone stands on administrative law may depend on where they most often interact with the administrative state.

2

A Deep Dive into Judicial Review

F ROM THE PREVIOUS CHAPTER, the reader will be familiar with
some key concepts in administrative law: jurisdiction, deference,
and legislative intent. Given that each is centrally important to the
story told in this chapter, it is worth reiterating what the terms mean.
"Jurisdiction" relates primarily to the simple notion that administrative
decision makers must remain within the four corners of the statutory
authority given to them by Parliament or a provincial legislature; the
boundaries set out in statutes comprise the jurisdiction of any decision
maker. "Deference" is the idea that generalist courts should pay due
respect to the views of specialist decision makers, either carving out
space for the specialists (and not interfering with their decisions unless
these are demonstrably unfounded) or giving weight to their analyses
(retaining the last word for themselves but with the specialists' views
weighing in the balance). And "legislative intent" highlights the relevance of statutory language – especially, in this chapter, in the form
of privative clauses – to the task of determining the boundaries of an
administrative decision maker's authority or the degree of deference
due to the decision maker (if any).

Most of the difficulties in contemporary Canadian administrative law
have arisen because of these different terms. What does "jurisdiction"
mean? What is "deference"? And when do "privative clauses" matter? As
we shall see, these difficulties, and the fault lines described in Chapter 1,

have arisen only in relation to substantive review – the realm of reasonableness review – not procedural fairness or remedies.

This chapter provides a brief overview of the development of a doctrine of deference by the Supreme Court of Canada, over a period spanning roughly from the 1970s to the 2010s. The discussion covers several topics: 1) an outline of the position that prevailed up to the mid-1970s; 2) the revolutionary decision of Justice Brian Dickson of the Supreme Court in the *New Brunswick Liquor* case; 3) the Supreme Court's development of a substantive test to define when deference is appropriate; and 4) the Supreme Court's *Dunsmuir* decision and its implications.

Up to the mid-1970s, Canadian courts adopted a highly formalistic approach, hostile to deference on questions of law specifically and, indeed, to administrative decision makers generally. This approach was strongly criticized by leading academics and practitioners in the Canadian legal community, especially those working in labour relations, where the courts were perceived as hostile to unions and happy to undo employee-friendly decisions by hook or by crook. In the *New Brunswick Liquor* case, Justice Dickson's analysis broke with past practice in judicial review. The Supreme Court announced a change of course, pursuant to which administrative decision makers who were protected by a privative clause and who possessed specialized expertise in a particular domain would be entitled to deference from the courts for their interpretations of law. The decision involved – as you may have guessed – a labour relations tribunal, and the Supreme Court confirmed its deferential approach in a series of decisions in the 1980s, again in cases about labour relations.

The Supreme Court then developed a substantive test to define the circumstances in which deference is appropriate. This pragmatic and functional analysis consisted of a general set of four factors, applicable to any type of administrative decision maker, designed to determine which matters should be left in the hands of the courts (on the "correctness" standard) and which should be left presumptively to administrative decision makers. Alas, as the years passed and the case law piled up, so too did criticism of the new approach: witty lawyers said – in private, of course, and out of earshot of Supreme Court judges – that it was neither pragmatic nor functional. There was growing demand for the Supreme Court to undertake a simplification exercise, which it did in the *Dunsmuir* decision in 2008. This decision merely stored up trouble for the future, however, despite the earnest desire of its drafters to simplify and clarify Canadian administrative law.

THE WORLD BEFORE DEFERENCE

Writing in the early 1970s, Professor Peter Hogg took the view that the Supreme Court of Canada's reasons for judgment were "often woefully inadequate" and decried the "lamentable" state of Canadian administrative law.[1] Lord Diplock famously said that "[a]ny judicial statements on matters of public law if made before 1950 are likely to be a misleading guide to what the law is today."[2] This is certainly true of Canada, where reference was made in the early years of that decade to the "twilight" of judicial review.[3] During these twilight years, administrative decision makers were free to make errors within jurisdiction. They had, one could say, the "right to be wrong."[4] Twilight evokes darkness, and in cases decided before the modern law of judicial review began to take shape, courts were indeed unwilling to shine a light on large swaths of the burgeoning administrative state.

To be sure, jurisdictional limits were guarded by the courts, sometimes jealously.[5] This is unsurprising when one considers how the Canadian "legal profession" was quick to "condemn" administrative decision makers as "usurpers" of the role of the courts.[6] In *Jarvis v Associated Medical Services Inc,*[7] an employer allegedly dismissed a manager for engaging in union activities. The Ontario Labour Relations Board ordered the employer to reinstate her. Neither the Ontario Court of Appeal nor the majority of the Supreme Court of Canada had great difficulty in striking down the board's decision. A manager was not an "employee," and the board lacked jurisdiction to order her reinstatement.

Yet inside these limits all was dark as far as courts were concerned: "[S]o long as an administrative authority has acted within its statutory jurisdiction a court will not interfere with its decision."[8] A good example is *Commission des relations ouvrières du Québec v Burlington Mills Hosiery Co of Canada*.[9] Here, Quebec's labour relations board had excluded employees under the age of sixteen from a bargaining unit, with the result that a negotiating group was certified. Justice Douglas Charles Abbott sharply rejected the employer's application for judicial review. Determining who is "to be included or excluded from a bargaining unit" was one of the board's "principal functions" and fell within its "exclusive jurisdiction": "Provided it exercises that discretion in good faith its decision is not subject to judicial review."[10]

But the limits of jurisdictional error were stretched by the Supreme Court's decision in *Metropolitan Life Insurance v International Union of Operating Engineers*,[11] the "high water mark" of "activist" judicial review of administrative action in Canada.[12] The court held that the Ontario Labour Relations Board had committed a reviewable error of law by misconstruing the statutory term "members of the trade union."[13] The board had developed a general policy of treating workers as "members" if they had manifested an intention to become members. The overall goal was to make it easier for unions to be accredited, as some workers might have been reluctant to formally join a union for fear of employer reprisals. But "[i]n proceeding in this manner the Board has failed to deal with the question remitted to it (i.e., whether the employees in question were members of the union at the relevant date) and instead has decided a question which was not remitted to it (i.e., whether in regard to those employees there has been fulfilment of the conditions stated above)."[14] The board was thus wrong and its decision could not stand.

In addition to its strong position on errors of law, the Supreme Court of Canada took an aggressive stance against erroneous findings of jurisdictional fact. The classic case here is *Bell v Ontario Human Rights Commission*,[15] where the commission was prevented from holding a public hearing into an allegation of racial discrimination by a landlord against a potential tenant on the basis that the premises were not a "self-contained dwelling unit" as required by the relevant statutory provisions. If the alleged discrimination had been in relation to a "self-contained dwelling unit," the commission could hold a hearing, but holding a hearing concerning racial discrimination in relation to other dwellings was not permissible and thus beyond the powers of the commission to rectify. To put it mildly, it was not at all clear that the courts should play such an active role in policing the commission's authority.

Although the distinction between jurisdictional and nonjurisdictional error accorded deference within limits, it became clear that those limits would be so strictly policed by courts that deference was largely illusory. No real space was carved out for administrative decision makers, whose autonomy ultimately depended on the good grace of the judges. Contemporary commentators were disquieted. In a survey of the Supreme Court of Canada's labour law jurisprudence, a large part of which consisted of judicial review cases, Professor Paul Weiler (later a professor at the Harvard Law School) ventured to suggest "that the tacit assumption concerning Canadian courts, especially among academic commentators, is that the judiciary as a whole is rather unsympathetic to both unions and administrative agencies in their decision-making."[16] Underneath the technical language of jurisdiction and error of law ran a current of hostility to administrative bodies. The approach was formal and nondeferential – and almost entirely based on respect for the authority of the legislature. There was nothing substantive about judicial review, the courts were not especially deferential toward administrative decision makers, and exercises of power (administrative or judicial) did not have to be reasoned to be effective.

The distinction between jurisdictional and nonjurisdictional errors of law and fact was "sufficiently vague – some would say meaningless – to offer a means of review of any erroneous finding of fact or law."[17] A broad conception of jurisdictional error allowed courts to reduce the autonomy of administrative decision makers and keep them within closely confined boundaries. Often, the Supreme Court in particular would be "utterly submerged by a mistaken zeal to 'correct' the agency's decision."[18] Professors Hogg and Weiler, who strongly criticized the courts, were two leading lights in the legal academy who went on to play starring roles in the late-twentieth-century formulation of constitutional law and labour relations law in Canada. With such forceful criticism ringing in their ears, Canadian courts were soon to recognize the difficulties with the concept of jurisdiction. They then had the difficult task of conjuring up a workable alternative.

DEFERENCE BEGINS

Commenting later on *Metropolitan Life*, Justice Bertha Wilson suggested that the decision reflected a failure to appreciate "1) that [administrative decision makers'] decisions are crafted by those with specialized knowledge of the subject matter before them; and 2) that there is value in limiting the extent to which their decisions may be frustrated through an expansive judicial review."[19] At least one judge had recognized this at a relatively early point. As Justice Ivan Rand of the Supreme Court of Canada put it, in dissent, in *Toronto Newspaper Guild v Globe Printing*: "It is to no purpose that judicial minds may be outraged by seemingly arbitrary if not irrational treatment of questions raised: these views are irrelevant where there is no *clear departure* from the field of action defined by the statute."[20] Here, the reference to "clear departure" suggests that the apparently exclusive spheres of authority might blur around the edges.

But it was not until the mid to late 1970s that a distinctly deferential approach began to emerge. In *Service Employees' International Union, Local No. 333 v Nipawin District Staff Nurses Association et al*,[21] Justice Dickson refused to quash a labour relations board's refusal to certify a union on the basis that it was a company-dominated organization. The domination in question was that of *another union*, not the employer. The Court of Appeal had concluded that the board had committed an error of law by failing to ask whether the union was dominated by the *employer*, an argument that did not appeal to Dickson. Judicial intervention would sometimes be appropriate, but "if the Board acts in good faith and its decision can be rationally supported on a construction which the relevant legislation may reasonably be considered to bear, then the Court will not intervene."[22]

A true landmark decision followed a few years later, with Dickson again the creator: *Canadian Union of Public Employees Local 963 v New*

Brunswick Liquor Corporation.[23] During a lawful strike, management replaced employees with management personnel, an apparent breach of labour relations legislation that provided that "the employer shall not replace the striking employees or fill their position with any other employee."[24] This provision was badly drafted: it "bristles with ambiguities," and one judge considered that there were four possible interpretations.[25] The board's conclusion was that replacing striking employees with management personnel was not permissible.

The Court of Appeal considered that the ambiguous provision was jurisdictional, and therefore that any error would justify judicial intervention.[26] Dickson did not reject the premise that jurisdictional error could justify judicial intervention, but he warned courts to be cautious about too lightly concluding that provisions are jurisdictional in nature: "The question of what is and is not jurisdictional is often very difficult to determine. The courts, in my view, should not be alert to brand as jurisdictional, and therefore subject to broader curial review, that which may be doubtfully so."[27] In the present case, the matter plainly fell within the broad authority of the board.

Moreover, there were good reasons for deference.[28] A privative clause protected decisions of the board, "a specialized tribunal which administers a comprehensive statute regulating labour relations," a task requiring it "not only to find facts and decide questions of law, but also to exercise its understanding of the body of jurisprudence that has developed around the collective bargaining system, as understood in Canada, and its labour relations sense acquired from accumulated experience in the area."[29] The legislation created a zone of protection, and the board was well equipped to use its expertise within the protected zone.

Given that the board was acting within its jurisdiction, a very high threshold had to be surpassed by the applicant for judicial review. The interpretation was not beyond review entirely, but intervention would be justifiable only in extreme cases of patent unreasonableness: "Put another way, was the Board's interpretation so patently unreasonable that its construction cannot be rationally supported by the relevant legislation and demands intervention by the court upon review?"[30]

Justice Dickson acknowledged that, "at first glance," the board's interpretation might seem unreasonable "if one draws too heavily upon private sector experience," but a "careful reading" of the pertinent materials revealed a sound basis for the board's conclusion: "At a minimum the Board's interpretation would seem at least as reasonable as the alternative interpretations suggested in the Court of Appeal."[31] This, a commentator wrote shortly after, was a "clear message" that the "rules of the game had been radically altered."[32] Where the legislature had created a specialized, expert tribunal and protected its decisions by way of a privative clause, courts could intervene only in extreme cases:

> The composition and institutional structure of the agencies, together with the expertise and the wide range of procedural tools available to them, apparently persuaded the courts that these bodies had indeed been given the primary statutory responsibility for implementing and elaborating the legislative mandate within their area of regulation.[33]

THE PRAGMATIC
AND FUNCTIONAL ANALYSIS

New Brunswick Liquor was a significant decision. For the first time, the Supreme Court of Canada clearly stated that administrative decision makers were entitled to deference in at least some circumstances. But in what circumstances precisely? And in what circumstances could the courts continue to police jurisdictional errors? These questions plagued Canadian courts in the following decades, as they sought to explain in terms of clear rules the attitudinal shift announced in *New Brunswick Liquor.*

Already in that decision it was evident that the rationale for deference had both substantive and formal elements. The substantive element of expertise was relevant, but so too was the formal element, the privative clause; but what of situations where there is expertise without a privative clause, or a privative clause without expertise? Do form and authority (the privative clause) trump substance and reason (expertise)? Meanwhile, the patent unreasonableness standard was deferential, but its scope and meaning were uncertain. In what cases would it apply, and in what circumstances would a decision fail to meet the standard for, say, want of convincing reasons? Where did deference begin and end, and was this to be assessed by formal or substantive criteria, drawn from an authoritative source or based in reason? In terms of the fault lines of form/substance, deference/nondeference, and reason/authority, *New Brunswick Liquor* was somewhat clumsily poised. With the landscape of judicial review shifting as more bodies became susceptible to court oversight on a growing range of issues, this was an uncomfortable posture: deference to labour boards, as a general principle, would presumably be extended by analogy to other bodies that perhaps did not deserve the same degree of judicial reticence.

The primary challenge following *New Brunswick Liquor* was determining the continuing relevance of jurisdiction. The difficulties presented by the concept of jurisdictional error are highlighted by the mid-1980s Supreme Court decision in *Syndicat des employés de production du Québec et de l'Acadie v Canada Labour Relations Board.*[34] The dispute turned on whether a refusal to work overtime amounted to an unlawful strike. The board concluded that it did. Two parts of the board's order were challenged. In one part, the board ordered immediate compliance by workers in two geographic areas, but not a third; and in another part, the board ordered the parties to submit to arbitration.

The union made an ambitious argument that the existence of a strike was a condition precedent to the board's jurisdiction. Justice Jean Beetz turned this argument aside with ease, describing "the question of the existence of a strike and of its legality" as falling "within the special expertise of the Board."[35] Absent a "manifestly unreasonable" error, the board's answer to these questions could not be disturbed by a court.[36]

Yet Beetz also acknowledged the continued vibrancy of the concept of jurisdictional error: "Such an error, even if committed in the best possible good faith, will result nonetheless in the decision containing it being set aside."[37] He quashed the second part of the board's order on the basis that the board's empowering statute did not vest in it the power to refer disputes to arbitration. Indeed, the board's order "infringe[d] the rules of interpretation" and led to a result "contrary to the intent of the legislator."[38] With jurisdictional error lurking in the background, more than an attitudinal shift was required.[39] A paradigm shift was necessary.

When it came, interestingly, the paradigm shift was effected by Beetz in *Union des employés de service, local 298 v Bibeault*,[40] yet another labour relations case. This time, the issue was whether a union's certification survived the award of a public contract to a different enterprise. Both a labour commissioner and a labour board found that it had. Beetz continued to accept that a decision maker who commits a jurisdictional error acts outside the powers granted to it and is thus liable to see its decision struck down on judicial review.[41] He acknowledged, however, the significant difficulties in applying the concept of jurisdictional error and decried its tendency to lead courts to ask themselves the wrong question in judicial review cases. Rather than asking: "Is this a preliminary or collateral question to the exercise of the tribunal's power?" a court should ask: "Did the legislator intend the question to be within the jurisdiction conferred on the tribunal?"[42]

It was necessary to formulate a workable test for determining whether a question was jurisdictional in nature. Beetz found a solution in the Supreme Court's growing acceptance of the relative institutional competence of administrative decision makers. The formal and substantive reasons for deference provided a way to answer the key question of legislative intent: Did the legislature intend that the decision maker, or the court, should make the decision at issue? To answer this question, Beetz held, a court should look at "the wording of the enactment conferring jurisdiction on the administrative tribunal ... the purpose of the statute creating the tribunal, the reason for its existence, the area of expertise of its members and the nature of the problem before the tribunal."[43] Formal and substantive reasons for deference would be revealed by this analysis.

Applying this new "pragmatic and functional" analysis,[44] Beetz identified a jurisdictional question. The decision makers had "no special expertise" in defining and applying "the concepts of alienation and operation by another" because these were "civil law concepts" falling within the judicial domain:[45] "[T]he legislative context ... and the area of expertise of the labour commissioner clearly indicate that the legislator did not intend the commissioner's decision as to the existence of an alienation or operation by another of an undertaking to be conclusive."[46] On the facts, the decision maker's desire to protect the union's certification could not overcome the plain language of the statute.

This opened Beetz up to the objection that the pragmatic and functional analysis was a wolf in sheep's clothing, simply a more complicated way to reach results that achieved the end of strictly confining the limits of administrative decision makers' authority.[47] However, requiring judges to apply a pragmatic and functional analysis had the benefit of requiring them to justify their decisions to intervene in light of the language of the whole of the statute and the relative expertise of the administrative decision maker in question.[48] Judges could no longer simply incant the magic words "jurisdictional error" and proceed to quash a decision with which they did not agree.[49] Short of the outright abolition of the concept of jurisdictional error, a pragmatic and functional analysis, the application of which focuses judicial attention on the formal and substantive reasons for deference, was the best way to secure autonomy for administrative bodies.

The pragmatic and functional analysis reached its logical conclusion in the Supreme Court's decision in *Pushpanathan v Canada (Minister of Citizenship and Immigration)*.[50] Justice Michel Bastarache outlined a multi-factor test designed to require justification for judicial intervention in terms of legislative intent, "a bold judicial venture designed to infuse jurisdiction with meaningful normative content."[51] Only those questions the legislature intended to reserve to the courts should be treated as jurisdictional, to be determined by reference to four factors: 1) the presence or absence of a privative clause or right of appeal;[52] 2) the relative expertise of the decision maker; 3) the purpose of the statutory framework; and 4) the nature of the question at issue. These four factors would point a court to the application of one of three standards: 1) the interventionist standard of "correctness," which would allow the court to substitute its judgment for that of the decision maker; 2) the deferential standard of "patent unreasonableness," where judicial intervention would be available only in extreme circumstances; and 3) the in-the-middle standard of "reasonableness *simpliciter,*" neither especially hands-on nor especially hands-off.

Jurisdictional error as a stand-alone concept was gutted.[53] "Jurisdiction" became "simply descriptive of a provision for which the proper standard of review is correctness, based on the outcome of the pragmatic and functional analysis": "In other words, 'jurisdictional error' is simply an error on an issue with respect to which, according to the outcome of the pragmatic and functional analysis, the tribunal must make a correct interpretation and to which no deference will be shown."[54] To say that a statutory provision was jurisdictional and required judicial review on a standard of correctness was simply to say that, on an application of the pragmatic and functional analysis, the question was one for the courts, not for the administrative decision maker. This was a triumph of substance over form.

Deference continued to be controversial, however. Questions of law were said to invite judicial intervention in some circumstances regardless of the merits of the administrative decision maker's interpretation.[55]

Consider the Supreme Court case of *Canada (Attorney General) v Mossop.*[56] The applicant here sought to take bereavement leave after the death of his partner's father. His request was refused. Both the applicant and his partner were male and the collective agreement in force at the applicant's place of work provided only for bereavement leave for opposite-sex unmarried couples. The applicant complained that the treatment of same-sex couples was discriminatory, a complaint upheld by the Canadian Human Rights Tribunal. The tribunal's view was that this amounted to discrimination based on "family status."[57]

A majority of the Supreme Court of Canada refused to defer to the tribunal. Writing for the majority on this point, Justice Gérard La Forest justified his position in the following terms:

> The superior expertise of a human rights tribunal relates to fact-finding and adjudication in a human rights context. It does not extend to general questions of law such as the one at issue in this case. These are ultimately matters within the province of the judiciary, and involve concepts of

statutory interpretation and general legal reasoning which the courts must be supposed competent to perform. The courts cannot abdicate this duty to the tribunal. They must, therefore, review the tribunal's decisions on questions of this kind on the basis of correctness, not on a standard of reasonability.[58]

There were features that distinguished *Mossop* from other cases: there was no privative clause protecting the tribunal, it was subject to review where it had "erred in law,"[59] and it operated in an area in which courts had long claimed a specialized expertise. Nonetheless, *Mossop* stood as an endorsement of judicial supremacy. General questions of law were in the judicial domain. On matters involving the "concepts of statutory interpretation," only a judicial writ would run.[60]

NEITHER PRAGMATIC NOR FUNCTIONAL

Implementing the pragmatic and functional approach proved very difficult. The failure to do so satisfactorily led to the Supreme Court's reformulation of judicial review doctrine in *Dunsmuir v New Brunswick*.[61]

As we have seen, the multi-factor test was eventually accompanied by multiple standards of review. Applying the pragmatic and functional analysis would indicate to a court whether to apply the correctness, reasonableness *simpliciter,* or patent unreasonableness standard. Correctness was always easy to define: it allowed the court to substitute its judgment for that of the administrative decision maker. Maintaining two distinct standards of reasonableness was a greater challenge.[62] Patent unreasonableness was said to be a "very strict test" met only by a decision that was "clearly irrational, that is to say evidently not in accordance with reason."[63] A decision would have to be "so flawed that no amount of curial deference can justify letting it stand," in which case, however, the defect "once identified, can be explained simply and easily, leaving no real possibility of doubting that the decision is defective."[64] Applying the standard of reasonableness *simpliciter* required a court to ask whether the decision maker had produced "reasons that can stand up to a somewhat probing examination."[65] Application of this standard was said to require "deferential self-discipline."[66] Intervention would be justifiable "only if there is no line of analysis within the given reasons that could reasonably lead the tribunal from the evidence before it to the conclusion at which it arrived."[67]

In a devastating set of concurring reasons in *Toronto (City) v Canadian Union of Public Employees, Local 79*,[68] Justice Louis LeBel identified "significant practical problems inherent in distinguishing meaningfully between the two standards."[69] It had been suggested that the magnitude of the error was the defining characteristic of a patently unreasonable decision. Yet, LeBel recalled, one judge queried "how helpful it is to substitute one adjectival phrase for another and define patent unreasonableness in terms of rational indefensibility. It seems to me that this simply injects one more opportunity for ambiguity into a test which is already fraught with ambiguity."[70] A purely linguistic test was thus liable to invite impressionistic conclusions from courts. It had also been suggested that patent unreasonableness depended on the obviousness of the error.[71] The suggestion would have to be that hidden or hard-to-find but very serious errors would not render a decision unreasonable. But, LeBel concluded, this would presumably require recourse to a minimally searching form of judicial review, which would in turn raise "a more theoretical quandary: the difficulty of articulating why a defect that is obvious on the face of a decision should present more of an imperative for court intervention than a latent defect."[72] Rule-of-law considerations counted against judicial laxity with respect to illogical or irrational decisions, however deeply the illogicalities or irrationalities were hidden.

As a trial judge put it,

attempting to follow the [Supreme] Court's distinctions between "patently unreasonable," "reasonable" and "correct," one feels at times as though one is watching a juggler juggle three transparent objects. Depending on the way the light falls, sometimes one thinks one can see the objects. Other times one cannot and, indeed, wonders whether there are really three distinct objects at all.[73]

A Federal Court judge complained:

> As is becoming increasingly common in administrative law cases, a prodigious amount of time was spent by the parties, at both the hearing before me and in their written submissions, regarding the correct standard of review to be applied. Although counsel did an admirable job of analysing the jurisprudence in order to delineate the fine and often obscure nuances between the concepts of patent unreasonableness and reasonableness *simpliciter,* it is obvious that what has developed in this field of law is an unwieldy framework which is unnecessarily complex and difficult to apply.[74]

Confusion about the multiple standards of review provided an impetus for reform. Substance had won over form but implementing it – identifying the deference that would replace jurisdiction and give effect to legislative intent – proved challenging, as did prising the viselike grip of jurisdiction from the case law.[75] In the lower courts in the *Dunsmuir* case itself, "no one could agree on the appropriate standard of review."[76]

The reforms that came in *Dunsmuir* were unannounced. David Dunsmuir was a lawyer (and part-time Elvis Presley impersonator)[77] who had been appointed as a court clerk in New Brunswick. His relationship with his superiors was not a happy one and he was eventually removed from his office. He successfully grieved his dismissal under provincial legislation: an adjudicator reinstated him on the basis that he had been treated procedurally unfairly. Before the New Brunswick courts, Dunsmuir had no such luck, but Clarence Bennett, the junior lawyer working on his file (now a very senior lawyer in the leading Atlantic law firm Stewart McKelvey LLP), saw an opportunity to seek leave to appeal to the Supreme Court due to the confusion about the standard of review. After "pestering" the senior lawyer, Gordon Petrie,

QC, with a barrage of memos, Bennett persuaded him that a trip to Ottawa was a realistic possibility.[78] Petrie had little interest in standard of review – he thought it was a distraction from the main issue – and avoided discussing it in oral argument:

> [He] did not intend to address the standard of review at all in his oral submission before the Supreme Court of Canada. He was more than 30 minutes into his submission when the issue was finally raised by the Hon. Justice Louise Charron who said: "*In your plea to get yourself before this court you suggested that the three standards of review were confusing. Could you help us on standard of review?*" Mr. Petrie wryly replied, "*Could I help you?*" After pausing for laughter he said, "*I'm sorry. You got yourself into it, you get ...*" invoking more laughter before making passing comments about the strength of the privative clause and moving on. Other members of the court attempted to pick up Justice Charron's line of questioning and Mr. Petrie simply provided cursory comments and went back to the issues he planned to argue.[79]

Undeterred, Justices Bastarache and LeBel announced in the opening paragraph of their joint majority reasons in *Dunsmuir v New Brunswick*[80] that it was time for a "reassessment" of the "troubling question" of judicial review of administrative action, for the court had failed to identify "solutions that provide real guidance for litigants, counsel, administrative decision makers or judicial review judges."[81] Substance's victory was, perhaps, short-lived.

The three standards were reduced to two, correctness and reasonableness. Reasonableness was described in elegant terms as requiring a court to inquire into "the existence of justification, transparency and intelligibility within the decision-making process" and "whether the decision falls within a range of possible, acceptable outcomes which are defensible in respect of the facts and law."[82]

The multi-factor pragmatic and functional analysis was also sidelined, in favour of a categorical "standard of review" analysis.[83] For example, "[d]eference will usually result where a tribunal is interpreting its own statute or statutes closely connected to its function, with which it will have particular familiarity."[84] In this way, *Dunsmuir* sought at first glance to draw sharp lines between the domains of deference and nondeference. Here, however, first impressions mislead.

Peppered throughout the Supreme Court's discussion in *Dunsmuir* of how courts should determine the appropriate standard of review are references to certain shortcuts or presumptions that should be borne in mind. For example, the presence of a privative clause would be a "strong indication of review pursuant to the reasonableness standard."[85] On the correctness side of the ledger, the court noted that previous jurisprudence had established that correctness would be the appropriate standard of review for several types of question. Nevertheless, the court expressly retained the four factors that comprised the standard of review analysis,[86] and even applied them to the facts of *Dunsmuir*.[87]

That there was some conceptual confusion underlying the court's analysis is suggested by its infelicitous observation that where a question of "fact, discretion or policy" is subject to review, "deference will usually apply automatically."[88] It is worth pausing for a moment to consider the linguistic wonder that is the thing that "usually happens automatically." A sliding door that "usually opens automatically" is likely to lead to puzzled pedestrians at best and bruised noses at worst. A company that "usually deposits paycheques automatically" is unlikely to gain the trust of its employees. At least with respect to this category of decision, it is rather unclear what the court was trying to say.

I do not raise this linguistic problem purely out of mischief. It points to deeper problems with *Dunsmuir*. As Justice Ian Binnie observed portentously in his concurring reasons:

> The judicial sensitivity to different levels of respect (or deference) required in different situations is quite legitimate. "Contextualizing" a single standard of review will shift the debate (slightly) from choosing *between* two standards of reasonableness that each represent a different level of deference to a debate *within* a single standard of reasonableness

to determine the appropriate level of deference. In practice, the result of today's decision may be like the bold innovations of a traffic engineer that in the end do no more than shift rush hour congestion from one road intersection to another without any overall saving to motorists in time or expense.[89]

At the same time that it purported to establish presumptive categories to which either reasonableness or correctness would be appropriately applied, the court maintained the four-factor standard of review analysis. It used the words "usually" and "generally" on several occasions.[90] It gave no guidance as to when the presumptions would be rebutted or displaced, or what weight the presumptions should be given, which is problematic: "Creating a presumption without providing guidance on how one could tell whether it has been rebutted does not ... provide any assistance to reviewing courts."[91] The Supreme Court gave no guidance either on the order in which a court should proceed. Should it consider the presumptions first and then the four factors? Or should it consider the four factors first and then the presumptions? On first sight, the second formulation might seem at odds with the court's overall approach, but there is a logic to it: first, the four-factor standard of review analysis would be applied, but if it produced an anomalous result, then reference to the presumptions would correct the anomaly. In some anomalous case, the four-factor analysis might suggest correctness, even with respect to a fact-laden decision, but the presumption that factual determinations attract deference would counsel reasonableness.[92] In any event, the Supreme Court did not specify which approach to follow. It sought to straddle the fault line between form and substance – but the merest tremor could cause the judges to lose their footing.[93]

The concept of reasonableness had its own problems. The doyen of Canada's administrative law community suggested, shortly after *Dunsmuir*, that the effect of the decision was to "simply postpone the complexity [of the multi-factor test] to a second stage, that of identifying where, on a spectrum of reasonableness, the reviewing court should locate itself in assessing the decision under attack."[94] Indeed, as reasonableness displaced correctness and became the dominant standard of review, such problems came to the fore. For all the many pages and paragraphs the Supreme Court had devoted over the years to the selection of the standard of review, it had much less to say about the content of reasonableness. What makes a decision reasonable or unreasonable? On what basis can a court say that a decision affecting Alexander Vavilov or Thanh Tam Tran should be set aside? All anyone had to go on were these two paragraphs from *Dunsmuir:*

> Reasonableness is a deferential standard animated by the principle that underlies the development of the two previous standards of reasonableness: certain questions that come before administrative tribunals do not lend themselves to one specific, particular result. Instead, they may give rise to a number of possible, reasonable conclusions. Tribunals have a margin of appreciation within the range of acceptable and rational solutions. A court conducting a review for reasonableness inquires into the qualities that make a decision reasonable, referring both to the process of articulating the reasons and to outcomes. In judicial review, reasonableness is concerned mostly with the existence of justification, transparency and intelligibility within the decision-making process. But it is also concerned with whether the decision falls within a range of possible, acceptable outcomes which are defensible in respect of the facts and law.
>
> ...
>
> What does deference mean in this context? Deference is both an attitude of the court and a requirement of the law of judicial review. It does not mean that courts are subservient to the determinations of decision makers, or that courts must show blind reverence to their interpretations, or that they may be content to pay lip service to the concept of reasonableness review while in fact imposing their own view. Rather, deference imports respect for the decision-making process of adjudicative bodies with regard to both the facts and the law ... We agree with David Dyzenhaus where he states that the concept of "deference as respect" requires of the courts "not submission but a respectful attention to the reasons offered or which could be offered in support of a decision": "The

Politics of Deference: Judicial Review and Democracy," in M. Taggart, ed, *The Province of Administrative Law* (1997), 279, at p. 286.[95]

This is all very elegant. But how much guidance does it give to judges deciding real-life cases? Justification, transparency, and intelligibility are fine in theory, but how would one go about operationalizing them in practice across the vast range of decision-making subject to administrative law principles? Here, the fault line between reason and authority is exposed. What of a decision where the reasoning lacks one or more of the hallmarks of justification, transparency, and intelligibility but nonetheless falls within the range of permissible, acceptable outcomes? Those on the authority side of the fault line would more readily uphold such a decision: all that matters is that it falls within the range and is made by the appropriate decision maker. On the reason side of the fault line, however, both the reasons and the outcome would have to be read together, and defective reasoning could lead to a finding that the decision was unlawful. Hence the comment that the lack of guidance on reasonableness review was "the most distressing part" of *Dunsmuir.*[96]

Moreover, the categorical approach soon hardened into an outright presumption that reasonableness will apply when a decision maker is interpreting its constitutive statute.[97] In the early post-*Dunsmuir* period, on each occasion that it granted leave to appeal a provincial court of appeal decision that had identified a question that attracted the correctness standard of review, the Supreme Court of Canada refused to apply the standard of correctness.[98] Even the tantalizing category of "true" jurisdictional error was kept shut. Reasonableness became the dominant standard of review.[99] The fault line between deference and nondeference almost disappeared entirely. Given that the meaning of "deference" was packed into a mere two paragraphs in *Dunsmuir,* trouble inevitably lay ahead.

The uncertain relationship between categories and context and the nebulous content of the reasonableness standard set the scene for the "*Dunsmuir* Decade," when the Supreme Court of Canada's approach to substantive review in administrative law fell into widespread disrepute.

CONCLUSION

In this chapter, we have taken a deep dive into Canadian judicial review. Beginning with the world before deference, we have observed how the concepts of "jurisdiction," "deference," and "legislative intent" have plagued generations of Canadian judges, practising lawyers, academics, students, and ordinary litigants. Deference began with a bang in the *New Brunswick Liquor* decision, but operationalizing deference and marginalizing jurisdiction proved difficult. The Supreme Court of Canada alighted on the so-called pragmatic and functional approach as an operational solution, but it proved neither pragmatic nor functional in its operation. Then there was *Dunsmuir,* but that decision was full of internal tensions and inconsistencies, which were aggravated by the dominance of reasonableness as the default standard of review, given the scanty details offered in *Dunsmuir* about the meaning of reasonableness.

Across these time periods, the fault lines of Canadian administrative law – form/substance, deference/nondeference, and reason/authority – were invariably clearly visible. The formalism of the pre-deference world gave way to the avowedly substantive pragmatic and functional analysis, but it was displaced (to some extent!) by *Dunsmuir.* Deference and nondeference ebbed and flowed, with the courts hesitant about the scope of deference on questions of law, before deference won what seemed like a decisive victory in *Dunsmuir.* Reason and authority were also visible, with the authority side of the fault line particularly well occupied throughout these periods. Privative clauses were an authoritative justification for deference historically, and became an important part of the reasoned approach to standard of review memorialized in the pragmatic and functional analysis. But *Dunsmuir* leaned too heavily on authority over reason, as we shall see in the next chapter. In brief, *Dunsmuir* was on the deference and authority side of those fault lines and precariously balanced over the form/substance fault line. This proved to be an unsustainable posture.

3

The *Dunsmuir* Decade

A S FORESHADOWED IN Chapter 2, the settlement effected
by the *Dunsmuir* decision[1] in 2008 did not provide a lasting
framework for Canadian administrative law.

First, the decision itself was plagued by internal tensions, neither
firmly formalist nor firmly substantivist in its approach to the selection
of the standard of review. The categories were not soundly based, as
became increasingly apparent over time. The Supreme Court of Canada
preferred form, but substance – like a ghoul in a horror movie – kept
rearing its head.

Second, the Supreme Court failed to give meaningful guidance
about reasonableness review, especially so far as the importance of reasons
was concerned. On the one hand, the court took a permissive approach,
upholding decisions on the basis of reasons that "could have been offered" in support of a decision, leading to doctrinal confusion and
morally suboptimal outcomes. On the other hand, judges took starkly
differing approaches to the application of the reasonableness standard,
without explaining, still less justifying, their divergent approaches.

Third, throughout the decade after *Dunsmuir,* the Supreme Court
regularly contradicted itself, or said one thing but then did another,
all to the consternation of courts and practitioners who were observ-
ing the jurisprudence. The lack of guidance on selecting and applying

the standard of review was bad enough, but it was exacerbated by the mounting contradictions and inconsistencies.

Fourth, there was disagreement among the judges on the question of preferring a formal or substantive approach and even on the question of whether deference on questions of law would ever be appropriate. The upshot was a significant lack of guidance to lower courts on how to use the increasingly mangled *Dunsmuir* framework, leading to significant uncertainty and even injustice. By 2018, the Canadian legal community was united in its support for a reformulation of Canadian administrative law.

Of course, the authors of *Dunsmuir* "were not naïve enough to think that it would be the last word on judicial review."[2] In many respects, the troubled decade resulted as much from the contributions of their successors as it did from the words used in *Dunsmuir*. Troubled the decade nonetheless was.

THE TENSIONS IN *DUNSMUIR*

As noted in the previous chapter, *Dunsmuir* had internal tensions, with the majority reasons poised precariously over the form/substance fault line. These tensions were resolved in two ways: first, the Supreme Court treated *Dunsmuir* as setting out a formal, categorical approach to the selection of the standard of review; and, second, the court developed a presumption of reasonableness review to alleviate the difficulties of choosing between the correctness and reasonableness standards. The result was that the court came down on the form side of the form/substance fault line and on the deference side of the deference/non-deference fault line. This represented more or less a complete reversal of the pre–*New Brunswick Liquor* position described in Chapter 2, and, analytically speaking, was accomplished in rather maladroit fashion.

Imperfect Categories

For a categorical approach to function – as it may certainly do in principle[3] – the categories must have sound bases. But the *Dunsmuir* categories were both over- and under-inclusive. The categories were set out by Justice Morris Fish in a 2011 Supreme Court decision, bringing a neat formalism to the *Dunsmuir* framework:

- Correctness applied to 1) constitutional issues; 2) questions of general law both of central importance to the legal system as a whole and outside the adjudicator's specialized area of expertise; 3) the drawing of jurisdictional lines between two or more competing specialized tribunals; and 4) true questions of jurisdiction or *vires*.
- Reasonableness, however, is normally the governing standard where the question at issue: 1) relates to the interpretation of the tribunal's home statute or statutes closely connected to its function, with which it will have particular familiarity; 2) raises issues of fact, discretion, or policy; or 3) involves inextricably intertwined legal and factual issues.[4]

Let us take a closer look at how the categories were over- and under-inclusive, starting with reasonableness category 1.[5] According deference to decision makers' interpretations of their home statutes carries significant appeal. Relative to a court staffed by generalists, a specialist administrative decision maker will often be better able to develop an interpretation of law that coheres with the principles and policies underpinning a statute. However, to state as a rule that *all* such interpretations should be reviewed on a reasonableness standard goes too far. There may be questions relating to the decision maker's home statute that are general in nature and thus not appropriate candidates for deference. As Justice Thomas Cromwell pointedly observed in the Supreme Court case *Alberta (Information and Privacy Commissioner) v Alberta Teachers' Association*,[6] there may be questions relating to the home statute that *should* be subject to review for correctness: "[I]t is hard to imagine where else the limits of a tribunal's delegated power are more likely to be set out."[7]

The approach of the Federal Court of Appeal in *Canada (Attorney General) v Mowat*[8] is instructive (though not authoritative in its result, as the Supreme Court took a different view on appeal, *sub nom Canada (Canadian Human Rights Commission) v Canada (Attorney General)*).[9]

Here, the question was whether the Canadian Human Rights Tribunal had the power to award legal costs to a successful complainant, under its authority to make awards in respect of "any expenses incurred by the victim as a result of the discriminatory practice."[10] The tribunal concluded that it had such power. On review by the Federal Court, a standard of reasonableness was applied to the tribunal's interpretation. However, the Federal Court of Appeal applied a standard of correctness, concluding that the question at issue had no factual component and required no human rights expertise; rather, the tribunal had to determine a "pure question of law, specifically, one that determines the bounds of its authority," with respect to which it had "no institutional or experiential advantage over the Court and [was] no better positioned than the Court."[11] The general approach of the Federal Court of Appeal shows how the "home statute" category was over-inclusive.

On the correctness side of the post-*Dunsmuir* ledger, the categories were also over-inclusive. Consider correctness category 2. With respect to general questions of law, a decision maker may sometimes be more expert than a court. For example, the question at issue in *Metropolitan Life Insurance v International Union of Operating Engineers*[12] – what constituted membership of a trade union – could easily be said to be a question of general law of central importance to the legal system.[13] The phrase "members of a trade union" appears in federal legislation and in numerous provincial statutes.[14] However, a large part of the reason that *Metropolitan Life* is now treated with such disdain[15] is that this is precisely the sort of question on which a labour relations board could easily be said to have more expertise than a generalist court.[16] First, a labour relations board will address such questions on a regular basis and, being staffed by experts in the field, will have an advantage relative to a court in determining which approach to take to the question of membership to best achieve its statutory objectives. Second, different labour relations boards can justifiably take different approaches to the question of membership: it is certainly not self-evident that the same conditions will be present in both Alberta and Newfoundland; different policies may be required to respond to the complexities present in different jurisdictions. Third, as practices in the labour relations community change, it may be prudent for labour relations boards to change their policies, perhaps with input from employer and employee representatives, a possibility foreclosed by national resolution of the question of membership.

It follows that the categories were also under-inclusive in important respects. Deference on a wider range of administrative decisions than that envisaged by the categories is appropriate. Most obviously, an administrative decision maker may be better able than a court to resolve questions of general law and jurisdictional questions. This implies that limiting the categories of decision to which deference should be accorded to factual questions, questions of mixed fact and law, and interpretations of a decision maker's home statute was inappropriate. Simply put, the categories were under-inclusive because they did not capture the full range of decisions on which a standard of review of reasonableness would be appropriate.

Accordingly, there was serious potential for conflict between the categories. *Canada (Canadian Human Rights Commission) v Canada (Attorney General)*[17] provides a good example. Recall that the Federal Court of Appeal held that the Canadian Human Rights Tribunal was not entitled to deference even though it was interpreting a provision in its home statute, because the question of whether the tribunal had the power to award costs was a question of general law. Following the categorical approach, however, it is difficult to see how the question at issue should be categorized. On the one hand, it clearly relates to an interpretation of the decision maker's home statute; on the other hand, it could be said to be a question of general law: many decision makers would be interested in the scope of their authority to award costs to successful claimants or participants.[18] At the Supreme Court of Canada, the conflict between the categories was ultimately resolved by reference to factors external to the categories. For the court, Justices Louis LeBel and Thomas Cromwell held that the question of whether legal costs incurred because of discriminatory conduct constituted expenses within the meaning of the home statute was one "within the core function and expertise" of the tribunal.[19] They noted that the question was "inextricably intertwined with the Tribunal's mandate and expertise to make factual findings relating to discrimination."[20] They added that given the tribunal's familiarity with the making of such factual determinations, the tribunal was well positioned to make assessments as to the necessity of awarding legal costs.[21] Finally, they emphasized that the question required a fact-sensitive inquiry.[22] In other words, to determine the appropriate standard of review, LeBel and Cromwell employed factors from the supposedly sidelined standard of review analysis: expertise, the factual nature of the question, and the purpose of the statutory provision in question.[23]

Thus, despite having been marginalized, the contextual factors of the standard of review analysis nonetheless played an important role in ensuring that decisions were assigned to the appropriate categories. On the face of it, form had triumphed over substance. On closer inspection, however, substance was the real winner.

The Hopeless Search for "True" Questions of Jurisdiction

The scope of some of the categories was also unclear. As Justice Marie Deschamps rightly protested in *Smith v Alliance Pipeline Ltd:* "[T]he development of any category of question that would tend to eliminate the need for a more fulsome analysis of the standard of review has to be grounded in a defensible rationale."[24] But the soundness of *Dunsmuir*'s categories was always dubious, "'true' questions of jurisdiction" chief among them.[25]

We have seen in the previous chapters that it has never been possible to define jurisdictional issues with any exactitude. In *Public Service Alliance of Canada v Canadian Federal Pilots Association,*[26] Justice John Evans of the Federal Court of Appeal attempted to narrow the category of jurisdictional questions established by *Dunsmuir* almost out of existence, with the powerful admonition that "it is too late in the development of administrative law in Canada for an applicant to invoke the ghost of jurisdiction past to inveigle the Court into reviewing for correctness a tribunal's interpretation of a provision in its enabling statute."[27] For good or ill, however, the judges expressly established a category of "'true' questions of jurisdiction or *vires*" in *Dunsmuir,* and then twice refused to abolish the category in the decade after *Dunsmuir.*

In *Alberta (Information and Privacy Commissioner) v Alberta Teachers' Association*,[28] Justice Marshall Rothstein, for the majority of the Supreme Court, indicated openness to the argument that the category of jurisdictional questions should be abolished entirely, but went no further. He pronounced himself "unable to provide a definition" of such a question[29] but emphasized that true jurisdictional questions are "exceptional"[30] and concluded without further explanation that this was not such an exceptional case.[31] In *Canada (Canadian Human Rights Commission) v Canada (Attorney General)*, Justice Clément Gascon described the category as "slippery" and as being "on life support," but declined to pull the plug.[32]

In a sense, this judicial reticence did not really matter. The decision in *Quebec (Attorney General) v Guérin* exemplifies the point.[33] Three members of the Supreme Court (Justices Russell Brown and Malcolm Rowe concurring, and Justice Suzanne Côté dissenting) purported to identify a jurisdictional question, but did not succeed in actually identifying one. At issue here was a classic labour arbitration problem. Ronald Guérin was a radiologist in the province of Quebec. The province had signed an agreement with the Fédération des médecins spécialistes du Québec, a body that represents consultant doctors. The *Health Insurance Act*[34] provided for the conclusion of such agreements and, in section 54, stated that a "dispute resulting from the interpretation or application of an agreement" would be a matter exclusively for arbitration. The agreement contained provisions relating to a "digitization fee," designed to incentivize innovation. Dr. Guérin asked an arbitrator to determine that certain radiology clinics fell within the scope of the agreement and were eligible to claim the digitization fee. The arbitrator declined, essentially on the basis that only the parties to the agreement – the province and the federation – had the power to designate laboratories that would be eligible for the digitization fee.

In times past (and in other countries), this might well have been characterized as a matter going to the arbitrator's jurisdiction. But as the majority explained, this turned on an interpretation of "enabling legislation and related documents," well within the presumption of reasonableness review.[35] Given that the decision maker was interpreting the Act and the agreement – and how often, do you think, a decision maker must stray further than its home statute – reasonableness review applied. As such, the standard of review was reasonableness and the arbitrator's conclusion was reasonable.[36] In addition, the arbitrator's conclusion that Dr. Guérin did not have standing to bring a claim to arbitration was reasonable.[37]

Justices Brown and Rowe concurred in the result but reached it by a different route. In their view, "[t]he question of whether the arbitrator had the authority to decide on Dr. Guérin's matter was ... clearly jurisdictional."[38] However, as is often the case in delineating matters that go to jurisdiction and those that do not, the conclusion is based more on assertion than on logic. Brown and Rowe's real reason and justification for identifying a "true" question of jurisdiction that had to be answered correctly can be found in the following passage:

> The matter raised by Dr. Guérin – specifically, a dispute concerning how the agreement between the Fédération des médecins spécialistes du Québec ("Fédération") and the Minister of Health and Social Services operated with respect to his facility – was *clearly* a "dispute resulting from the interpretation or application of an agreement."[39]

For Brown and Rowe, the question before the arbitrator *required* a particular answer. But the concept of jurisdiction is not doing any analytical work here. Their conclusion was driven by their *interpretation* of the statute and agreement: only one answer was possible and, as a result, the arbitrator had to give the correct answer. Again, however, this does not demonstrate that the question was jurisdictional. It simply demonstrates that, on the concurring judges' approach, the range of possible, acceptable outcomes contained only one interpretation. Indeed, it would have been possible for Brown and Rowe to have come to precisely the same conclusion by applying a reasonableness standard: that the range of reasonable outcomes contained only one possible, acceptable interpretation. So what, then, *would* a "true" jurisdictional error look like? We will never know.

The "Black Hole" of Reasonableness Review

At the risk of jolting the reader, it can be said that the coherence of the categories did not matter all that much.[40] This is because of the presumption of reasonableness review that applied to interpretations of home statutes. Reasonableness review of decisions taken under a decision maker's home statute was the "black hole" of the categorical approach, its gravitational pull so powerful that it almost swallowed whole the other categories, especially those of "true" questions of jurisdiction and questions of general law of central importance to the legal system.

Consider *Alberta Teachers':* the Information and Privacy Commissioner commenced an investigation into complaints that data had been unlawfully disclosed, an investigation that was to be completed within ninety days.[41] Between the commencement of the investigation and the completion of the inquiry, the commissioner employed its power to extend the ninety-day timeline. This was done, however, only some twenty-two months after the initial complaint had been received.

It is difficult to imagine a truer question of jurisdiction or *vires.* If the commissioner failed to comply with the statutory preconditions, it seemed to follow that jurisdiction was lost. Yet Justice Rothstein, for the majority of the Supreme Court, did not classify the question as one falling in the jurisdictional category.[42] He noted that the decision was "squarely" within the "specialized expertise" of the decision maker; that the decision maker had "significant familiarity" with the issue, which was "specific" to the commissioner's home statute; and that the interests of the parties in the conclusion of inquiries in a timely manner, in being kept informed, and in the effect of automatic termination of privacy investigations fell within the commissioner's role, which "centres upon balancing" the rights of individuals to privacy against organizations' needs to disclose information in certain circumstances.[43]

Yet what was true of the commissioner will be true of all other decision makers. Supposedly jurisdictional questions will almost always be part of a decision maker's home statute, for where else would one expect to find limits on a decision maker's powers? And the Supreme Court emphasized in *Dunsmuir* that even where the decision maker is interpreting a statute "closely connected" to its home statute, deference should be accorded.[44]

It might be argued that no deference should be accorded to a decision maker's interpretation of a statute far removed from its core expertise,[45] and that such interpretive questions are "jurisdictional" in nature. This argument is doomed to failure, however.[46] Once it has interpreted a "foreign" statute, an administrative decision maker will then have to apply it in its own regulatory domain. This application will necessarily turn on the decision maker's interpretation of its home statute and its consideration of the facts placed before it. It is singularly unlikely to "involve any readily extricable question of more general application" requiring judicial intervention on a standard of correctness.[47]

Furthermore, where a decision maker interprets a statute that is not its own, its starting point will always be its home statute. If it interprets its home statute as requiring it to look to another statute, that interpretation is entitled to deference. If the other statute is thus in turn "closely connected" to the decision maker's home statute, the decision maker's interpretation of the other statute is entitled to deference. Once a decision maker decides that a statute is closely connected to its function, it must surely follow that the statute *is* closely connected to its function – and therefore the interpretation of it is also entitled to deference – *unless* the interpretation of its home statute is unreasonable. There was no way to escape the black hole created by the presumption of deference.

A similar problem plagued the category of questions of general law of central importance to the legal system. Most of the time, a question said to be of general importance – because of its effect on a large number of people,[48] or because it is common to multiple regulatory regimes[49] – will also arise within the specialized jurisdiction of the decision maker in question. Some questions sneaked into this category – solicitor-client privilege,[50] parliamentary privilege,[51] the state's obligation of religious neutrality[52] – but they were few and far between. In each of these situations, indeed, uniformity is absolutely critical: for example, if legal advice is protected before a labour arbitrator but not before a freedom of information commissioner, such that the scope of privilege depends on the identity of the decision maker, lawyers would be much more cautious about giving advice, undermining the very purpose of solicitor-client privilege. But this was a narrow set of questions.

Moreover, the category of constitutional questions offered no means of escape either. Consider *Doré v Barreau du Québec*,[53] a Supreme Court case involving a disciplinary sanction issued against a lawyer by his law society. The lawyer contended that his freedom of expression had been infringed and that the decision to sanction him was unconstitutional because it did not satisfy the exigencies of the "*Oakes* test."[54] The court rejected this argument, however, concluding that a decision maker need only reach a "proportionate balancing" between its statutory objectives and an individual's Charter rights in the exercise of its functions.[55] Deference was to be accorded to the decision maker in its application of constitutional principles in the context of its regulatory mandate.[56] In subsequent cases, the court leavened the application of reasonableness review in the constitutional domain with the exhortation that, in such circumstances, "reasonableness requires proportionality."[57] Indeed, "if there was an option or avenue *reasonably* open to the decision maker that would reduce the impact on the protected right while still permitting him or her to sufficiently further the relevant statutory objectives, the decision would not fall within a range of reasonable outcomes."[58] Nonetheless, despite a more generous application of the reasonableness standard, even the Charter did not escape the black hole of reasonableness review.

It was only at the very highest level of generality that constitutional questions were reserved to the courts. For example, in *Saskatchewan (Human Rights Commission) v Whatcott*,[59] the Supreme Court interpreted the anti-hate-speech provision of the *Saskatchewan Human Rights Code*[60] to render it compliant with the constitutional guarantee of freedom of expression.[61] This was a pure question of constitutional interpretation. When it came, however, to the application of the reinterpreted provision to the facts of the case, a reasonableness standard applied. In determining whether William Whatcott's homophobic pamphlets breached the statutory prohibition on hate speech, the decision maker was entitled to deference.[62]

Even legislatures ended up being consumed by the black hole of reasonableness review. As we saw in Chapter 2, it had long been accepted that deference could sometimes be appropriate on statutory appeals from specialist decision makers. But what about appeals that were limited to points of law or jurisdiction, involving questions well within the judicial wheelhouse? In a system of judicial review respectful of a legislature's considered choices, one would expect correctness review to apply in such circumstances. But the presumption of reasonableness review was so powerful as to overcome even narrowly tailored appeal clauses.

The key case here was *Edmonton (City) v Edmonton East (Capilano) Shopping Centres Ltd.*[63] The underlying question was catnip for common law courts: whether an Assessment Review Board could increase the value of a property assessment where a taxpayer had applied for a decrease in the assessed value. Here, the assessment was almost doubled (from $22 million to $41 million), an outcome greeted no doubt with consternation by the taxpayer, who may also have legitimately observed that in the common law tradition, the appeal rights of state bodies are often more limited than those of the individuals subject to their authority. In the Alberta Court of Appeal, Justice Frans Slatter had insisted that a "mechanical and formalistic" approach to judicial review was inappropriate, preferring to identify several contextual factors (including, obviously, the existence of an appeal clause) that justified the application of a correctness standard. In his view, the property assessment could not be increased: "There is no room in the complaint procedure for a municipality to effectively mount a cross-complaint and seek an increase in the assessment."[64]

At the Supreme Court, a five-judge majority defended the *Dunsmuir* framework, and in particular the presumption of reasonableness review that had been grafted onto it, against an attack by four dissenters. For Justice Andromache Karakatsanis, who wrote the majority reasons, "the principles in *Dunsmuir* should provide the foundation for any future direction," although "any recalibration of our jurisprudence should await full submissions."[65]

Here, there was no reason not to apply the presumption of reasonableness review, because the board was interpreting its home statute.

Indeed, "recognizing issues arising on statutory appeals as a new category to which the correctness standard applies – as the Court of Appeal did in this case – would go against strong jurisprudence from this Court."[66] Karakatsanis took a firm line on the primacy of the categorical approach: "The contextual approach can generate uncertainty and endless litigation concerning the standard of review."[67] That may be so, but the wholesale reliance on presumed expertise was troubling to many observers.[68]

The dissenters, for whom Justices Brown and Côté wrote, were more expansive. Correctness was the appropriate standard based on a contextual approach: "An approach to the standard of review analysis that relies exclusively on categories and eschews any role for context risks introducing the vice of formalism into the law of judicial review."[69] In administrative law cases, it is always necessary to ask "what the appropriate standard of review is for *this* question decided by *this* decision maker":[70] "The contextual standard of review analysis ensures that legislative intent is respected and the rule of law is protected when courts review decisions of administrative actors."[71] Moreover, "[a]n administrative decision maker is entitled to deference on the basis of expertise only if the question before it falls within the scope of its expertise, whether specific or institutional."[72] The presumption of reasonableness review for interpretations of a decision maker's home statute, however, assumes that expertise is ever present, and "in strengthening the presumption by ignoring or explaining away any factors that might rebut it, the majority risks making this presumption irrebuttable."[73]

Here, "the wording of this statutory appeal clause, in combination with the legislative scheme, points to the conclusion that the legislature intended that a more exacting standard of review be applied to questions appealed to the [courts]."[74] The statute provided for an appeal with leave, on questions of law or jurisdiction of sufficient importance and with sufficient prospects of success to merit a hearing.[75] In addition, the accompanying remedial powers indicated that the courts were to have the capacity to correct legal or jurisdictional errors,[76] and the legislative scheme was designed to provide unity of interpretation across municipalities.[77] Finally, the board did not have expertise in statutory interpretation but rather in "complex matters of valuation of property," a point underscored by the form of the statutory appeal clause: "While the Board may have familiarity with the application of the assessment provisions of the Act, the legislature has recognized that the Board's specialized expertise does not necessarily extend to general questions of law and jurisdiction."[78]

Edmonton East was a key moment in the *Dunsmuir* decade. The majority prevailed only narrowly, and the composition of the Supreme Court was rapidly changing. Of the nine judges who had decided *Dunsmuir,* only Chief Justice Beverley McLachlin (who would retire in 2018) and Justice Rosalie Abella remained. Change in personnel made jurisprudential change more plausible. And *Edmonton East* itself was problematic, not just because the black hole of reasonableness review swallowed up a considered legislative choice about judicial oversight of the administrative state (where it joined true questions of jurisdiction, most general questions of law, and a large number of constitutional questions) but also because of how the reasonableness standard was applied.

The majority and minority groups took different views on the underlying question, the dissenters agreeing with the Alberta Court of Appeal that the authorities may not ask the board to increase the assessment. The majority preferred the view that the board's interpretation was reasonable – but the board had never given reasons for its interpretation! As Justice Karakatsanis explained, "it is hardly surprising the Board did not explain why it was of the view that it could increase the assessment: the Company expressly conceded the point."[79]

There followed[80] a detailed discussion of "the reasons which *could be* offered in support of" the board's interpretation.[81] Karakatsanis pointed to multiple features of the elaborate statutory scheme that might be said to support the alternative interpretation, and explained how each of them was nonetheless consistent with the board's interpretation (if one can call it that), much of which was supported by reference to a decision made by another body that "formerly" had appellate jurisdiction from the board.[82] This, frankly, was quite bizarre. Who knows what the board would have said if these points had been made to it.

This leads to the second major theme of the *Dunsmuir* decade: the Supreme Court's confused approach to reasonableness review.

CONFUSION LAYERED UPON CONFUSION

So much for the tensions internal to *Dunsmuir*. Rather than resolve the tensions, the Supreme Court in the post-*Dunsmuir* period layered confusion upon confusion by introducing further difficulties into the selection and application of the standard of review.[83] Given the strength of the presumption of reasonableness review, and *Dunsmuir*'s ambiguous position in relation to the reason/authority fault line, trouble lay ahead.

Lack of Guidance on Reasonableness Review: What Are Reasons?

Paragraph 47 of *Dunsmuir* was instantly well known for its elaboration of a unified standard of reasonableness, with two prongs. Administrative decision makers must make decisions that bear the hallmarks of "justification, transparency and intelligibility" and that fall within a "range of reasonable outcomes."

Less well known, at least initially, was the rhetorical flourish in the following paragraph. Citing Professor David Dyzenhaus, Justices Michel Bastarache and Louis LeBel noted that courts should pay "respectful attention to the reasons offered or which could be offered in support of a decision."[84] Dyzenhaus's concern was that courts should not intervene in situations where a decision maker had not necessarily joined all the dots in its reasoning in a way satisfactory to a judicial mind. And the Supreme Court signalled its understanding of this concern in *Newfoundland and Labrador Nurses' Union v Newfoundland and Labrador (Treasury Board)*.[85] Writing for a unanimous court, Justice Abella noted that "decision makers routinely render decisions in their respective spheres of expertise, using concepts and language often unique to their areas and rendering decisions that are often counter-intuitive to a generalist."[86] Her appreciation of context led her to a sensible doctrinal prescription:

Reasons may not include all the arguments, statutory provisions, jurisprudence or other details the reviewing judge would have preferred,
but that does not impugn the validity of either the reasons or the result
under a reasonableness analysis.[87]

This passage is unobjectionable. It comports with the spirit of Dyzenhaus's essay on deference. This passage also does not invite judicial
abdication. As explained by Justice Donald Rennie of the Federal Court
in *Komolafe v Canada (Citizenship and Immigration):*

Newfoundland Nurses is not an open invitation to the Court to provide
reasons that were not given, nor is it licence to guess what findings
might have been made or to speculate as to what the tribunal might
have been thinking. This is particularly so where the reasons are silent
on a critical issue. It is ironic that *Newfoundland Nurses,* a case which
at its core is about deference and standard of review, is urged as authority
for the supervisory court to do the task that the decision maker did not
do, to supply the reasons that might have been given and make findings
of fact that were not made. This is to turn the jurisprudence on its head.
Newfoundland Nurses allows courts to connect the dots on the page
where the lines, and the direction they are headed, may be readily drawn.
Here, there were no dots on the page.[88]

Regrettably, the Supreme Court went much further, departing radically
from the spirit of "deference as respect," which treats reasoned decision-making as the *sine qua non* of deference.[89]

In *Alberta Teachers',* described in more detail earlier in this chapter,
the Information and Privacy Commissioner had not formally given a
decision on the timeline issue, though, as Justice Rothstein concluded,
a finding that the failure to invoke the power was not fatal to jurisdiction was necessarily implicit in the commissioner's decision.[90] The key
factor here was the existence of a plausible basis for the commissioner's
implicit decision. In related decisions of the commissioner with respect
to legislation within the commissioner's purview, a consistent approach
had been taken to the timelines issue. In the circumstances, the absence

of a set of formal reasons did not inhibit the court from subjecting the commissioner's approach to reasonableness review.[91]

This is relatively unobjectionable. One would rarely expect an administrative decision maker to give reasons for a decision not to use a power. It was a decision that it had not taken. Moreover, its position had been laid out in other decisions, and the individuals could doubtless have complained (thereby seeking and receiving a reasoned decision) had they wanted to.

In *McLean v British Columbia (Securities Commission)*,[92] however, paragraph 48 of *Dunsmuir* was stretched to the breaking point. Patricia McLean had misconducted herself in the Ontario securities market in the early 2000s. She and the Ontario Securities Commission eventually arrived at a settlement in 2008. McLean was barred from activities in Ontario. Subsequently, the British Columbia Securities Commission took action against her under a statutory provision that allows it to impose sanctions on a person who "has agreed with a securities regulatory authority, a self-regulatory body or an exchange, in Canada or elsewhere, to be subject to sanctions, conditions, restrictions or requirements."[93]

The difficulty raised by McLean was that the commission could not commence proceedings "more than 6 years after the date of the events that give rise to the proceedings."[94] The key question was the meaning of the term "events": if the term referred to the underlying misconduct, the limitation period had expired before the commission imposed the sanctions on McLean; if the term included the conclusion of the settlement agreement, then the commission's action was timely. The parties more or less lined up behind these alternative interpretations.

In its very brief order[95] (so brief that the British Columbia Court of Appeal considered appellate review "impossible" and remanded the matter for further reasons[96]), the commission did not explain its interpretation of the limitation period provision. It simply made an order barring McLean from activities in British Columbia for the same periods she was barred from activities in Ontario.

The fact that the commission did not explain its interpretation of the term "events" did not particularly trouble the Supreme Court:

Unlike *Alberta Teachers,* in the case at bar, we do not have the benefit
of the Commission's reasoning from its decisions in other cases involving
the same issue ... However, a basis for the Commission's interpretation
is apparent from the arguments advanced by the respondent, who is
also empowered to make orders under (and thus to interpret) ss. 161(1)
and (6). These arguments follow from established principles of statutory
interpretation. Accordingly, though reasons would have been preferable,
there is nothing to be gained here from requiring the Commission to
explain on remand what is readily apparent now.[97]

Canadian courts post-*Dunsmuir* took a somewhat laissez-faire atti-
tude toward after-the-fact rationalizations of administrative decisions.
In *Saskatchewan (Energy and Resources) v Areva Resources Canada Inc,*[98]
the Ministry of Energy and Resources did not offer any interpretation
of the provision at issue at the time it made a decision on the amount
of royalties due on uranium sales. After a judicial review application
had been commenced, the ministry duly filed a supporting affidavit
explaining its position. Even though this was "an after-the-fact explanation" and "largely argumentative," the Court of Appeal expressed the
view that these features "need not detain" the court, because of *Dunsmuir's* reference to reasons that could be offered in support of a decision.[99] One could imagine the applicant thinking it rather unfair that
the ministry won the case based on an argument elaborated only after
the dispute between the parties had arisen. A particularly angst-ridden
applicant would doubtless think that maybe, just maybe, it could have
mounted a better argument in its discussions with the ministry if only
it had had the full details of the ministry's position.

On any view, far too much leeway was given to judges and administrative decision makers by the admonition in *Dunsmuir* to pay
attention to reasons that could have been offered for a decision. The
individual subject to the authority of the administrative decision maker
should have the opportunity to argue his or her case on the record in
full knowledge of the decision maker's position on the relevant interpretive questions.[100] Allowing a decision maker to put a thumb on the
scales after the event is unfair and prevents a full airing of all relevant

issues. To ask courts to adopt a permissive approach on judicial review of a fully reasoned decision reached after an adjudicative process is one thing. To allow after-the-fact rationalizations for decisions that might have been reached on entirely different grounds is quite another. Thanh Tam Tran, whom we met in the Introduction, would certainly have agreed.

Allowing after-the-fact rationalizations has the potential to cause other difficulties. Where the decision maker has said nothing at all, judicial-review judges are left to guess at its thinking and even to ask counterfactuals about whether the decision would have been the same had the decision maker put its mind to a particular point. Indeed, in *Alberta Teachers'*, Justice Rothstein warned that respectful attention to reasons that could have been offered should not be treated as a "*carte blanche* to reformulate a tribunal's decision in a way that casts aside an unreasonable chain of analysis in favour of the court's own rationale for the result."[101]

Consider now the facts of *Agraira v Canada (Public Safety and Emergency Preparedness)*.[102] The applicant, Muhsen Ahmed Ramadan Agraira, was a Libyan national. Claiming that he had been a member of the Libyan National Salvation Front, he sought refugee status but was refused for want of sufficient involvement. This caused problems for him down the line. When he applied to become a permanent resident of Canada, he was deemed inadmissible because of his involvement in a terrorist organization. In short, he was not involved enough to be a refugee, but too involved to be admissible.

At that point, Agraira requested ministerial relief on the basis of his unusual circumstances. Section 34(2) of the *Immigration and Refugee Protection Act* (which has now been repealed) provided that although otherwise inadmissible, "a permanent resident or a foreign national who satisfies the Minister that their presence in Canada would not be detrimental to the national interest" will be treated as admissible.[103]

An immigration officer prepared a report in his favour. A briefing note from the Canada Border Services Agency also argued that the minister should exercise his discretion in favour of the applicant. Yet the minister did not follow this advice, concluding instead: "It is not in the national interest to admit individuals who have had sustained contact with known terrorist and/or terrorist-connected organizations."[104] Evidently – though his interpretation was not spelled out – the minister considered involvement with terrorist organizations to be detrimental to Canada's "national interest." Judging by the decision, the minister put determinative weight on terrorist involvement in determining whether it would be in the "national interest" to admit the applicant.[105]

The Supreme Court, however, imputed to the minister an implied interpretation that he plainly did not hold. It was evident from the minister's decision that almost exclusive emphasis was placed on the applicant's alleged terrorist connections. The court's interpretation was much more subtle. Although it was not problematic that the minister's interpretation "related predominantly to national security and public safety,"[106] it also had to include considerations set out in soft law guidelines, considerations including such matters as the individual's activities in Canada and family situation.[107] Had the more subtle interpretation that the court considered reasonable been adopted by the minister, the outcome of the case could well have been very different. Yet poor Mr. Agraira lost the case, because the court concluded that the minister's decision (based on the implied interpretation that the court arrived at after the fact) was reasonable.[108]

How can a court see into the mind of an administrative decision maker and answer counterfactuals about what the decision maker would have done had different arguments been made? The answer is that they cannot. The *McLean/Agraira* approach posed fairly obvious practical problems.[109] And, again, the combination of a presumption of deference with heavy reliance on authority rather than reason in the application of the reasonableness standard was poorly designed, leading to morally suboptimal outcomes.

Lack of Guidance on Reasonableness Review: What Is Reasonable?

The difficulties the Supreme Court created in its elaboration of the reasonableness standard were the product of a failure to think in broad terms about the meaning of reasonableness. Instead of a sustained attempt to articulate the reason and structure of review for reasonableness, the court instead offered bromides about reasonableness taking colour from its "context," a context created by "all relevant factors."[110] These masked important differences in the way the judges approached judicial review cases, which in turn diminished the guidance the court provided.

Consider the *Irving Paper* case,[111] which raises in stark form the difficulty of distinguishing clearly between a decision maker's reasoning process and the substantive outcomes arrived at. Both the court of first instance[112] and the New Brunswick Court of Appeal[113] quashed the decision. The employer here owned a large paper mill located in downtown Saint John, New Brunswick. It had unilaterally imposed mandatory random alcohol testing for employees holding safety-sensitive positions. Labour law principles are clear here: a test of reasonableness applies to any such imposition. In the present case, a majority of the arbitration board concluded that the invasion of employee privacy rights was not justified by the evidence presented to it. A particular bone of contention was a distinction made by the board between "ultra-dangerous" and merely "dangerous" workplaces. Surely, Justice Joseph Robertson held at the Court of Appeal, once it is accepted that catastrophic harm can result from a breakdown at a particular facility, any such distinction is flawed.[114]

By way of a majority decision by Justice Abella, the Supreme Court restored the arbitration board's decision, though taking care not to endorse the distinction between the dangerous and the ultra-dangerous. As she explained, relying on the arbitral jurisprudence, a balancing exercise is necessary: employees' privacy rights, on one side, versus risks to safety, on the other.[115] On the facts, there were eight incidents over a fifteen-year period. Abella concluded that the arbitrator was entitled reasonably to come to the conclusion that this evidence did not outweigh the invasion of the employees' privacy interests. Justice Rothstein and Justice Michael Moldaver filed a lengthy set of dissenting reasons. Their quibble was that the board had imposed an unduly onerous evidentiary standard, one that did not reflect "the arbitral consensus"[116] because it instead required a "significant or serious problem" with alcohol use and a causal connection between such use "and a workplace incident."[117]

One reading of cases like this on the application of the nominally invariant reasonableness standard is that two distinct approaches are present: the restorative (in which courts strive to present a decision in the best possible light, so as to uphold it) and the restrictive (in which courts approach decisions with skepticism and look closely for error).[118] Here, it was as if the majority and dissenting judges read two entirely different arbitral decisions.

More broadly, both the majority and dissenting justices were happy to allow the arbitral jurisprudence to set the parameters of the board's decision.[119] There was no question of the court revising or doing away with important parts of a body of labour law that has long been in the making by expert decision makers. The difficulty with this approach is that although there may be serious flaws in a decision maker's reasoning, its reasoning will nonetheless set the framework for future decision makers. On the one hand, courts could not intervene because administrative decision makers are not held to a standard of perfection.[120] On the other hand, without intervention (judicial or otherwise), decisions could become progressively less and less reasonable. In this case, the troublesome ultra-dangerous/dangerous distinction would have been at large in the arbitral jurisprudence. One can understand (without necessarily agreeing) why Justices Moldaver and Rothstein – or any other judges – might have been concerned about this prospect. But the issue was never discussed in those terms, nor in any detail at all by the Supreme Court. This was regrettable: "It is hard for public officials to know what standard they are expected to meet for their decisions to be safe from review, and hard for courts to articulate why they feel compelled to intervene."[121] On its own, disagreement on how to apply an open-textured standard like "reasonableness" to a complex set of facts is nothing to fret too much about. But coupled with the Supreme Court's lack of guidance on the meaning of "reasonableness," the sort of disagreement in *Irving Paper* only heightened the confusion of administrative law aficionados.

In short, the problems outlined thus far in this chapter are what led to the problematic *Tran* decision[122] described in the Introduction: a virtually irrebuttable presumption of reasonableness review, coupled with a fairly loose approach by the courts to reasonableness review. *Irving Paper* indicates that courts might take a tighter or looser approach in a particular context, without any indication in advance of when or why this might be so. Indeed, as we shall now see, things got worse as the Supreme Court preached one thing but often practised something else entirely.

Contradiction

As we saw in Chapter 1, the general principles of administrative law have to be applied in a variety of specific areas.[123] This gives rise to a problem. As the judicial body of last resort, the Supreme Court is expected to give authoritative guidance on matters of substantive Canadian law to other actors (individuals, politicians, lawyers, and lower-court judges). But according deference to administrative decision makers means permitting those decision makers to put their own spin on rules of substantive and procedural law. Yet as Canada's apex court, the Supreme Court has an institutional obligation to set down clear substantive and procedural rules for courts and decision makers across the country.

Few of the judicial review cases the court agreed to hear post-*Dunsmuir* provided meaningful guidance to lower courts on how to apply the general principles of administrative law.

In the *Tran* case,[124] the Supreme Court simply ignored, without so much as a word, the fact that it was hearing a judicial review. There was no discussion of standard of review. The minister's delegate's reasons did not warrant a mention, even in passing. As it turned out, this was good news for Tran, who won his appeal. But it was bad news for others in his situation: if their case made it to the Supreme Court, they might have a chance of victory, but lower courts would almost certainly do what the Federal Court of Appeal had done, and conclude that the decision was a permissible one on the basis of the Supreme Court's limited, and confusing, guidance about reasonableness review.

Sometimes the court ignored the role of the administrative decision maker entirely. *Febles v Canada (Citizenship and Immigration)*,[125] which involved an important question of immigration law touching on the interpretation of the United Nations *Convention Relating to the Status of Refugees*, is an example. Sometimes it dressed up its authoritative exposition of the law in the guise of reasonableness review – so-called "disguised correctness review," in which it said it was applying a reasonableness standard but in fact performed its own analysis of the law and the facts to reach an independent conclusion that it labelled "reasonable" or "unreasonable."[126] At other times, it undermined deference in its drive for coherence.[127] The techniques are not mutually exclusive, of course, and they were often deployed in combination.[128] These techniques might have permitted the court to provide authoritative guidance on important questions of substantive law, but their use raised inevitable questions about their impact on the general principles of judicial review. When the court ignored administrative law, engaged in disguised correctness review, or otherwise played fast and loose with administrative law doctrine to enable it to give guidance to the wider community on substantive law, it risked warping the administrative law framework and creating confusion.

Consider *Quebec (Commission des droits de la personne et des droits de la jeunesse) v Bombardier Inc (Bombardier Aerospace Training Center)*,[129] a case that was resolved decisively in favour of the exposition of national rules of substantive and procedural law.

Javed Latif was a Pakistani pilot who was denied training by Bombardier in 2004. The denial was based on a national security decision of the American authorities, a decision Bombardier applied because it did not want to imperil its standing with the Federal Aviation Authority. The Quebec Human Rights Tribunal found that Bombardier had discriminated against Latif. Although there was no direct evidence of discrimination by Bombardier, the tribunal based its decision on an expert report and circumstantial evidence about racial profiling in the United States after 9/11.

At first blush, this looks like a straightforward administrative law case that required the tribunal to weigh evidence and come to a conclusion.

Moreover, it conducted the weighing exercise in a very particular context, one in which an individual like Latif is powerless in the face of an unreviewable decision.[130] In this sort of context, one can understand why the tribunal was not especially impressed by Bombardier's automatic application of the American decision, and why the tribunal thought Bombardier should have been more proactive.[131] As a large institution, it was certainly in a better position than Latif to follow up with the American authorities.

Why, then, did the Supreme Court decide to grant leave to hear this case? Of course, except for the *Vavilov/Bell/NFL* leave decisions discussed in the Introduction,[132] the judges never give reasons. But there are two large clues in the joint reasons of Justices Richard Wagner and Côté for a unanimous Supreme Court.

First, this was the first opportunity for the court to consider "a form of discrimination allegedly arising out of the decision of a foreign authority."[133] Second, the court had "never clearly enunciated the degree of proof associated with the plaintiff's burden" of making out a *prima facie* case of discrimination.[134] Unsurprisingly, the bulk of the reasons are devoted to giving administrative decision makers and lower courts guidance on these interrelated issues. The guidance is that the civil standard of the burden of proof always applies.[135]

What about deference? Wagner and Côté accepted that tribunals have the authority to adapt their rules of procedure and admissibility of evidence to their particular regulatory context.[136] But not the burden of proof, "in order to maintain the uniformity, integrity and predictability of the law."[137] It is difficult to see a justification here for according the burden of proof a special status different from rules of procedure and evidence. Wagner and Côté said only "that the application of a given legal test must be based on the same elements and the same degree of proof in every case,"[138] but this is difficult to square with the court's openness to allowing administrative decision makers to mould rules of substantive law to better achieve their regulatory purposes. As Justice Fish put it in *Nor-Man Regional Health Authority Inc v Manitoba Association of Health Care Professionals,* an administrative decision maker "may properly develop doctrines and fashion remedies appropriate in their field, drawing inspiration from general legal principles, the objectives and purposes of the statutory scheme," and other contextual considerations.[139]

There then followed an intrusive analysis of the tribunal's appreciation of the facts, which looked suspiciously like correctness review even though it was adorned with the language of reasonableness.[140] At one point, Wagner and Côté commented that the "practical" effect of the tribunal's decision was to reverse the burden of proof they had previously established,[141] but in their analysis they also carefully picked apart the tribunal's reasons, using different expressions: insufficient evidence,[142] evidence not "tangibly related,"[143] evidence "not sufficiently related,"[144] or simply "no evidence."[145] But whether the evidence is adequate or not is a matter for the administrative decision maker. As has been said many times, it is emphatically *not* "the function of the reviewing court to reweigh the evidence."[146]

Further, the evidence was insufficient on only one of the three grounds Latif needed to prove to make out a *prima facie* case of discrimination. Does this mean that a court is entitled to pick apart a human rights tribunal's decision and examine the sufficiency of the evidence on each ground independently? Readers of Supreme Court cases had previously been told, however, that judicial review is not a "line-by-line treasure hunt for error."[147]

Inasmuch as there was any meaningful guidance to lower courts here about the general principles of administrative law, the unfortunate effect would be to license intrusive judicial review of tribunals' appreciation of facts and evidence.

The lack of congruence between the "law in the books" and the "law in action" did not escape the notice of the judges. In *Kanthasamy v Canada (Citizenship and Immigration),*[148] the dissenting judges took aim at what they perceived to be nondeferential reasonableness review of a highly discretionary decision made by an immigration officer. Accusing the majority of parsing the officer's decision for errors, resolving ambiguities against the officer, and reweighing the evidence (much as occurred, I have suggested, in *Bombardier*), Justice Moldaver commented sternly that the judges could "be accused of adopting a 'do as we say, not what we do' approach to reasonableness review."[149] Not only was *Dunsmuir* riven by internal tensions and lacking in guidance on reasonableness review (features exacerbated by subsequent decisions) but the *Dunsmuir* framework was being implemented in slipshod fashion.

Fault Lines and Revolution

If anything, the foregoing analysis of the difficulties of the *Dunsmuir* decade understates just how bad things were. In the cases I have mentioned – and many more – the judges of the Supreme Court sharply divided on the selection and application of the standard of review. *Edmonton East* is a neat snapshot: some judges preferred a more contextual approach (substantivists!), while others preferred the neat formalism of the presumption of reasonableness review (formalists!); some favoured deference, others saw a nice question of law ripe for judicial resolution; and a bare majority relied on reasons that could have been offered in support of a decision (authority!), with the minority disparaging such an approach (reason!). These fault lines, present throughout the evolution of Canadian administrative law, were present even on the country's highest court.[150]

With changes in the court's composition came changes in the alignment of the judges in relation to the fault lines. In *Wilson v Atomic Energy of Canada,*[151] three judges (Moldaver, appointed in 2011; Côté, appointed in 2015; and Brown, appointed in 2015) would have applied the correctness standard on the basis that there were two conflicting lines of labour arbitrator authority on the underlying question (the protection of federally regulated employees from being terminated for cause). Côté was particularly fond of correctness review,[152] as was Justice Rowe, who joined the court in 2016.[153] In the high-profile *Trinity Western University* cases – where the university's proposed law school had been refused accreditation by two provincial law societies – the Côté-Brown-Rowe troika took aim at the application of a deferential standard of review on constitutional questions, worrying that it created underpowered judicial review of interference with fundamental rights.[154]

Meanwhile, there was widespread revolt in the lower courts. A respected appellate judge described Canadian administrative law as a "never ending construction site."[155] By 2019, things had boiled over. In *Atlantic Mining NS Corp (DDV Gold Limited) v Oakley*, which involved a complaint by the corporation about the nonpecuniary losses it was obliged to cover in connection with an expropriation of property, Justice Peter Bryson of the Nova Scotia Court of Appeal was strongly critical of the Supreme Court's prevailing approach to appeal clauses:

> Respectfully, the reasons of the majority in [*Edmonton (City) v Edmonton East (Capilano) Shopping Centres Ltd*[156]] for such an indulgent standard of review as reasonableness, are unconvincing. Respect for legislative preferences cannot explain deference in a statutory appeal on a question of law when that right of appeal long predates later Supreme Court decisions on deference. In such cases, the legislature would have understood the law to require review on a correctness standard. So a reasonableness standard does not respect legislative intent. Legislated deference on questions of fact within a specialized tribunal's area of expertise is a weak basis for supposing a superior expertise on questions of law which is the every day business of Superior Courts to which no such deference is given. That is especially so where presumed expertise may be more generous than the limited resources of some tribunals may justify. A strong "rule of law" argument can be made that on questions of law, the Superior Courts should have the final say because consistency is a hallmark of that rule.[157]

With evident distaste, Justice Bryson applied the reasonableness standard but concluded that the Utility and Review Board's interpretation was unreasonable and, indeed, that interpreting losses as pecuniary only was the sole reasonable interpretation of the provincial *Expropriation Act*.[158] The effect was to deny Wayne Oakley compensation for (unquantifiable) discomfort and anxiety.

By contrast, writing for the majority in *Nova Scotia (Attorney General) v S&D Smith Central Supplies Limited*, another case involving the Utility and Review Board, Justice Joel Fichaud of the same court had no hesitation in applying a reasonableness standard to the board's interpretation of the *Expropriation Act*. As he observed: "The Supreme Court has explained its reasons for the textured, rather than a linear approach to deference. Whether that approach should be revisited is for the Supreme Court, not this Court."[159] In dissent, however, Justice Duncan Beveridge applied correctness, writing pointedly: "The last ten years of judicial debate has, with respect, lost its focus on the key issue of legislative intent."[160] Of *Edmonton East* he wrote that "reliance on a presumption of legislative intent in favour of deference ... spurns well-established norms of statutory interpretation."[161]

This strong dissent indicated deep disagreement among the judges on the Nova Scotia Court of Appeal and, as with Justice Bryson, a willingness to challenge the authority of the Supreme Court.

With concerns that the Supreme Court's writ might not be running *a mari usque ad mare,* it became inevitable that the court would have to undertake a major revision of its approach to administrative law.

CONCLUSION

The purpose of this chapter has been to explain the tumultuous *Dunsmuir* decade. Ultimately, those years proved that the *Dunsmuir* framework was not up to the task of handling the complexity of administrative law. As early as 2016, a majority of the Supreme Court of Canada had appreciated the desirability of modifying the current standard of review framework. In *Wilson,*[162] Justice Abella aired "in *obiter*" a "proposal" on how to "simplify the standard of review labyrinth we currently find ourselves in," with a view to "starting the conversation about the way forward."[163] Four of her colleagues welcomed her "efforts to stimulate a discussion on how to clarify or simplify our standard of review jurisprudence to better promote certainty and predictability."[164] The dissenting judges welcomed the "constructive spirit" in which Abella's suggestions were offered, although they "harbour[ed] concerns about their merits."[165]

The debates continued on the court, with sharp divisions on the scope of correctness review and fundamental disagreement about where the court should position itself in relation to the various fault lines that have been present throughout the evolution of Canada's law of judicial review.[166]

Then, in 2018, Chief Justice McLachlin retired and was replaced by Chief Justice Wagner. Soon after, the Court issued its fateful leave to appeal reasons in which it invited submissions on a wholesale reform of Canadian administrative law.

4

The Big Bang

I T W A S A D I V I D E D Supreme Court of Canada that invited the parties in cases involving citizenship and the Super Bowl to make submissions about the standard of review. The prior decade had been tumultuous, with the inadequacies of the *Dunsmuir* framework gradually laid bare. The changing composition of the court exacerbated divisions along the classic form/substance, deference/nondeference, and reason/authority fault lines. With continuing debates about the standard of review and growing unrest in the Canadian legal community, the time was ripe for change – but it was doubtful that the judges would be able to agree on the changes.

The parties in the cases were very much taken by surprise by the court's invitation. I acted as a consultant to the lawyers for Bell Canada and the National Football League. Professional obligations preclude me from saying much more about my involvement, but I think I can say (and that it would be fair to say) that the parties were not overjoyed by the invitation. Lawyers are interested in winning cases for their clients more than they are interested in reforming the law. Of course, most good lawyers will find ways to propose reforms that would both improve the law and guarantee victory for their client. But this is the very point of common law adjudication: in general, the best way to move the law forward is thought to be in increments – rather than by wholesale reform – motivated by the resolution of individual cases in a coherent way over time.[1] The parties here were being asked to play quite a different role. That said, the incrementalism of the *Dunsmuir* decade had led to anything but coherence.

The parties were carefully selected to cover a fairly broad range of the vast expanse of the administrative state: an individual (Alexander Vavilov) and powerful economic entities (Bell Canada and the National Football League) versus a front-line government decision maker (a delegate of the Registrar of Canadian Citizenship) and a sophisticated regulator (the CRTC). Furthermore, the parties themselves could be relied on to make well-crafted submissions: Bell Canada and the National Football League were represented by eminent appellate lawyers (who didn't really need my help, to be honest!), the Attorney General of Canada's significant institutional expertise in judicial review proceedings was available as his office represented both the Registrar and the CRTC, and although Vavilov himself did not have comparable resources, it was a fair bet that immigration lawyers (who are uniquely passionate about administrative law and its failings) would freely offer advice to his counsel about the best way to approach the appeal.

These parties were supplemented by the *amici curiae* – Daniel Jutras and Audrey Boctor – appointed by the court to provide a fresh perspective on the state of play. Dozens of interveners were permitted to make submissions, on behalf of groups ranging from attorneys general to economic regulators and administrative tribunals, to advocacy groups for marginalized constituencies (and even a group of students from the University of Cambridge, one of whom was my PhD supervisee, although I did not discuss the matter with him). The court set aside three days in December 2018 to hear arguments, and over the next year the judges debated the issues among themselves, with a majority eventually hammering out a compromise that enabled them to establish a new framework for Canadian administrative law.

What ultimately emerged was the decision in *Vavilov*, which set out a general framework for Canadian administrative law.[2] (The *Bell Canada/ National Football League* cases ended up merely being occasions for applying the *Vavilov* framework.) Seven of the nine judges – Chief Justice Richard Wagner, and Justices Michael Moldaver, Clément

Gascon, Suzanne Côté, Russell Brown, Malcolm Rowe, and Sheilah Martin – signed the majority reasons. Immediately, one will see that this coalition included some judicial review hawks (Côté, Brown, and Rowe), some doves (Wagner and Gascon), and two judges who are probably best described as nonaligned (Moldaver, who sometimes found himself with the hawks, sometimes with the doves, and Martin, the court's newest member). Justices Rosalie Abella and Andromache Karakatsanis, both judicial review doves, delivered concurring reasons that, in reality, were reasons dissenting from the majority's new framework. As you can probably guess, there was a significant amount of compromise in the majority reasons: broadly speaking, the hawks would have been happier with the section on selecting the standard of review, the doves with the articulation of reasonableness review.[3]

The majority explained that they sought "to bring greater coherence and predictability" to the selection of the standard of review[4] and "to more clearly articulate what [the reasonableness standard] entails and how it should be applied in practice."[5] The goals of *Vavilov* were therefore to simplify and to clarify.[6] How did the judges achieve those goals? In this chapter, I will first discuss the framework for selecting the standard of review, based on the (wafer-thin) principles of "institutional design" and "the rule of law," and then move to the rich conception of reasonableness review, based on the principle of "responsive justification." Before concluding, I will also address, but more briefly, the role of precedent and remedial discretion in the *Vavilov* framework.

SELECTING THE STANDARD OF REVIEW

Imagine you are in a corridor. Dead ahead in front of you is a door marked "reasonableness review." On your left are three narrow doors, labelled "constitutional questions," "overlapping jurisdiction," and "central importance." On your right are two regular-sized doors – "appeals" and "legislated standard of review" – that can be unlocked only with special keys. Welcome to the *Vavilov* framework for selecting the standard of review. Much of the time, you will head to reasonableness review, but sometimes you will be able to squeeze through one of the narrow doors on your left, and on other occasions, you will have a key to unlock the doors on your right (if so, you will find that special rules apply for selecting the standard of review). Let me explain in non-metaphorical terms.

Under the *Vavilov* framework, reasonableness review is the presumptive starting point, but there is an important exception for statutory appeals, which attract correctness review on extricable questions of law; and standards of review specified by legislation. And in three other nonexhaustive scenarios, correctness review is required by the rule of law: the resolution of constitutional questions, questions of central importance to the legal system as a whole, and issues of overlapping jurisdiction. Jurisdictional questions, even in their purest form, will no longer attract correctness review.

All trace of nuance and context was swept from this area by *Vavilov*. As the majority forthrightly stated: "[T]his decision conclusively closes the door on the application of a contextual analysis to determine the applicable standard, and in doing so streamlines and simplifies the standard of review framework."[7] Where once the contextual pragmatic and functional approach, with its four interlocking factors, reigned supreme until dethroned by a presumption of reasonableness review rebuttable by reference to contextual factors, context will no longer play any role in the selection of the standard of review. Rather, the standard applied "must reflect the legislature's intent with respect to the role of the reviewing court, except where giving effect to that intent is precluded by the rule of law."[8] Form, not substance, will determine the standard of review.

Institutional Design
The starting point is a presumption of reasonableness review. Significantly, this presumption is based on the brute fact of a legislative choice to delegate decision-making authority to an administrative decision maker. Other justifications, such as the expertise of the decision maker in question, are irrelevant to the selection of the standard of review: "[I]t is the *very fact* that the legislature has chosen to delegate authority which justifies a default position of reasonableness review."[9] This is dressed up as respect for an "institutional design choice"[10] by

the legislature, but in reality reflects a judicial choice to do away with the complexities of a contextual approach. Hence my observation that form trumps substance on the selection of the standard of review.[11]

Accordingly, where the legislature has legislated a standard of review[12] or, more commonly, provided for an appeal, the courts must respect this institutional design choice. Most importantly, where there is a right of appeal of any sort, the appellate review regime laid out in *Housen v Nikolaisen*[13] applies in all circumstances:

> Where a legislature has provided that parties may appeal from an administrative decision to a court, either as of right or with leave, it has subjected the administrative regime to appellate oversight and indicated that it expects the court to scrutinize such administrative decisions on an appellate basis.[14]

This means that extricable questions of law are reviewed on a correctness standard. If there is a general issue of principle within a decision, it can be extracted and the court can substitute its judgment for that of the decision maker. When I say "general issue of principle," I mean, first, that the decision maker interpreted a general norm, such as a statutory or regulatory provision, or a principle contained in a previous decision; second, that the interpretation has precedential value, in that it could be applied to subsequent decisions; and, third, that the interpretation is material to the outcome of the case.

By contrast, a mixed question of law and fact (i.e., an application of a legal standard to the facts as found) or a question of fact (i.e., a finding as to whether an event occurred) will be reviewed on the palpable and overriding error standard. Judicial intervention for palpable and overriding error will be rare:

> Palpable and overriding error is a highly deferential standard of review ... "Palpable" means an error that is obvious. "Overriding" means an error that goes to the very core of the outcome of the case. When arguing palpable and overriding error, it is not enough to pull at leaves and branches and leave the tree standing. The entire tree must fall.[15]

This is a significant change. Some areas, admittedly, were only recently colonized by the marauding presumption of reasonableness review. Accordingly, *Vavilov* will represent a welcome return to the pre– *Edmonton East* status quo ante in areas where the presumption was regarded as an invader.[16] More broadly, however, as Justices Abella and Karakatsanis noted, "the majority's reasons strip away deference from hundreds of administrative actors subject to statutory rights of appeal."[17] Decisions of economic regulators, such as the federal CRTC[18] and the provincial securities commissions,[19] are typically subject to appeal clauses, as are the decisions of professional disciplinary tribunals.[20] Of course, the courts had managed, with respect to some bodies (the Competition Tribunal springs to mind[21]), to reason their way to correctness review notwithstanding the strong doctrinal currents that dragged them toward deference. But these are exceptions, not the rule, and in general such entities have long been used to deference, even on questions of law. This has not been especially controversial, given widespread recognition that matters on which regulators have expertise can bleed into the interpretation of terms in their parent statutes.[22] With expertise shunted to the margins, however, deference will no longer be the starting point with respect to these bodies.

The majority's rejoinder is essentially that there is "no principled rationale for ignoring statutory appeal mechanisms."[23] With respect, however, this rejoinder is aimed at a straw man. The balance of the academic and judicial criticism cited by the majority[24] was not that statutory appeal provisions should *never* be taken into account. It has been more common to propose a nuanced approach that would take account of the difference between, say, an appeal on a point of law with leave of a court and a full *de novo* appeal right. As the *amici* observed in their factum, "not all rights of appeal are created equal."[25] Such nuances are, in the majority's view, irrelevant: "While the existence of a leave requirement will affect whether a court will hear an appeal from a particular decision, it does not affect the standard to be applied if leave is given and the appeal is heard."[26] In the *Vavilov* framework, appeal rights equal correctness review on questions of law, context and nuance be damned, all in the name of the institutional design principle.

This principle is, however, wafer-thin, almost an entirely formal construct. Its thinness is illustrated by the fate of privative clauses in the *Vavilov* framework. That fate is brutal. Privative clauses count for nothing. A presumption of reasonableness review will apply whether or not there is a privative clause in an administrative decision maker's home statute. Only a right of appeal matters for the purposes of the *Vavilov* framework. The point is even sharper when one analyzes a limited right of appeal that is *combined* with a clause having privative effect.

In section 31 of the *Broadcasting Act*, for example, briefly considered in *Bell Canada v Canada (Attorney General)*,[27] there is an appeal (with leave) from the CRTC to the Federal Court of Appeal on a question of law or jurisdiction. But there is also a clause stating that decisions of the CRTC are "final and conclusive."[28] Final and conclusive clauses were treated, in earlier eras, as indications that the legislature intended courts to engage in deferential judicial review.[29] Do they mean anything now? In the *Vavilov* majority's view, "the existence of a circumscribed right of appeal in a statutory scheme does not on its own preclude applications for judicial review of decisions, or of aspects of decisions, to which the appeal mechanism does not apply, or by individuals who have no right of appeal."[30] This seems to mean that the final and conclusive clause in the *Broadcasting Act* excludes *appeals* on questions of fact but not *judicial review* on questions of fact. But then factual issues would be considered under the "robust" reasonableness standard, not the "palpable and overriding error" standard.

This creates something of a puzzle. Although the appellate standard of review framework set out in *Housen v Nikolaisen* calls for correctness on questions of law, it calls for the deferential standard of palpable and overriding error on everything else, including mixed questions of law and fact. Where there is a statutory appeal, any issue of fact, discretion, or mixed law and fact will be subject to the palpable and overriding error standard. On judicial review, by contrast, robust reasonableness review will be applied to any such issue and will, in some respects, go further than palpable and overriding error. Furthermore, whereas the animating principle of *Vavilovian* reasonableness review is responsive justification, the animating principle of the *Housen v Nikolaisen* framework is judicial economy, designed to minimize appellate oversight.[31] More deference would be due, in other words, in situations where an appeal has been provided for. With respect to section 31 of the *Broadcasting Act*, for example, by trying to confine the scope of judicial oversight, the legislature – perversely – has ended up expanding it.[32] In *Vavilov*, the majority was unrepentant: "[A]ny such application for judicial review is distinct from an appeal, and the presumption of reasonableness review that applies on judicial review cannot then be rebutted by reference to the statutory appeal mechanism."[33] This will make little sense in practice to, say, a securities trader whose livelihood is put at risk by a regulatory decision – good luck explaining to her why her prospects on appeal are less than her prospects would have been on judicial review; references to "institutional design" are unlikely to be compelling.[34] If the institutional design principle were thicker, such anomalies could be avoided, but the majority consciously chose a thin principle. A substantive approach would allow courts to iron out such anomalies: they are precisely the sorts of bugs that emerge when courts take formal approaches to judicial review of administrative action.

The Rule of Law

Any other departures from the starting point of the presumption of reasonableness review are justifiable only by reference to the rule of law. These are the categories set out in *Dunsmuir v New Brunswick*,[35] minus true questions of jurisdiction: "[R]espect for the rule of law requires courts to apply the standard of correctness for certain types of legal questions: constitutional questions, general questions of law of central importance to the legal system as a whole and questions regarding the jurisdictional boundaries between two or more administrative bodies."[36] The majority's conception of the oft-controversial concept of the rule of law is as wafer-thin as its conception of institutional design: the rule of law is engaged only in situations where "consistency" and thus "a final, determinate answer" to a legal question is necessary.[37] There is no hint here of a broad conception of the rule of law as a tool for enhancing human autonomy or ensuring respect for human dignity or advancing equality. This despite the fact that such a broad conception is a common feature of other Supreme Court decisions and the voluminous academic literature on the rule of law.

Three points are notable here: 1) the potential expansion of the central questions category, 2) the elimination of jurisdictional questions, and 3) the letting of the door ever-so-slightly ajar to the possibility that a new rule-of-law category will be recognized in the future.

With expertise now out of the way, it no longer performs a limiting function in the definition of "questions of central importance to the legal system."[38] The concurring judges warned that this "inevitably" widens the scope for intrusive judicial oversight of expert bodies: "Issues of discrimination, labour rights, and economic regulation of the securities markets (among many others) theoretically raise questions of vital importance for Canada and its legal system [and could require correctness review]."[39] As it happened, the first application of the *Vavilov* framework by a Canadian court involved (among other things) the application of correctness review to a question of human rights law.[40] However, the majority insisted that "questions of central importance are not transformed into a broad catch-all category for correctness review" simply "because expertise no longer plays a role in the selection of the standard of review."[41] The thin conception of the rule of law employed by the *Vavilov* majority, triggered only by questions requiring a final, determinate answer to be furnished by the courts, supports this view. Notably, issues of international law are not, apparently, questions falling within this category.[42] On balance, given the narrow foundations – a thin conception of the rule of law – on which this category rests, it is unlikely to be expanded.[43]

Jurisdictional questions seem to have been finally consigned to the dustbin of history. For the majority, it was not "necessary to maintain this category of correctness review" as the concerns about decision makers overstepping the boundaries of their authority can be addressed by suitably robust reasonableness review.[44] Herein lies the rub. Jurisdictional questions have such a stubborn hold on the legal imagination that any measure short of a stake through the heart cannot be assured of success. In future cases, some members of the *Vavilov* majority coalition might use the insistence that reasonableness review "does not give [administrative decision makers] licence to enlarge their powers beyond what the legislature intended," and that the "governing statutory scheme will *always* operate as a constraint on administrative decision makers and as a limit on their authority,"[45] as justification for nondeferential reasonableness review to achieve the same results as a correctness standard for jurisdictional issues.

Portentously, the rule-of-law door was left slightly ajar. The majority "would not definitively foreclose the possibility that another category could be recognized as requiring a derogation from the presumption of reasonableness review in a future case."[46] In language reminiscent of *Alberta (Information and Privacy Commissioner) v Alberta Teachers' Association*[47] and *Canada (Canadian Human Rights Commission) v Canada (Attorney General)*,[48] the reader is warned that any new category would be "exceptional."[49] If history is any guide, however, such equivocation will be treated by lawyers as a wedge with which to open another door to correctness review. Only time will tell whether the coalition can hold and whether lower courts resist the temptation to take a peek behind the rule-of-law door.[50]

Notably, the majority rejected the suggestion of one of the *amici* that reviewing courts should engage in correctness review whenever there is "persistent discord" on an issue within an administrative decision-making body.[51] Readers will recall from Chapter 3 that this had split the court in 2016, in the *Wilson* case, with three judges taking the view that persistent discord requires correctness review to preserve the rule of law. This is a notable feature of the majority reasons because it illustrates how the dissenters in *Wilson* – Moldaver, Côté, and Brown – were willing to compromise in the interests of establishing a workable general framework for administrative law. We shall see below that there was more to the compromise, as the underlying issue of discord was addressed by the majority in *Vavilov* as part of its elaboration of a contextual approach to reasonableness review, but the point for present purposes is to illustrate the narrowness of the correctness categories and further demonstrate the thinness of the majority's rule-of-law principle.

Summary

The removal of the "vexing" contextual factors[52] is the most important contribution of *Vavilov* on selecting the standard of review. This leads to an avowedly formal, rules-based approach to identifying the applicable standard, with substance removed entirely from the equation. This is, moreover, an approach based on authority rather than on reason, inasmuch as all that matters are brute facts relating to the creation of an administrative decision maker and rights of appeal (or legislated standards of review), rather than reasoned arguments for or against deference. The approach to selecting the standard of review is, therefore, formal (not substantive) and based on authority (not reason). Also, despite the presumptive deferential starting point, this approach significantly reduces the scope for deference on questions of law in many areas where deference was well entrenched, especially economic regulation and professional discipline. There is perhaps the merest hint of overstatement in Abella and Karakatsanis's description of the majority's approach to selecting the standard of review as an "encomium for correctness and a eulogy for deference,"[53] but there is no doubt that on its face the *Vavilov* majority made a significant alteration to the status quo.

It is, nonetheless, difficult to be categorical about the likely consequences of *Vavilov* for economic regulation and professional discipline, where the expertise of decision makers is well established as a matter of social fact even if it is henceforth irrelevant as a matter of legal doctrine. Much will depend, therefore, on the willingness of first-instance judges to categorize matters coming within the expertise of regulators as questions of law (subject to correctness review) or as mixed questions (subject to review for palpable and overriding error). And one wonders whether, despite the injunction to perform correctness review on extricable questions of law, courts hearing appeals from specialized administrative decision makers will nevertheless give significant or perhaps even dispositive weight to the decision makers' views on matters within their expertise.[54] Deference might not be dead yet. I will return to this issue in Chapter 5.

For what it is worth, I think the majority's conception of the rule of law (thin and all as it is) would have been a more effective organizing principle for the selection of the standard of review than the principle of institutional design. Rather than holding that *all* appeal clauses call for the application of the *Housen v Nikolaisen* framework, the majority could have held that *some* appeal clauses – such as those allowing for appeals on issues of law or jurisdiction – require the courts to give a final, definitive answer. In this way, the Supreme Court could have retained its presumption of reasonableness review, subject to exceptions justified by a thin conception of the rule of law. Such an approach would have had a stronger theoretical basis as it would not have the weaknesses of the thin institutional design principle. I did not have to rally a majority of judges to my side, however. It seems clear that the formal, nondeferential, authority-based approach to selecting the standard of review was traded off against the very different approach to reasonableness review. As we shall see next, this approach is substantive, deferential, and based on reason.

The most important question, if we are to judge the majority in *Vavilov* by their own lights, is whether the approach to selecting the standard of review provides simplicity and clarity. Notwithstanding my sympathy for the position of Justices Abella and Karakatsanis, I do not think there is any doubt that it does. Can the same be said of reasonableness review?

REASONABLENESS REVIEW

Despite all the fuss about selecting the standard of review, empirical studies have revealed that most of the time, Canadian courts apply the reasonableness standard of review.[55] But what does "reasonableness" mean? The Supreme Court had not provided much guidance in this area. Indeed, as more fully described in Chapter 3, the Supreme Court had said little other than that "reasonableness depends on the context." Other courts, particularly the Federal Court of Appeal, where Justice David Stratas was an influential and eloquent voice for reform, had tried to flesh out what this might mean, perhaps broader or narrower ranges depending on the interplay of contextual factors (not unlike the 1988–2008 approach to selecting the standard of review), and a requirement to identify "badges" of unreasonableness tainting the decision complained of.[56] In the application of reasonableness review to questions of statutory interpretation, though the Supreme Court had said next to nothing. The result was that some lower courts (like the British Columbia Court of Appeal) insisted that the principles of statutory interpretation must be applied rigorously to set a benchmark against which to measure the administrative decision maker's interpretation of law, whereas others (like the Federal Court of Appeal) preached a more restrained approach, in which statutory interpretation principles play a secondary role in determining whether the decision at issue was indeed demonstrably unreasonable. There was support for both of these wildly divergent approaches in the Supreme Court's recent administrative law jurisprudence.[57] Against this unpromising backdrop, the Supreme Court set out in *Vavilov* to provide "better guidance ... on the proper application of the reasonableness standard."[58]

The Approach in *Vavilov*

As the majority acknowledged, in its prior administrative law decisions the Supreme Court had provided "relatively little guidance on how to conduct reasonableness review in practice."[59] It made up for this in *Vavilov*, setting out a detailed methodology for first-instance judges required to apply the reasonableness standard.[60] In their hard-hitting concurring reasons, Justices Abella and Karakatsanis charged the majority with "reviv[ing] the kind of search for errors that dominated the pre-*C.U.P.E. v. N.B. Liquor Corporation* era."[61] Although there are some differences in detail, and some internal tensions in the majority's articulation of a new methodology for reasonableness review, on balance the majority was right that the dissent's approach was not "fundamentally dissimilar."[62]

Methodology of Reasonableness Review

On the key propositions underpinning the methodology of reasonableness review, all nine judges were in fact in agreement: reasonableness review is robust; reasons are fundamental to the legitimacy of administrative decision-making; unreasonableness must be demonstrated by the applicant; reasonableness review should begin with the reasons given by the administrative decision maker; reasonableness review is contextual; and reasonableness review should be conducted with a healthy appreciation that "'[a]dministrative justice' will not always look like 'judicial justice'":[63]

- "Reasonableness review is ... a robust form of review"[64]
- "[W]here reasons are required, they are the primary mechanism by which administrative decision makers show that their decisions are reasonable – both to the affected parties and to the reviewing courts"[65]
- "The burden is on the party challenging the decision to show that it is unreasonable"[66]
- "[A] court applying the reasonableness standard does not ask what decision it would have made in place of that of the administrative decision maker, attempt to ascertain the 'range' of possible conclusions that would have been open to the decision maker, conduct a *de novo* analysis or seek to determine the 'correct' solution to the problem ... A principled approach to reasonableness review is one which puts [the decision maker's] reasons first"[67]
- "[W]hat is reasonable in a given situation will always depend on the constraints imposed by the legal and factual context of the particular decision under review"[68]
- "In conducting reasonableness review, judges should be attentive to the application by decision makers of specialized knowledge, as demonstrated by their reasons. Respectful attention to a decision maker's demonstrated expertise may reveal to a reviewing court that an outcome that might be puzzling or counterintuitive on its face nevertheless accords with the purposes and practical realities of the relevant administrative regime and represents a reasonable approach given the consequences and the operational impact of the decision."[69]

In addition, the majority insisted that where reasons are defective, a reviewing court is not "to fashion its own reasons in order to buttress the administrative decision."[70] Admittedly, Justices Abella and Karakatsanis did not accept this proposition,[71] but it is surely fair to say that even if it did not quite attract a consensus, it nonetheless reflects the recent direction of travel. *Alberta Teachers'*, notably, was limited to its particular facts,[72] and there was no repetition of some of the more permissive language of the most recent leading precedent on defective reasons, *Delta Air Lines Inc v Lukács*,[73] which was cited instead for the principle that "it is not open to a reviewing court to disregard the flawed basis for a decision and substitute its own justification for the outcome."[74]

In some situations, the majority explained, reasons need not be given. For instance, with respect to legislative-type decisions like regulations or municipal bylaws, reasons are either not given at all or do not resemble the reasons received for adjudicative or discretionary decisions.[75] In such scenarios, the majority explained in *Vavilov*, reasonableness review remains possible, although the application of the legal and factual constraints will focus on the outcome rather than on the reasons.[76] The message here is that administrative decision makers are more likely to see their legislative-type decisions upheld if they provide reasoned explanations for the consideration of the courts.[77] At the very least, they are more likely to have a degree of control over the focus of the reviewing court's attention.

On the whole, the methodology of reasonableness review set out in *Vavilov* is inherently deferential. Of course, reasonableness review is robust and no page of the record will be left unturned, but judicial analysis *must* begin with the reasons for the decision and *respect* the expertise of the administrative decision maker, with intervention *only* to be countenanced if the decision is *demonstrated* to be unreasonable. This is the essence of deference.

Fundamental Flaws and Contextual Considerations
Having set out the methodology of reasonableness review, the majority

went on, at some length, "to consider two types of fundamental flaws," but emphasized that these flaws are simply "a convenient way to discuss the types of issues that may show a decision to be unreasonable,"[78] that is, where "there are sufficiently serious shortcomings in the decision such that it cannot be said to exhibit the requisite degree of justification, intelligibility and transparency."[79] First, the absence of "reasoning that is both rational and logical,"[80] such as reasons that "fail to reveal a rational chain of analysis," ones that "read in conjunction with the record do not make it possible to understand the decision maker's reasoning on a critical point,"[81] or ones that "exhibit clear logical fallacies, such as circular reasoning, false dilemmas, unfounded generalizations or an absurd premise."[82] Plainly, these are intended as examples that illustrate a general point – the absence of logic and reason – and not as a set of categories into which dubious administrative decisions can be pigeonholed by reviewing courts.[83]

Second, a decision must be "justified in relation to the constellation of law and facts that are relevant to the decision."[84] The majority emphasized that it is impossible to "catalogue" all the considerations that will be relevant to the constellation of particular individual cases, but presented a set that will "generally be relevant":

> the governing statutory scheme; other relevant statutory or common law [including international law]; the principles of statutory interpretation; the evidence before the decision maker and facts of which the decision maker may take notice; the submissions of the parties; the past practices and decisions of the administrative body; and the potential impact of the decision on the individual to whom it applies.[85]

That these elements are not intended as "a checklist for conducting reasonableness review"[86] clearly emerges from the ensuing discussion, where the formulation "may be unreasonable" is repeatedly employed. And, of course, they must be read against the clear guidance set out by the majority (and accepted by the concurring judges) on the inherently deferential methodology of reasonableness review.

Reasonableness review as articulated in *Vavilov* is much thicker than the thin principles of institutional design and rule of law used to support the framework for selecting the standard of review. *Vavilovian* reasonableness is substantive, deferential, and reasoned. First, context is of primary importance, with the legal and factual constraints on administrative decision makers tighter or looser depending on the circumstances, chief among them the language of the decision maker's statute. Vague statutory terms or discretionary powers – e.g., to regulate in the "national interest" – empower; prescriptive statutory schemes setting out detailed requirements inhibit:

> If a legislature wishes to precisely circumscribe an administrative decision maker's power in some respect, it can do so by using precise and narrow language and delineating the power in detail, thereby tightly constraining the decision maker's ability to interpret the provision. Conversely, where the legislature chooses to use broad, open-ended or highly qualitative language – for example, "in the public interest" – it clearly contemplates that the decision maker is to have greater flexibility in interpreting the meaning of such language. Other language will fall in the middle of this spectrum.[87]

Second, the requirement to start with the reasons for decision and work from there to a conclusion of unreasonableness should stand in the way of overly aggressive review and makes *Vavilovian* reasonableness review inherently deferential (especially on questions of fact[88]). Indeed, the majority was clear that administrative decision makers are not bound to apply legal precedents or principles the way courts would apply them, but can mould those precedents or principles to their own ends if they provide adequate reasons to justify doing so (itself a contextual inquiry):

> It is evident that both statutory and common law will impose constraints on how and what an administrative decision maker can lawfully decide ... Any precedents on the issue before the administrative decision maker

or on a similar issue will act as a constraint on what the decision maker can reasonably decide. An administrative body's decision may be unreasonable on the basis that the body failed to explain or justify a departure from a binding precedent in which the same provision had been interpreted. Where, for example, there is a relevant case in which a court considered a statutory provision, it would be unreasonable for an administrative decision maker to interpret or apply the provision without regard to that precedent. The decision maker would have to be able to explain why a different interpretation is preferable by, for example, explaining why the court's interpretation does not work in the administrative context ... That being said, administrative decision makers will not necessarily be required to apply equitable and common law principles in the same manner as courts in order for their decisions to be reasonable. For example, it may be reasonable for a decision maker to adapt a common law or equitable doctrine to its administrative context ... Conversely, a decision maker that rigidly applies a common law doctrine without adapting it to the relevant administrative context may be acting unreasonably.[89]

Third, however, deference must be earned through reasons. Decision makers must grapple with the arguments presented, be responsive to the parties and demonstrate that they listened to what was said, and discharge a heavier burden of justification in situations where important individual interests are at stake:

The principles of justification and transparency require that an administrative decision maker's reasons meaningfully account for the central issues and concerns raised by the parties ... The concept of responsive reasons is inherently bound up with this principle, because reasons are the primary mechanism by which decision makers demonstrate that they have actually *listened* to the parties ... [A] decision maker's failure to meaningfully grapple with key issues or central arguments raised by the parties may call into question whether the decision maker was actually alert and sensitive to the matter before it. In addition to assuring parties that their concerns have been heard, the process of drafting reasons with care and attention can alert the decision maker to inadvertent gaps and other flaws in its reasoning ... Central to the necessity of adequate justification is the perspective of the individual or party over whom authority is being exercised. Where the impact of a decision on an individual's rights and interests is severe, the reasons provided to that individual must reflect the stakes. The principle of responsive justification means that if a decision has particularly harsh consequences for the affected individual, the decision maker must explain why its decision best reflects the legislature's intention. This includes decisions with consequences that threaten an individual's life, liberty, dignity or livelihood.[90]

Vavilovian reasonableness review is deferential, but it is deference based on reason, not on brute force. Responsive justification is the key principle. This is a conception of deference much more congenial to those seeking to challenge administrative decisions, such as lawyers practising in the area of immigration and refugee law, than those who would prefer a high degree of deference to administrative decisions. Progressive labour relations lawyers who contributed to the foundations of deference in Canadian administrative law might well be shifting uneasily in their graves, even though on matters of politics they would mostly make common cause with members of the immigration and refugee bar. In *Vavilov*, interveners representing the environment, prisoners, immigration-status claimants, tenants and First Nations children all advocated for more intrusive judicial review and expressed skepticism about the inherent expertise of administrative decision makers. It is difficult to avoid the conclusion that these interventions weighed heavily on the majority. The key difference between the minority judges and the majority judges is that Abella and Karakatsanis worried that setting out a context-sensitive approach to reasonableness review would encourage judges to meddle in areas best left to experts. On this, as we will see in the next chapter, they may well have been right: *Vavilov* has certainly imposed higher standards in some areas of public administration. But for the majority, this was plainly a feature, not a bug.[91]

The contrast between the two primary parts of *Vavilov* – selecting the standard of review and the reasonableness standard – is striking. As for the fault lines of form/substance, deference/nondeference, and authority/reason, reasonableness review is the mirror image of selecting the standard of review. Where the selection of the standard of review is formalist, nondeferential, and based on authority, the articulation of reasonableness is substantive, deferential, and based on reason. Plainly, this was a compromise hammered out between judges who aligned very differently relative to the fault lines of Canadian administrative law.

The Limits of Compromise?

In that regard, it is worth taking a deep dive into the idea of persistent discord. As mentioned above, the majority did not accept that disagreement between administrative decision makers could justify correctness review. The treatment of reasonableness review as it applies to persistent discord is doubly telling: first, it underscores how the judges compromised to achieve an (almost) unified front; and second, it underscores the substantive, deferential, and reasoned basis of *Vavilovian* reasonableness review.

While rejecting the proposition that correctness review should be applied whenever there is persistent discord about a particular problem, the majority accepted that situations in which the outcome of the administrative process depends on the identity of the administrative decision maker an individual happens to encounter are not tolerable. Mindful, though, of the "practical difficulties" of identifying exactly when and where disagreement within an administrative decision-making body has risen to the level of "persistent discord," the majority concluded that recognizing a correctness category would be inappropriate.[92] Rather, "the more robust reasonableness review" enunciated in *Vavilov* would be an adequate safeguard against the risk of intolerable arbitrariness, "guarding against threats to the rule of law" created by inconsistent outputs from the administrative process.[93] That said, citizens "are entitled to expect that like cases will generally be treated alike and that outcomes will not depend merely on the identity of the individual decision maker."[94] Accordingly, "[w]here a decision maker *does* depart from longstanding practices or established internal authority, it bears the justificatory burden of explaining that departure in its reasons."[95]

Again, the approach is substantive, deferential, and reasoned. Whether a burden exists and the weight it has is invariably contextual. The approach is deferential inasmuch as it starts with the reasons of the administrative decision maker, not with a judge's external perception of matters, and entertains the possibility (perhaps even the likelihood) that an apparent discord can be satisfactorily explained such that a court has no basis to intervene. And the approach is reasoned: neither the administrative decision maker nor the reviewing court has the inherent authority to decide the matter one way or another, but rather the key question is whether the administrative decision maker has adequately discharged any burden of justification it bears.

Elsewhere in the majority reasons, however, the potential for future tensions between the different camps who compromised to create the *Vavilov* framework is clear.

Whereas with respect to the other contextual considerations considered by the majority the permissive term "may" was almost invariably used, it was replaced by the imperative "must" with respect to the governing statutory scheme.[96] A decision maker *must*, therefore, comply with the "rationale and purview of the statutory scheme";[97] a decision "must comport with any more specific constraints imposed by the governing legislative scheme, such as the statutory definitions, principles or formulas that prescribe the exercise of a discretion";[98] and a decision maker should not fetter a discretionary power.[99] Thus, "[a]lthough a decision maker's interpretation of its statutory grant of authority is generally entitled to deference, the decision maker *must* nonetheless properly justify that interpretation."[100] *Must*, not may. This is form, not substance and may even mischievously be said to involve "true" questions of jurisdiction.

Tension is also evident in respect of the so-called nominate grounds of review. In most other Commonwealth jurisdictions, the exercise of discretionary powers is reviewable on a variety of bases, such as improper purposes, irrelevant considerations, fettering of discretion, subdelegation, and bad faith. These relate, in the argot of *Vavilov*, to the "governing statutory scheme." The difficulty this creates is that the Supreme Court held in the early 2000s that while such grounds of review are "still useful as familiar landmarks," it emphasized that they "no longer dictate the journey" to a conclusion of unreasonableness:[101] it is insufficient "merely to identify a categorical or nominate error, such as bad faith, error on collateral or preliminary matters, ulterior or improper purpose, no evidence, or the consideration of an irrelevant factor."[102] Since then, however, many judges have considered that the establishment of at least some of the nominate grounds of review renders an administrative decision *per se* unreasonable: they are hard, formal limits.[103] Again, the formulation in *Vavilov* might be thought to favour form over substance.

It is apparent, however, that with respect to some of the nominate grounds of review, a holistic reasonableness analysis will be appropriate and even unavoidable. Take, for example, fettering of discretion, where the question for a reviewing court will not be: "Was discretion fettered?" but rather: "Was it reasonable, given the context, to issue a detailed directive to front-line decision makers?"[104] Sometimes, discretion might indeed be fettered, at least to some extent, but the question for the reviewing court will be whether this was justifiable, given the decision-making context.[105] Therefore, justifying a decision will be easier in circumstances where the decision maker has been empowered in broad terms, but more difficult where the statute leaves little room for interpretive maneuver. This is a substantive rather than formal approach to nominate grounds of review. *Vavilov* is open to both a pro-form and a pro-substance reading.

In terms of the tensions in *Vavilov*, the discussion of statutory interpretation is the neatest example. The majority made clear that a reviewing court is not to conduct its own statutory interpretation exercise to establish a benchmark or yardstick against which to measure an administrative decision maker's interpretation of law.[106]

However, the finer details of how to approach the review of a decision based on a statutory interpretation exercise undertaken by the decision maker are murky. On the one hand, the reader is told: "Administrative decision makers are not required to engage in a formalistic statutory interpretation exercise in every case."[107] On the other hand, a few paragraphs later, the administrative decision maker's task is said to be to "interpret the contested provision in a manner consistent with the text, context and purpose, applying its particular insight into the statutory scheme at issue."[108]

The latter statement looks awfully like a "formalistic statutory interpretation exercise," one that judges suspicious of an administrative decision maker's ability to make interpretations of law might well require. Such judges should take particular note of the majority's insistence that sometimes an administrative decision maker need "touch upon only the most salient aspects of the text, context or purpose."[109] But there is a risk that judges opposed to deference will nonetheless fasten upon the emphasis on text, context, and purpose to constrain administrative interpretations of law. Put another way, the *Vavilov* compromise does not eliminate the fault lines or the fact that judges align themselves differently in relation to form/substance, deference/nondeference, and authority/reason. Indeed, in some respects, *Vavilovian* reasonableness review merely papers over these cracks.

Summary

In the next chapter, we will explore the reception of *Vavilov* by Canada's legal community. The compromise achieved in *Vavilov* may not hold; the coalition may fracture, with different members emphasizing different aspects of the decision. The basic compromise is clear, however: 1) form over substance on selecting the standard of review, but a reversal of roles when it comes to articulating the reasonableness standard; 2) nondeference over deference in deciding between deferential review and correctness review, but deference over nondeference on reasonableness review; and 3) authority trumping reason on the selection of the standard of review, with reason turning the tables in the articulation of reasonableness review.

There is, moreover, reason to be optimistic that the *Vavilov* framework is capable of responding adequately to the underlying complexity of administrative law. Most of all, the framework is relatively easy to grasp: "jurisdiction" has been eliminated as an organizing principle; "legislative intent" has been replaced by the thin conception of "institutional design"; and "deference" has been defined in detail. Certainly the reasonableness standard is sufficiently flexible to be of general applicability, with the various contextual considerations carrying greater or lesser force in particular areas. Even with respect to statutory appeals, there may be enough play in the joints of the framework to accommodate the nuances of different areas of law (by classifying matters within the expertise of economic regulators or professional disciplinary bodies as factual or mixed questions), thereby meeting some of the concerns powerfully articulated by Justices Abella and Karakatsanis in their concurring reasons. In summary, "jurisdiction" has been sidelined, "legislative intent" has been redefined, and the meaning of "deference" is no longer obscure.

PRECEDENT

The *Vavilov* framework is intended to be a clear break with the past: "A court seeking to determine what standard is appropriate in a case before it should look to these reasons first in order to determine how this general framework applies to that case."[110] Given the reformulations effected in *Vavilov*, some precedents will now carry less force: decisions on jurisdictional questions or statutory appeal mechanisms, for instance, will henceforth be of little relevance.[111] Prior decisions on overlapping jurisdiction, by contrast, will continue to be relevant.[112] The majority suggested, or perhaps expressed the hope, that the Supreme Court's jurisprudence on questions of central importance to the legal system will "continue to apply essentially without modification."[113]

More ominously, the majority acknowledged that retrofitting precedents to the *Vavilov* framework "may" require reviewing courts to "resolve subsidiary questions" about the compatibility of prior decisions with the new framework.[114] There is, again, a suggestion/expression of hope that the Supreme Court's precedents will "continue to provide helpful guidance."[115] But the majority – to its credit – appreciated that matters will not always be so simple: "Where a reviewing court is not certain how these reasons relate to the case before it, it may find it prudent to request submissions from the parties on both the appropriate standard and the application of that standard."[116] *Vavilov* was the big bang, and everything can be pieced back together again only by using the framework *Vavilov* created.

REMEDIAL DISCRETION

Even where a court has determined that a decision is unreasonable or procedurally unfair, it retains the power to refuse to grant a remedy, or to grant a remedy subject to conditions. Remedial discretion is a key feature of contemporary administrative law. In *Vavilov*, the majority discussed the issue at surprising length – surprising because although remedial discretion is by now a well-developed phenomenon, it is rarely the subject of detailed discussion.

The majority set out a variety of factors that are influential in the exercise of remedial discretion:

> Elements like concern for delay, fairness to the parties, urgency of providing a resolution to the dispute, the nature of the particular regulatory regime, whether the administrative decision maker had a genuine opportunity to weigh in on the issue in question, costs to the parties, and the efficient use of public resources ...[117]

The particular aspect discussed in *Vavilov* is the discretion of the reviewing court that has quashed an administrative decision to "remit the matter to the decision maker for reconsideration with the benefit of the court's reasons."[118]

Remitting the matter will "most often"[119] be the appropriate course of action, as "the legislature has entrusted the matter to the administrative decision maker, and not to the court, to decide."[120] Considerations of efficient and effective administration will also be relevant,[121] and although these will typically also militate in favour of remitting a matter for fresh consideration by a specialized, expert decision maker, there are "limited scenarios in which remitting the matter would stymie the timely and effective resolution of matters."[122] It may, for instance, not be appropriate to remit where "it becomes evident to the court, in the course of its review, that a particular outcome is inevitable and that remitting the case would therefore serve no useful purpose."[123]

There is nothing particularly objectionable about any of this. Indeed, it is salutary to have remedial discretion out in the open, as a subject of discussion rather than exercised (as is often the case) without much analysis.

That said, the discussion in *Vavilov* falls short in two respects. The first is that the framework for exercising remedial discretion does not really follow from any set of guiding principles. The majority stated that "the choice of remedy must be guided by the rationale for applying that standard to begin with."[124] But given that the selection of the standard of review is now based on a context- and nuance-free assessment of whether the legislature created a right of appeal, it is difficult to identify a "rationale" that can offer much assistance to a judge struggling to decide whether to remit a matter. There is a much richer, principle- and value-laden analysis in *D'Errico v Canada (Attorney General)*,[125] a Federal Court of Appeal case that the majority cites and that emphasizes the important additional factor – glossed over by the majority – of the rights of the individual who has been deprived of a benefit he or she is entitled to. Perhaps in the future *D'Errico* will get more attention.

The second is the failure to appreciate that exercises of judicial discretion can have systemic consequences. If judicial willingness to quash decisions for unreasonableness is combined with judicial unwillingness to remit matters to the administrative decision makers whose responsibility it is to address them, the result will be to transfer decision-making authority from administrative decision makers to the courts. Over time, there is even a risk that administrative decision makers will come to take their responsibilities less seriously, in the knowledge that if any problems arise, the courts will sort them out in due course. By contrast, if matters are routinely remitted, the effect will be very quickly to make clear to administrative decision makers that they really have to get it right the first time, otherwise, the matters will keep returning to their desks, embossed with a judicial stamp to the effect of "not good enough." Where the discussion in *Vavilov* falls short is in its failure to appreciate the systemic consequences of exercises of judicial discretion.

Nonetheless, the application of robust reasonableness review should generally lead to decisions regularly being remitted, given the majority's warning about *ex post facto* supplementation of sparse administrative decisions, as it will rarely be possible for a reviewing court to refuse to remit a sparse decision without engaging in extensive supplementation.[126] And the more dynamic and responsive the reasonableness review is, the more difficult it will be to say that if the matter were sent back, the outcome would be inevitable. Of course, the law here will have to be built from the ground up,[127] and lower courts may pay more attention to the systemic consequences of exercises of judicial discretion than the majority did in *Vavilov*.

CONCLUSION

Concerned about the complexity that existed in terms of selecting the standard of review (correctness or reasonableness) and the lack of clarity on how to apply the reasonableness standard, the majority in *Vavilov* set out to simplify the selection of the standard of review and clarify the application of the reasonableness standard.

In terms of the former, the majority relied on a simple, rules-based formula provided by "institutional design" and the "rule of law." By virtue of the institutional choice to delegate decision-making authority to an administrative decision maker, the presumptive standard of review is reasonableness; deviations from reasonableness review are justifiable only where there is a statutory right of appeal or legislated standard of review – institutional design choices – or where the rule of law requires the courts to furnish a final, definitive answer on a question of transcendent importance for the integrity of the legal system – constitutional questions, questions of central importance to the legal system, and questions of overlapping jurisdiction. Statutory appeal rights henceforth attract the well-established framework of *Housen v Nikolaisen*:[128] extricable questions of law are for the courts, but determinations of fact or mixed law and fact can be interfered with only if the appellant can demonstrate a palpable and overriding error on the part of the decision maker. Notably, although the concepts of institutional design and the rule of law are potentially capacious, for the purposes of *Vavilovian* judicial review, they contain only limited content: statutory appeals, legislated standards of review, and questions that demand a uniform answer. The "vexing" contextual factors,[129] such as expertise, have been excised from the standard of review selection exercise, replaced by wafer-thin principles.

Whereas the concepts underpinning the new approach to selecting the standard of review are thin, the conception of reasonableness review developed by the majority in *Vavilov* is thick. Reasonableness review is at once robust in policing the limits of administrative decision-making authority and respectful in appreciating that "'[a]dministrative justice' will not always look like 'judicial justice.'"[130] Although *Vavilovian* reasonableness review is inherently deferential, it is nonetheless more demanding than the articulation of the reasonableness standard developed in previous cases: decisions must be justified, not merely justifiable; decision makers must demonstrate their expertise; a decision must be responsive to the particularities of, and presented by, the parties; and only contemporaneous reasons can be offered in support of the reasonableness of a decision.[131] On balance, I believe that the *Vavilov* majority was on firmer footing than Justices Abella and Karakatsanis. As long as the correctness categories are narrowly confined and the standard of reasonableness is applied in the inherently deferential manner set out by the majority, *Vavilov* is better suited to contemporary judicial review – with its broad reach into all aspects of public admin-istration – than a hands-off approach. If some decision makers have to up their game, so be it.

Vavilov is the product of sustained deliberation by the country's apex court. Judges who had rarely agreed on any administrative law matters prior to *Vavilov* coalesced around the solution outlined in the majority reasons: a thin approach to selecting the standard of review; a thick approach to reasonableness review. To achieve this consensus, judges who prefer clear categories (forms) and nondeferential review on questions of law had to water down their wine; so, too, did their colleagues who have a penchant for contextual (substantive) analysis and accept that on many issues administrative decision makers deserve deference on the basis of the meaningful advantages specialists on the front lines of public administration have relative to generalist judges.[132] Rather than reasoning on every issue, in every case, from first principles, these judges coalesced around the consensus memorialized in the majority reasons in *Vavilov*.

5

Vavilov Hits the Road

THIS CHAPTER DISCUSSES FOUR aspects of the reception and application of the *Vavilov* framework by courts around Canada:

1 Reasonableness review has become a culture of justification in action. Decision makers, such as ministers and labour relations arbitrators, who historically benefitted from significant judicial deference, have had to adjust their practices to take account of the new normal ushered in by the "big bang."

2 The area of statutory appeals has been considerably modified, with very important and significant decisions demonstrating that courts are much less likely to defer to expert regulators on matters relating to the interpretation of the statutes they administer, occasioning a significant transfer of power from regulators to the courts.

3 Judges have generally remained deferential in exercising their remedial discretion, and have favoured sending matters back to the decision maker for a fresh decision after finding that a decision was unreasonable. However, there are signs that in some cases judges are willing to take a more muscular approach.

4 There has been little interest in adding new correctness categories to the *Vavilov* framework, although the Supreme Court of Canada itself added such a category shortly before this book went to

press. The reasoning in this decision was questionable, however, and does not augur well for the future operation of the *Vavilov* framework.

APPLYING THE REASONABLENESS STANDARD

The methodology of reasonableness review set out in *Vavilov* is inherently deferential and in that regard "does not constitute a significant change in the law of judicial review with respect to the review of the reasons of administrative tribunals."[1] Justice Simon Ruel of the Quebec Court of Appeal provided a sharp reminder of the inherently deferential nature of judicial review on the reasonableness standard in *MO c Société de l'assurance automobile du Québec,* criticizing counsel for essentially repeating arguments made not just before the lower court but also before multiple administrative decision makers.[2]

Administrative decisions are to be read fairly; courts are not to prowl the reasons and record looking for any small error on which they can pounce:[3]

> In *Vavilov,* the Supreme Court tells us that we should not be too hasty to find [material] flaws. Vavilov's requirement of a reasoned explanation cannot be applied in a way that transforms reasonableness review into correctness review. If reviewing courts are too fussy and adopt the attitude of a literary critic all too willing to find shortcomings, they will be conducting correctness review, not reasonableness review. That would return us to the bad old days in the 1960's and 1970's when reviewing courts would come up with any old excuse to strike down decisions they disliked – and often did.[4]

Canada Post Corp v Canadian Union of Postal Workers,[5] handed down by the Supreme Court a day after *Vavilov,* is instructive. At issue here was the scope of paragraph 125(1)(z.12) of the *Canada Labour Code,* pursuant to which an employer shall inspect a workplace at least once a year, even in areas "not controlled by the employer."[6]

A complaint was filed about Canada Post's compliance with this duty, in relation to employees in Burlington, Ontario. Canada Post took the view that the duty under the *Code* extended only to its local depot, not to all of the highways and byways its employees traipse to reach letter boxes all around Burlington. The union favoured a more liberal interpretation, which would encompass the routes and the letter boxes. The stakes were high, as a determination in favour of the union would, in principle, have nationwide repercussions. Canada Post would have to inspect every letter box from coast to coast to coast at least once a year. A health and safety officer agreed with the union, but an appeals officer took Canada Post's side at the Occupational Health and Safety Tribunal Canada.

A majority of the Supreme Court upheld the appeals officer's decision. Here, Justice Malcolm Rowe noted, the appeals officer had provided "detailed reasons" that were, indeed, "exemplary"[7] and "contended with the submissions of the parties throughout his analysis."[8] Crucially, these reasons "amply" demonstrated that the appeals officer "considered the text, context, purpose, as well as the practical implications of his interpretation."[9]

The appeals officer had not considered, because he had not been referred to it, another provision of the *Code* that dealt with the concept of control. This, Rowe held, was not fatal, not least because the appeals officer had not been referred to it but also because, more generally, "[f]ailure to consider a particular piece of the statutory context that does not support a decision maker's statutory interpretation analysis will not necessarily render the interpretation unreasonable."[10] From there, the conclusion that the appeals officer's decision was reasonable was unsurprising and perhaps inevitable.

In dissent, Justice Rosalie Abella (with whom Justice Sheilah Martin agreed) took the view that paragraph 125(1)(z.12) was "an unambiguous dual legislative direction to employers that their safety obligations – including the inspection duty – apply both to *workplaces* they control *and*, if they do not control the actual workplace, to every *work activity* that they do control to the extent of that control."[11] There would be much to be said for this approach if the court were indeed interpreting the provision *de novo,* without the benefit of the appeals officer's reasons. Given, however, that the appeals officer had provided detailed reasons that responded amply to the fulsome submissions made by Canada Post and the union, those reasons were properly the starting point for the Supreme Court's analysis, not the text of the provision.

Thus *Vavilov* teaches that judicial review should be neither a line-by-line treasure hunt for error nor an effort in redoing the work of the administrative decision maker. Reasons for administrative decisions should be read fairly, with due attention to the decision-making context and the arguments made before the decision maker. Some serious error or violation of the legal and factual constraints on the decision maker must be demonstrated.[12]

But *Vavilov* has set a higher bar for decision makers than the pre-*Vavilov* regime, with respect to justification, demonstrated expertise, responsiveness, and contemporaneity.[13] While most respectable administrative tribunals are likely to continue to scale this bar with ease, other bodies might find it more imposing. Those operating in high-volume areas of decision-making (such as immigration) and those used to receiving a high degree of deference on the basis of their expertise (such as labour arbitrators) or electoral legitimacy (such as ministers) have had to learn to jump higher than they have in the past.

Justification

A decision must be justified in light of the legal and factual constraints on the decision maker. As Justice Alan Diner of the Federal Court explained in *Ortiz v Canada (Citizenship and Immigration),* whereas previously courts began with the outcome and then looked back at the reasons, *Vavilov* instructs them "to start with the reasons, and assess whether they justify the outcome."[14] There has been, as Justice Richard Elson of the Saskatchewan Court of Queen's Bench remarked in *Pierson v Estevan Board of Police Commissioners,* "a shift in focus from the *justifiability* of the decision maker's conclusion to whether it is actually *justified* by a rational and coherent chain of analysis."[15] A decision maker must therefore explain how its decisions are justified, by laying out the legal framework and the relevant facts before reaching a conclusion that is intelligible and cogent in light of the law and the facts.

Demonstrated Expertise

The decision must be the product of the demonstrated expertise of the decision maker. Prior to *Vavilov,* decision makers benefitted from a thoroughgoing presumption of expertise.[16] However, a decision maker must henceforth demonstrate that it has applied its expertise, by explaining how its specialized knowledge of the field leads or guides it to the conclusions underpinning its decisions.

The decision of the Ontario Court of Appeal in *Romania v Boros*[17] warrants a special mention. This decision was issued in the context of extradition proceedings, where the ministers have typically been given wide latitude, because extradition involves international relations, in which the executive branch has particular expertise. Although the minister had provided a lengthy, twenty-page letter ordering the surrender of the applicant to Romania, he did not provide an adequate justification for an eight-year delay in seeking the extradition. The applicant had been convicted *in absentia* in 2000; there was a dispute about the state of knowledge of the Romanian authorities, particularly whether they knew in 1998 that the applicant was, or was soon to arrive, in Canada, long before making the extradition request in 2008. That the "combined Canadian delay of nearly 8 years is not addressed beyond an implicit general claim that these matters take a long time" meant that the decision was not "adequate."[18] Strikingly, although the Supreme Court held in *Sriskandarajah v United States of America*[19] that procedural fairness does not require extradition authorities to seek out evidence that may be helpful to an applicant, the Ontario Court of Appeal held in light of *Vavilov* that it was "incumbent upon the Minister to make inquiries" about the point at which the Romanian authorities knew or ought to have known that the applicant was in Canada.[20] Both procedure and substance were considered together, holistically, to justify the conclusion that the decision should be struck down:

The delay between [1998] and the issuance of the summons on November 15, 2016 – more than 18 years – has not been properly investigated, nor properly explained. In the circumstances, the surrender order cannot stand. On the existing record, we are unable to determine whether the decision to order Ms. Boros' surrender was reasonable. More information is required before we can properly conduct this analysis.[21]

In sum, the minister did not benefit here from the deference typically afforded elected officials in the sensitive area of deportation, with its implications for Canada's international relations. This is a marker of the significant shift *Vavilov* has required with respect to some types of decision maker.

Responsiveness

The decision must be responsive to the central points raised before the decision maker, who must, indeed, grapple with key arguments and evidence. Where, moreover, the decision would have harsh consequences for the individual concerned, there is a "heightened responsibility" of responsiveness on the decision maker.[22]

For example, in *Langlais c Collège des médecins du Québec*, it was unreasonable for the Collège to fail to address the regulatory provision that a doctor invoked to support his application for recognition as a specialist in internal medicine (necessary because, in 2012, the Collège had introduced more stringent standards in this regard).[23] This thinking has been echoed in several Federal Court decisions. In *Patel v Canada (Citizenship and Immigration)*, Justice Alan Diner noted that *Vavilov* requires "basic responsiveness" to the evidence presented (and found it lacking).[24] In *Samra v Canada (Citizenship and Immigration)*, Justice Paul Favel found a decision unreasonable because it "lacked analysis": "the officer's decision is merely a recitation of the evidence before him followed by a conclusion."[25] In *Li v Canada (Citizenship and Immigration)*, Justice Janet Fuhrer struck down a sparsely reasoned study permit decision issued by a line officer who failed to "engage" with the applicant's evidence.[26] In *Slemko v Canada (Public Safety and Emergency*

Preparedness), Justice Elizabeth Walker held that brief reasons for refusing a humanitarian and compassionate application were unreasonable as they failed to consider and weigh all of the applicant's submissions.[27] And in *Albrifcani v Canada (Citizenship and Immigration)*, Justice Cecily Strickland noted that key findings were not justified by reference to the record, with an undefined term "QA" playing an important role.[28]

These Federal Court cases all addressed decisions made by front-line decision makers processing hundreds or thousands of applications. In *Rodriguez Martinez v Canada (Citizenship and Immigration)*, Justice Nicholas McHaffie explained that while institutional constraints "must inform the assessment of reasonableness,"[29] a decision maker – even a line decision maker – must nonetheless respond to the evidence.[30] Thus boilerplate statements are now treated with suspicion by the courts. For example, Diner concluded in *Osun v Canada (Citizenship and Immigration)* that a boilerplate comment to the effect that the decision maker had given a piece of evidence "careful consideration" was insufficient, as the decision lacked an "assessment" of the evidence.[31]

In terms of responsiveness to harsh consequences, the importance of the decision for the individual tends to play an understated role, because where there would be harsh consequences, these will usually form part of the argument and evidence that the decision maker is, in any event, obliged to respond to. The revocation of a passport in *Alsaloussi v Canada (Attorney General)*, was unreasonable because the consequences were "severe and harsh" but the decision lacked a "proper analysis" of the effect on the applicant.[32] In *Downey v Nova Scotia (Attorney General)*, the harsh consequences related to the applicant's property interests: he had occupied land for close to twenty years and sought to have the title clarified.[33] The effect on his property interests bolstered the court's conclusion that it was unreasonable to interpret the provincial land titles clarification legislation as requiring the applicant to demonstrate adverse possession with respect to land to which title was unclear. Here, however, the analysis of harsh consequences simply supported a conclusion of unreasonableness reached on other grounds, which has been a common feature of the post-*Vavilov* jurisprudence.[34]

Responsive decisions need not be lengthy. Brief explanations can satisfy the responsiveness requirement.[35] In *Mao v Canada (Citizenship and Immigration)*, Justice Favel of the Federal Court noted that "there is no need for a decision maker to engage with every argument – it is enough that they are alive [to] and aware of them."[36] In *Vavilov*, the requirement to "meaningfully grapple" with an individual's submissions applies only to those that are "key."[37] Thus, the Alberta Court of Appeal upheld against a reasonableness challenge a labour relations decision that took only five paragraphs to address a key issue.[38] Responsive decisions do need to engage with the arguments and evidence, may do so briefly.

Contemporaneity

There is now a strong requirement of contemporaneity. Consistent with the majority reasons in *Vavilov*, courts are to refrain from bolstering defective administrative decisions with post-hoc reasoning supplied by the decision maker in an affidavit, by clever counsel at the lectern, or by the court itself.[39] A court should not "fashion its own reasons in order to buttress the administrative decision."[40] If justification, responsiveness, and demonstrated expertise are not present in the reasons given to the affected individual or parties, a court should ordinarily not permit them to be "coopered up" later on, to borrow an elegant phrase from Justice David Stratas of the Federal Court of Appeal.[41] Courts are no longer able or willing to "infer" that an argument or evidence was considered in the absence of reasons dealing with the argument or evidence.[42]

Judicial rewriting of defective decisions has been definitively ruled out.[43] Remember Justice Johanne Gauthier's evident distaste for the Supreme Court's judicial review doctrine in the *Tran* case?[44] Contrast the same judge's conclusion in *Farrier v Canada (Attorney General)*.[45] Quashing as unreasonable a one-page decision from the Parole Board that failed to engage with the applicant's arguments, Gauthier commented, with evident relish:

> Before *Vavilov* I would probably have found, as did the Federal Court, that, in light of the presumption that the decision maker considered all

of the arguments and the case law before it and after having read the record, the decision was reasonable. The absence of reasons dealing with the first two issues before the Appeal Division was not at the time sufficient to set aside the decision. It was implicit that the Appeal Division did not accept that the Board's interpretation of the Act was erroneous, particularly considering subsection 143(1) of the Act. Under the circumstances, the administrative decision maker was presumed to have rejected Mr. Farrier's arguments regarding any prejudice caused by the lack of a recording regardless of whether the Act provides for such a recording or whether there was simply a breach of the Manual. Such a finding was one of the possible outcomes given the Supreme Court's decision in *CUPE*, even if that decision was not cited by the Appeal Division.[46]

In the absence of any internal policies, previous Parole Board jurisprudence, or other explanations for not addressing the applicant's arguments,[47] the conclusion that the decision was unreasonable was irresistible.[48] There may be situations where it is obvious from the background context that a decision maker did not address a particular point because the decision maker considered it unnecessary to do so (which, on occasion, may be due to the existence of established jurisprudence or publicly available administrative policies, or simply the way the matter was presented to the decision maker), but this is just another way of saying that administrative decisions should be read fairly and in their whole context, to borrow again from Justice Stratas, judges are not "literary critics" or Monday-morning quarterbacks critiquing the way a decision maker formulated its reasons.[49]

The Tensions in *Vavilov*

Clearly, then, the lower courts have heard one of the messages of *Vavilov* loud and clear: the need for a decision maker to demonstrate responsive justification in order to gain deference.

It would be remiss of me, however, to discuss the rollout of the *Vavilov* framework without acknowledging that some of the tensions in the decision have been visible in lower-court decisions. This is especially true with respect to statutory interpretation.

Consider *Canadian National Railway Company v Richardson International Limited.*[50] The standard of review here was correctness, as the matter came before the Federal Court of Appeal as a statutory appeal from a decision of the Canadian Transportation Agency relating to railways. But Justice Marc Nadon also commented, in *obiter dicta,* that he would have struck the decision down for unreasonableness in any event, "because it failed to consider both context and the legislative scheme as a whole."[51] Citing paragraph 118 of *Vavilov* – but not the more equivocal language of paragraphs 119 and 122 – Nadon commented that the agency's failure to "observe the fundamental principles of statutory interpretation"[52] was "fatal to its decision."[53] This might be thought to betray a predilection for an interventionist standard of reasonableness review on issues of statutory interpretation (although, to be fair, Nadon remitted the matter to the agency and took pains not to "rule out the possibility that the Agency might come to an interpretation that differs from the one it arrived at in the present matter").[54]

A more moderate approach was taken by Justice Daniel Boone of the Newfoundland and Labrador Supreme Court in *Salmonid Association of Eastern Newfoundland v Her Majesty the Queen in Right of Newfoundland and Labrador,* where the key flaw was that the minister "did not explain his reasons for his adoption of an interpretation that he was aware was one of two valid but opposite readings,"[55] and by Justice Robert Barnes of the Federal Court in *Glaxosmithkline Biologicals SA v Canada (Health),* noting that the minister had failed to have regard to the obligation to interpret Canadian law implementing the *Canada-Europe Trade Agreement* in conformity with the agreement[56] (albeit the minister prevailed on appeal[57]). By contrast, in *Natco Pharma (Canada) Inc v Canada (Health),* the minister prevailed but it was a close-run thing:[58] the message for ministerial decision-making from this and other post-*Vavilov* decisions is that ministers must make a sincere effort to justify their decisions in terms of statutory text, context, and purpose.

And there is also a clear message for all other decision makers: a statutory interpretation analysis should not be reverse-engineered to achieve a desired outcome on policy grounds.[59]

Justice Nadon's *obiter* comments certainly underscore how some portions of *Vavilov* are liable to become battlegrounds between different factions of judges – those who favour more intrusive review on questions of law in one camp, their more deferential colleagues in the other. For a similar approach, almost demanding panoptic qualities on the part of an administrative decision maker, see the comments of Justice John Bodurtha of the Nova Scotia Supreme Court in *Beals v Nova Scotia (Attorney General)*: "[T]he legislature and applicants ... are entitled to presume that the person making a decision about an application under [legislation] knows the occasion and necessity for the enactment, the circumstances existing at the time it was passed, the mischief to be remedied, and the object to be attained, without that information necessarily appearing in the record."[60] This would set a high bar, higher than the majority in *Vavilov* intended. Justice Christa Brothers of the same court was quite right, in my view, to comment, in *Bancroft v Nova Scotia (Lands and Forests)*, that *Vavilov*'s approach to statutory interpretation involves a "balancing act."[61]

In terms of that balancing act, it is instructive to consider some cases involving judicial review of legislative-type decisions for which contemporaneous reasons were not provided. In *Vavilov*, the Supreme Court left the door open to focusing on the outcome of a decision-making process in situations where reasons are not provided.[62] Accordingly, in *1120732 BC Ltd v Whistler (Resort Municipality)*, Justice David Tysoe of the British Columbia Court of Appeal held that the enactment of a municipal bylaw was reasonable on the basis that there were "at least three ways in which the Municipality's council could have reasonably concluded" that it had the necessary statutory authority.[63] Contrast, however, the relatively intensive review undertaken in *Wilson v Cowichan Valley (Regional District)*, where there the municipality sought to use a regulation to prohibit when the relevant legislative provisions permitted it only to regulate.[64] The best way to understand these contrasting decisions is that, in some instances, the governing statutory scheme[65] will give municipalities (and other makers of regulations) a large margin of appreciation, whereas in others, municipalities will be more tightly constrained by prescriptive statutory language.[66]

Summing Up

The analysis in the Ontario Divisional Court case of *Scarborough Health Network v Canadian Union of Public Employees, Local 5852* is instructive.[67] This concerned an interest arbitration, which arose in the context of a merger of hospital units and the constitution of a new bargaining unit. Several outstanding issues relating to a new collective agreement could not be resolved and became the subject of a labour relations matter. The most important issue was wage harmonization. After hearing argument from the union and the employer, the arbitration board determined that it would harmonize like classifications to the higher or highest of the applicable pre-existing wage rates. The entirety of the board's substantive analysis of this issue was contained in a single paragraph:

> There is a well-established pattern in the hospital sector of post-merger harmonization of wages to the higher rate. This pattern is reflected in numerous voluntary settlements, and Arbitrators have adopted this approach on the basis of replication (See, e.g., *The Niagara Health System and Service Employees International Union, Local 204*, July 5, 2002 (Kaplan) at p. 2–4, *Participating Hospitals and Canadian Union of Public Employees*, March 4, 2011 (Petryshen), *Trillium Health Partners and CUPE*, December 9, 2015 (Kaplan)). Having reviewed and carefully considered the parties' materials and submissions, and on the basis of the principles identified in the opening section of our main local issues award, including my determination of the pay equity jurisdictional argument, I am satisfied that it is appropriate to replicate the established approach to post-merger wage harmonization.

The Divisional Court quashed the arbitration decision as it lacked the attributes of reasonableness.

First, the decision was not justified:

There is nothing to show that the Board considered the particular circumstances of this case. There is no analysis of the Hospital's argument that this case is distinguishable from past cases. Past practice may be a relevant consideration, but there is no explanation why past practice, in this case, is so dispositive that other considerations need not be addressed at all.[68]

Second, the decision was not the product of demonstrated expertise, but rather was based on "conclusory" statements about the factors the arbitration board took into account and the decision it reached: "It does not explain why the Board of Arbitration did what it did."[69]

Third, the decision was not responsive to the arguments made, especially the employer's argument that the factual matrix of this case was unusual: "The employer sought evaluation of the particular context of the hospital and the affected employees."[70] Post-*Vavilov*, however, judicial review requires reasons that "demonstrate analysis of the submissions and positions of the parties. It is not enough to summarize the parties' positions. Only through reasons can the parties know that the issues of concern to them have been the subject of reasoned consideration."[71]

And, fourth, in view of the contemporaneity requirement imposed by *Vavilov*, counsel's attempt to supplement the defective reasons was rejected by the Divisional Court: "It is not a question of whether the decision could be justified on the evidence, but rather whether the decision was justified in the Board's reasons, that is, whether the Board used evidence and analysis to come to a logical, transparent and, thus, reasonable decision."[72] Given the high degree of deference that has typically been accorded to labour relations determinations (by arbitrators or by labour boards), this decision is especially notable,[73] and the same logic can be seen to apply to front-line decision makers[74] and ministers,[75] other bodies that have traditionally benefitted from significant deference.

SELECTING THE STANDARD OF REVIEW

Evidently, *Vavilov* made significant changes to the selection of the standard of review, leveraging the principle of institutional design to create a new regime for the treatment of statutory appeals and using the rule of law in a very thin sense to create limited categories of correctness review. It has significantly simplified the selection of the standard of review by using a formal, rules-based approach that eliminates contextual factors. Context may still play a role – for example, in helping courts classify questions for the purposes of statutory appeals – but it operates in the background and occupies much less of the time of judges, lawyers, and litigants than it did in earlier eras of Canadian judicial review.

Institutional Design

As discussed in Chapter 4, *Vavilov* made major changes to the treatment of statutory appeals. However, the extent of the change depends on the classification of the questions raised on appeal: Are they questions of law, mixed questions of fact and law, or questions of fact? Correctness review applies only to extricable questions of law, and so far courts have been relatively parsimonious in identifying such questions, especially in professional disciplinary cases.[76] Where concepts familiar to common law courts are in play, however, appellate oversight can be expected to be rigorous.[77] Much therefore depends on the willingness of judges to categorize matters coming within the expertise of regulators as questions of law (subject to correctness review) or as mixed questions (subject to review for palpable and overriding error). There is a classification game, and courts around the country have begun to play it.

The Classification Game

One way in which deference might persist on statutory appeals post-*Vavilov* is in the classification of matters falling within a decision maker's expertise as factual questions or mixed questions of fact and law.[78] As Justice Jack Watson of the Alberta Court of Appeal rightly insisted in *Canadian Natural Resources Limited v Elizabeth Métis Settlement,* a question of law must be extricable to be subject to correctness review: "It must go to the defining elements of the relevant legal test and not merely to how the tribunal assesses the evidence before applying the test."[79] There are inherent requirements of generality, precedential force, and materiality.[80] Relatedly, Justice Frans Slatter of the same court observed in *Yee v Chartered Professional Accountants of Alberta* that "i) the standard of practice the profession expects in any particular case, and ii) whether, on the facts, the professional subject to discipline has met that standard" are questions of mixed fact and law calling for deferential review.[81]

If so, the scope for appellate oversight of professional disciplinary decisions will be quite limited and the change wrought by *Vavilov* not especially dramatic.[82] Perhaps for this reason, the New Brunswick Court of Appeal suggested in *Longphee v Workplace Health, Safety and Compensation Commission* that *Vavilov*'s new teachings on statutory appeals do "not fundamentally change" the approach to the decisions of (at least some) administrative tribunals.[83] Indeed, in a case relating to discipline in the legal profession, the same court wondered in *obiter dicta* whether the pre-*Vavilov* argument that "[p]ractising lawyers are uniquely positioned to identify professional misconduct and to appreciate its severity"[84] might continue to have force even on appeals.[85]

Expertise

Even where a matter has been classified as a question of law subject to the correctness standard on a statutory appeal, respect for the expertise of the decision maker might still influence the outcome. The following comment from Justice Katherine Swinton of the Ontario Superior Court is notable:

> While the Court will ultimately review the interpretation of the Act on a standard of correctness, respect for the specialized function of the Board still remains important. One of the important messages in *Vavilov* is the need for the courts to respect the institutional design chosen by the Legislature when it has established an administrative tribunal (at para 36). In the present case, the Court would be greatly assisted with its interpretive task if it had the assistance of the Board's interpretation respecting the words of the Act, the general scheme of the Act and the policy objectives behind the provision.[86]

If judges continue to consider and give weight to administrative interpretations of law on statutory appeals, deference could continue to have force even on statutory appeals, though it is clear from *Vavilov* that even where an administrative decision maker's jurisprudence is considered, the appellate court retains the final word on questions of law and is not bound to follow administrative jurisprudence.[87]

Appeals on Questions of Law or Jurisdiction

In situations where the statute provides for an appeal on a question of law or jurisdiction, it is patently obvious that *Vavilov* has effected a significant change. One such situation arose in the companion case to *Vavilov, Bell Canada v Canada (Attorney General).*[88] Section 31 of the *Broadcasting Act* provides for an appeal, with leave, on questions of law or jurisdiction, from orders of the CRTC to the Federal Court of Appeal. As the question at issue – whether the CRTC had the authority to target the Super Bowl for special treatment – "plainly" fell "within the scope of the statutory appeal mechanism," correctness was the appropriate standard.[89]

What is a question of law or jurisdiction for the purposes of such an appeal clause? It is likely that appellate courts will take the view that "law or jurisdiction" is to be read conjunctively, to apply to any extricable question of law that materially affected the outcome of the matter under appeal.[90] Skillful advocacy is required to get within a limited appeal clause,[91] but once an appellant has succeeded in demonstrating that the appeal falls within the confines of such a clause, arguments for deference seem likely to be ignored, as the courts are significantly less likely to take part in a classification game.

Consider the decision of the Manitoba Court of Appeal in *Manitoba (Hydro-Electric Board) v Manitoba (Public Utilities Board) et al.*[92] Here, the Public Utilities Board sought to create a special zero electricity rate for First Nations residential customers on reserves, looking to alleviate poverty in one of the province's most disadvantaged groups. But the Court of Appeal held that the board erred in concluding that it had the power to create a differential rate for First Nations customers.

The Court of Appeal's analysis was based on two building blocks, one about the board's ability to create a class of customers who would benefit from a reduced rate, and the other about the extent to which the board could wander into the realm of social policy-making. Both building blocks would have proved much more brittle on a deferential standard of review.

First, section 39(2.1) of the *Manitoba Hydro Act*[93] provides that "[t]he rates charged for power supplied to a class of grid customers within the province shall be the same throughout the province." For further clarity, section 39(2.2)(b) adds that "customers shall not be classified based *solely* on the region of the province in which they are located or on the population density of the area in which they are located" [emphasis added]. Creating a special rate for First Nations, based on their location on reserves, fell outside the scope of section 39, as even though the board "created the on-reserve class to address poverty concerns, treaty members who do not reside on reserve are not eligible, even if they are living in similar circumstances," such that "the defining circumstance for class membership is geographic location, not poverty or treaty status," a criterion "based solely on a geographic region of the province in which certain customers are located."[94]

In defence of the board, I would observe that the perfect need not be made the enemy of the good. Striking a rate for members of First Nations, regardless of their location within the province, would be administratively difficult, if not impossible.[95] That the board was not able to proceed with surgical precision should not necessarily mean that no procedure could be undertaken at all. This defence of the board can be grounded in the language of the statute: section 39(2.2) prohibits making a class where geographical location is the *sole* criterion. But the board was evidently not motivated *solely* by geography in setting a special rate for First Nations. Rather, the geographical locations – reserve lands – were convenient proxies for the alleviation of disadvantage the board wished to achieve. Had the board's decision been reviewed on a standard of reasonableness, the result might well have been different, as it is at least arguable that section 39(2.2) can reasonably bear the board's interpretation.

Second, section 43(3) of the Act provides for a limitation on the use and allocation of Manitoba Hydro's funds: they "shall not be employed for the purposes of the government." The Court of Appeal accepted that the board had broad authority to consider "social policy and any other factors it considers relevant in fulfilling its mandate,"[96] as befits a body required to set rates that are just and reasonable, all things considered. In pursuing the goal of poverty alleviation, however, the board failed to respect the limitation contained in section 43(3), because "the ability to consider factors such as social policy and bill affordability in approving and fixing rates for service does not equate to the authority to direct the creation of customer classifications implementing broader social policy aimed at poverty reduction and which have the effect of redistributing Manitoba Hydro's funds and revenues to alleviate such conditions."[97] Whereas the board preferred to follow the majority of the Ontario Divisional Court in *Advocacy Centre For Tenants-Ontario v Ontario Energy Board*,[98] the Court of Appeal found Justice Swinton's dissent more persuasive on this point.

Again, it is at least arguable that section 43(3) does not stand in the way of making a special rate for customers residing on First Nations lands. It can be read more narrowly, but no less purposively, as an anti-commandeering principle that prevents the government from directing Manitoba Hydro's resources to its political ends. Nothing of the sort was happening here. Rather, the board was attempting to achieve the broad goal of poverty alleviation, in the context of a nationwide effort to promote reconciliation between Canada and First Nations.

The point is not that the board was right and the Court of Appeal wrong, or vice versa. The point is that in a deferential regime, the outcome in this case would quite probably have been different. It is true that Canadian courts have policed the boundaries of rate-setting authority with some vigour.[99] But the pre-*Vavilov* law was very favourable to expert economic regulators. This case demonstrates that *Vavilov* is much less friendly, at least where there is a statutory right of appeal on a question of law or jurisdiction.

The Rule of Law

Any other departures from the starting point of the presumption of reasonableness review are justifiable only by reference to the rule of law. As explained in Chapter 4, the doors to correctness review are very narrow, as the thin conception of the rule of law set out in *Vavilov* is engaged only in situations where "consistency," and thus "a final, determinate answer" to a legal question, is necessary.[100]

Constitutional Questions

In *Doré v Barreau du Québec*,[101] the Supreme Court of Canada held that alleged infringements of Charter rights by administrative decision makers should be reviewed on the deferential reasonableness standard. What matters is not whether the decision survives the rigours of the proportionality test but whether it represents an appropriate balance between Charter values and the decision maker's statutory objectives. *Vavilov* does not discuss *Doré* in terms, but the emerging judicial consensus is that the two decisions are consistent.

The conceptual framework of *Vavilov* supports the continued application of *Doré*. Exceptions to the presumption of reasonableness review can be based only on legislative intent or the rule of law. In the absence of federal or provincial legislation requiring correctness review for Charter questions, it is only where the rule of law is engaged that Charter issues will be subject to correctness review under the *Vavilov* framework. But recall again that the rule of law, as defined in *Vavilov*, is engaged only where a "final and determinate" judicial interpretation is necessary to ensure "consistency."[102]

The first post-*Vavilov* decision, the Alberta Court of Queen's Bench's *Peter v Public Health Appeal Board of Alberta*,[103] did embrace correctness review on constitutional issues. By contrast, in *Syndicat des employé(e)s de l'école Vanguard ltée (CSN) c Mercier*, Justice Marc St-Pierre of the Quebec Superior Court applied the reasonableness standard even in the face of an argument based on the quasi-constitutional Quebec *Charter of Human Rights and Freedoms*.[104] St-Pierre's position is more persuasive given the narrow conceptual basis provided for the correctness categories in *Vavilov*.[105]

Direct challenges to the constitutionality of statutes or similarly general norms will continue to attract correctness review,[106] as will decisions touching on the borderline between provincial and federal regulation[107] and those setting the boundaries of constitutional rights or obligations.[108] Facial challenges to statutes, the borderline between provincial and federal regulation, and the determination of the scope of constitutional rights or obligations demand a uniform answer, inasmuch as the answer should not depend on the identity of the administrative decision maker providing it. Here, the integrity of the legal system is at stake and correctness review rests comfortably on the narrow rule-of-law basis provided in *Vavilov.* However, individualized decisions about the appropriate application of the *Canadian Charter of Rights and Freedoms* in a particular regulatory setting do not compromise the integrity of the legal system: different balances may legitimately be struck in different areas of regulation between individual rights and the public interest. I will return to this issue in Chapter 6.

Overlapping Jurisdiction

In the interests of uniformity and the integrity of the legal system, courts must "resolve questions regarding the jurisdictional boundaries between two or more administrative bodies."[109] These questions have most commonly arisen in the context of labour relations disputes, where a collective agreement arguably gives an arbitrator the authority to adjudicate the dispute. In *Regina Police Assn Inc v Regina (City) Board of Police Commissioners,*[110] an arbitrator declined to hear a matter, reasoning that it could be dealt with under a police disciplinary procedure established by statute. By contrast, in *Quebec (Commission des droits de la personne et des droits de la jeunesse) v Quebec (Attorney General),*[111] the Quebec Human Rights Tribunal could hear a human rights complaint with respect to alleged discrimination even though such matters related to the complainants' employment. In these cases, there was no conflict as such between competing jurisdictions: in the former, the arbitrator had declined jurisdiction; in the latter, the tribunal had asserted jurisdiction. But in both cases there was no competing decision from the body said to have the authority to hear the matter. Nonetheless, the Supreme Court resolved the question of jurisdictional boundaries on a correctness standard in these cases. As explained in *Vavilov,* "[m]embers of the public must know where to turn in order to resolve a dispute."[112]

The issue returned to the Supreme Court in *Northern Regional Health Authority v Horrocks,*[113] a case about the competing jurisdictions of a labour arbitrator and a human rights adjudicator. For the majority, Justice Russell Brown applied correctness review (and Justice Andromache Karakatsanis in dissent did not take issue with the choice of standard of review). Linda Horrocks had been a unionized worker. She had problems with alcohol addiction and, having once been reinstated after her union intervened, she was eventually dismissed. Instead of grieving her dismissal under the collective agreement before a labour arbitrator, she brought a complaint to a human rights adjudicator. Accordingly, a decision had to be made "concerning the jurisdictional lines between two or more administrative bodies."[114] To the argument that a fact-specific determination had to be made here about the "essential character" of Horrocks's complaint – was it truly a labour relations grievance or was it a human rights claim? – responded that the standard remains correctness:

> [C]orrectly determining the jurisdictional lines between two administrative bodies requires that a decision maker correctly identify the essential character of the dispute. Applying a reasonableness standard to this component of the analysis would undermine the objective of ensuring that one adjudicative body does not trespass on the jurisdiction of the other ... [Other appellate courts have explained] that this is so notwithstanding the fact-specific nature of the essential character inquiry, because it grounds a determination of jurisdiction.[115]

When determining whether a decision about competing jurisdictional boundaries was lawful, the decision maker must be correct *and* the court must satisfy itself, based on the record, that the decision maker came to the correct conclusion. Therefore, there was no room for deference to the first-instance judge:

As indicated, the adjudicator's finding that she had jurisdiction is reviewable for correctness. And if the adjudicator was bound to correctly determine her own jurisdiction, it follows that the reviewing judge was also bound to apply the same standard in reviewing the adjudicator's decision. Concluding otherwise would allow an incorrect determination of jurisdictional lines to stand, which would undermine the values of certainty and predictability that justified the application of the correctness standard in the first instance.[116]

It was possible that the court might take *Horrocks* as an opportunity to narrow the category of overlapping jurisdiction. In *The Owners, Strata Plan BCS 435 v Wong*, for example, Justice Lindsay Lyster of the British Columbia Supreme Court declined to apply correctness review on the basis that there was only a potential for jurisdictional overlap and no "operational conflict" between two tribunals.[117] In my view, Lyster's approach better fits the narrow basis for *Vavilov's* correctness categories. It is nonetheless unsurprising that correctness review was reaffirmed in *Horrocks*, as this particular question has traditionally been subject to the most intrusive standard. Notably, Karakatsanis, who was the sole dissenter (and who co-wrote skeptical concurring reasons in *Vavilov*), did not advocate the application of the reasonableness standard here.

Questions of Central Importance to the Legal System

The category most apt to be expanded after *Vavilov* is surely the "questions of central importance to the legal system" category. The narrow rule-of-law basis for the correctness categories does not provide a solid foundation for such arguments, however.

In *Bank of Montreal v Li*,[118] for example, the issue was whether an employee who had signed a release on conclusion of her employment could nonetheless make an unjust dismissal claim. An adjudicator held that she could and, on judicial review, the company sought to persuade the courts to apply correctness review on the basis that the issue of whether an individual can waive a statutory entitlement is a general one requiring definitive judicial resolution. Justice Yves De Montigny of the Federal Court of Appeal was not persuaded, concluding that the waiver issue would not have systemic or constitutional implications and noting that "framing an issue in a general or abstract sense is not sufficient to make it a question of central importance to the legal system as a whole."[119]

There is some disagreement on this point, however. Consider the decision of the Alberta Court of Appeal in *United Nurses of Alberta v Alberta Health Services*.[120] The underlying issue in this labour relations matter was the test for making out a *prima facie* case for discrimination on the basis of family status. A majority of the arbitration board had applied the Federal Court of Appeal's *Johnstone* test and rejected the griever's discrimination claim. But the first-instance judge and the Alberta Court of Appeal rejected the *Johnstone* test. For the Court of Appeal, the quasi-constitutional status of human rights legislation – the backdrop against which the collective agreement here fell to be interpreted – meant that correctness simply had to be the applicable standard of review as a "general question of law of central importance to the legal system" arose:

> The interpretation of the same human rights protections in collective agreements and in human rights legislation must be consistent, as these provisions provide some of the most important protections in our society. Labour arbitration boards, human rights tribunals, and superior courts on review are regularly called upon to consider discrimination cases and to interpret similar or identical human rights protections in keeping with human rights legislation, which has quasi-constitutional status in Canada.[121]

In following such an approach, the Court of Appeal traversed a well-trodden path in Canadian administrative law, using language that recalls decisions of the 1990s reserving human rights concepts to courts. But is such an approach appropriate today? *Vavilov* teaches that expertise is no longer a factor in selecting the standard of review, and that the public importance of a question does not turn it into a general question of law of central importance to the legal system. The fact that human rights statutes might be interpreted by different bodies does not change the analysis, in my view. To begin with, these statutory creations are provincial and federal in nature: they are not pan-Canadian concepts; there is no inherent need for Alberta and Ontario, for example, to maintain precisely the same anti-discrimination provisions. Variation between provinces is part of life in a federation. Moreover, different decision makers might legitimately interpret the concepts differently: the fact that the courts can intervene in situations of "overlapping jurisdiction" already ensures that differentiated decision-making does not undermine the coherence of the legal system. Experience teaches that significant judicial humility is required before concluding that the correctness standard must be applied, setting courts' interpretations of human rights law in stone.[122]

Although I am not persuaded by the Court of Appeal's analysis, it is undoubtedly the most thorough and interesting consideration of the implications of *Vavilov* for human rights concepts specifically and quasi-constitutional statutes generally. However, this is as broad a view of the scope of this correctness category as has been taken post-*Vavilov*.[123]

Further Correctness Categories?

In *Vavilov*, the rule-of-law door was left slightly ajar, as the majority did "not definitively foreclose the possibility that another category could be recognized as requiring a derogation from the presumption of reasonableness review in a future case."[124] It did not take long for the Supreme Court itself to push through that door. In *Society of Composers, Authors and Music Publishers of Canada v Entertainment Software Association*,[125] Justice Rowe held that shared jurisdiction between the Federal Court and the Copyright Board of Canada over the interpretation of Canadian copyright law was a "rare and exceptional" case where it was "appropriate to recognize a new category of correctness review," namely, "when courts and administrative bodies have concurrent first instance jurisdiction over a legal issue in a statute."[126] The implications of this decision are unclear at the time of writing: perhaps *Entertainment Software Association* will prove to be a ticket good for the Copyright Board of Canada only rather than a lever to create additional correctness categories.[127]

Otherwise, there has been little judicial appetite to expand the realm of correctness review. The most significant post-*Vavilov* controversy about additional correctness categories relates to judicial review of legislative-type decisions. Some doubts have been expressed about whether *Vavilovian* reasonableness review can be applied to such decisions. The reason for doubt is as follows. On the one hand, the question of whether a particular regulation is within the scope of its parent statute might be said to require a final, definitive answer from the courts, engaging *Vavilov*'s rule-of-law justification for correctness review. Just as the constitutionality of a statutory or regulatory provision should not depend on the identity of the tribunal (or of the tribunal member presiding) so too the lawfulness of a regulation should be the same across the board. And there are settled principles concerning judicial review of regulations. In *Hudson's Bay Company ULC v Ontario (Attorney General)*, the Ontario Divisional Court stated that "[t]he test for challenging a regulation as *ultra vires* is well settled,"[128] and went on to enumerate the general principles set out by the Supreme Court in *Katz Group Canada Inc v Ontario (Health and Long-Term Care)*,[129] not the principles from *Vavilov*.[130]

On the other hand, reasonableness is the presumptive standard of review when it comes to the merits of administrative action. The most obvious justification for correctness review of regulations – that they relate to jurisdiction – was eliminated by *Vavilov*. There is consequently no equivalence between the lawfulness of regulations and the constitutionality of statutory or regulatory provisions: constitutional questions represent a (narrow) category of cases in which correctness review is appropriate, but the category into which regulations might previously have fitted was expressly abolished by the Supreme Court. This point has been recognized by courts around the country.[131]

Indeed, as Justice Anna Loparco of the Alberta Court of Queen's Bench observed in *Morris v Law Society of Alberta (Trust Safety Committee)*, the Supreme Court spoke explicitly to the issue of jurisdiction or *vires* in *Vavilov* by abolishing "true" questions of jurisdiction as a correctness category:

[T]he Supreme Court concluded that the question of whether or not a delegated decision maker should "be free to determine the scope of its own authority [can] be addressed adequately by applying the framework for conducting reasonableness review." The Court specifically endorsed use of [the] reasonableness review standard in cases "where the legislature has delegated broad authority to an administrative decision maker that allows the latter to make regulations in pursuit of the objects of its enabling statute": *Ibid* at para 66[132]

Notably, Loparco applied the reasonableness standard even though the rule at issue touched on matters relating to solicitor-client privilege (which are subject to correctness review), reasoning that the relevant issue was whether the Law Society had the authority to enact the rule in question.[133]

I would also observe that key precedents concerning judicial review of regulations were incorporated into the Supreme Court's framework for reasonableness review in *Vavilov,* forming part of the legal and factual constraints on the decision maker whose decision is challenged on judicial review.[134] There is, thus, no need for a separate correctness category for legislative-type decisions.

Reasons are, of course, central to reasonableness review as articulated in *Vavilov.* Often, however, reasons for legislative-type decisions will be absent. Nonetheless, it is possible to judicially review the reasonableness of regulations in the absence of reasons. After all, the Supreme Court made it clear in *Vavilov* that judicial review could be conducted in the absence of reasons.[135] Of course, it will not invariably be the case that reasons or reasoning are entirely absent in cases involving legislative-type decisions; if so, the judicial review will look quite conventional.[136]

Ultimately, given that the Supreme Court's goal was to create a "coherent and unified approach to judicial review,"[137] it is difficult to avoid the conclusion that *Vavilovian* reasonableness review applies when regulations are challenged. In *Portnov v Canada (Attorney General),*[138] the Federal Court of Appeal came to the same conclusion. As Justice David Stratas explained, *Katz* has been "overtaken" by developments in the law, especially the Supreme Court's rearticulation of administrative law in *Vavilov*.[139] To begin with, the approach articulated in *Katz* had its origins in a much earlier era, where judicial review of legislative-type decisions was available only on the basis of "some rare and significant error" of a jurisdictional nature.[140] But we no longer draw such sharp distinctions between legislative-type and nonlegislative-type decisions. Regulations "are nothing more than binding legal instruments that administrative officials decide to make – in other words, they are the product of administrative decision-making."[141] Furthermore, the Supreme Court set out a "sweeping and comprehensive" framework for judicial review in *Vavilov*.[142] There is no "special rule for regulations,"[143] as the Supreme Court has instructed Canadian courts "to conduct reasonableness review of all administrative decision-making unless one of three exceptions leading to correctness review applies."[144] None of these exceptions was present here.[145] Accordingly, *Vavilov* supplies the analytical framework for judicial review of regulations made by the federal Cabinet (or, for that matter, a provincial Cabinet or any other decision maker with the authority to adopt regulations or other general rules).

Finally, concerns that the promulgators of regulations will receive too much deference under *Vavilov* should not be overblown. The approach to judicial review of regulations in *Katz* is extremely deferential. *Hudson's Bay* is an example. Rejecting the argument of counsel for the applicant that *Vavilov* requires more intrusive review,[146] the Ontario Divisional Court drew on the general principles set out in *Katz* to state that the "wisdom or efficacy" of regulations was not something that fell for consideration on judicial review.[147] The challenge to the COVID-19 lockdown regulations brought by the Hudson's Bay Company thus failed. At the municipal level, the Supreme Court's decision in *Catalyst Paper Corp v North Cowichan (District)*[148] involves a similarly deferential approach to judicial review of bylaws. It is difficult to see, therefore, how regulations would be reviewed more deferentially after *Vavilov* than they were before.

Prior decisions on judicial review of regulations provide valuable guidance on the application of the reasonableness standard. As Justice Paul Jeffrey of the Alberta Court of Queen's Bench observed in the course of an extremely persuasive analysis in *Terrigno v Calgary (City)*, past jurisprudence has not been "ousted."[149] Rather, it helps to shape the relative tightness or looseness of the factual and legal constraints on the decision maker. Indeed, both *Catalyst* and *Katz* were expressly referenced by the Supreme Court as shaping the factual and legal constraints in a given case: *Catalyst* as to the governing statutory scheme[150] and *Katz* as to applicable common law principles.[151] The irresistible inference is that the teachings found in those cases are to form part of the application of the reasonableness standard rather than to apply as stand-alone principles. This may mean a significant degree of deference in some cases involving legislative-type decisions, but this would depend on a comprehensive consideration of contextual factors, not the formal classification of a decision into a category where special, hyperdeferential rules apply.

Moreover, this approach allows for the factual and legal constraints to be tightened in appropriate cases. Rather than applying the hyper-deferential approach of *Katz* and *Catalyst* in all cases, the courts can look to other contextual considerations to constrain (or liberate) decision makers: the available evidence, arguments submitted prior to the adoption of the regulation, past regulatory practice, and the harsh consequences of a regulation on a particular group might be relevant in charting the scope of a decision maker's freedom of action in any given case. This is a much more flexible approach to judicial review of regulations, which meshes well with the articulation of contextual reasonableness review in *Vavilov*.

REMEDIES

Initially, judges did not seem overly anxious to jump on the suggestion that they might refuse to remit a matter consequent on a finding of unlawfulness where it is "evident" that a "particular outcome is inevitable."[152] In *Canadian Broadcasting Corporation v Ferrier*, for example, Justice Robert Sharpe of the Ontario Court of Appeal remitted to the decision maker the question of the applicability of the open court principle to police board hearings (here, a preliminary hearing on whether the time period for reporting alleged police misconduct should be extended).[153] Sharpe remitted the question even though much of his analysis was conducted on a standard of correctness,[154] he had little doubt that a recent Ontario Court of Appeal decision on the application of the open court principle to police board hearings was dispositive,[155] and the judicial review proceedings had already slowed down a process that was moving quite slowly.[156] On balance, Sharpe concluded, the decision maker "should be permitted to take another look at the matter with the benefit" of another recent decision of the Court of Appeal in a case called *Langenfeld*.[157] I think Sharpe was quite right to remit the matter, especially because the issues in *Ferrier* and *Langenfeld* arose in different contexts. Where a file is factually and legally complex, the better course is to remit it for further consideration by the decision maker, in light of the court's analysis. Indeed, it will be very rare to find a case "where the evidence can lead only to one result" and refusal to remit would thus be appropriate.[158]

I would single out *Downey v Nova Scotia (Attorney General)* for special attention as an example of how to resist the attraction of exercising the remedial discretion identified in *Vavilov*. Here a relatively simple land titles matter was remitted to the minister even though the factual record before the court would have enabled the judge to issue a definitive order as to the applicant's entitlements under the provincial land titles clarification legislation.[159]

However, the examples of judges taking a muscular approach to refusal to remit unreasonable decisions quickly multiplied. In *Alexis v Alberta (Environment and Parks)*, the majority of the Alberta Court of Appeal was convinced (in spite of a spirited dissent from one of their colleagues), on a thin factual record from which reasons were absent, that the outcome of any remittal was preordained.[160] Justice Dawn Pentelechuk's partially concurring and partially dissenting observations about the thinness of the record and inadequacy of the decision-making process should have given the majority pause.[161] Consider also *JE and KE v Children's Aid Society of the Niagara Region*, where the import of the Ontario Divisional Court's order was to place a child for adoption with a family in circumstances where another family had sought to adopt the child.[162]

The issue in *Nation Rise Wind Farm Limited Partnership v Minister of the Environment, Conservation and Parks* was the minister's decision to cancel a major wind farm project on appeal from the Environmental Review Tribunal.[163] The sole reason for the cancellation decision was the effect the project would have on the colonies of bats. But the effect on bats had not been raised by any of the parties to the tribunal decision or the appeal. It was unreasonable for the minister to raise the effects on his own initiative.[164] The implication was that there would be "no utility" in sending the matter back to the minister[165] because the minister had made clear that the effect on bats was the "only basis" for revoking the permission for the project;[166] moreover, the minister's findings on this point were unreasonable.[167] There was also "evidence of urgency," in the form of a "real risk" that the project would be cancelled if the matter were sent back for further redetermination by the minister.[168] I wish I could share the Ontario Divisional Court's confidence in the inevitability of the outcome of a complex regulatory process. If the minister were to do it all again, with the effect on bats out of the picture, would the appeal process have unfolded as it did? Even on the understanding of remedial discretion laid out in *Vavilov*, inevitability is a high bar and I am not sure it was reached here.

Finally, in *Oberg v Saskatchewan (Board of Education of the South East Cornerstone School Division No 209),*[169] Justice Meghan McCreary of the Saskatchewan Court of Queen's Bench quashed a decision removing the applicant as the principal of a high school and ordered that the applicant be reinstated: it was unreasonable for the board to have demoted the applicant and the only other option open to the board was the status quo. The Court of Appeal endorsed McCreary's analysis.[170] This is, I suppose, logical enough so far as it goes, but when one considers how reluctant common law courts traditionally have been to make mandatory orders (especially in employment-related matters[171]), it is a striking example of the potentially radical results *Vavilov's* discussion of remedies might lead to.

CONCLUSION

To echo Chairman Mao's quip about the French Revolution, it is too early to make a definitive judgment about the importance of *Vavilov* for the future of Canadian administrative law: "Landmark judicial decisions should be viewed as a starting point, not the end point in legal evolution or, to change the metaphor, they close one chapter and open another."[172] However, it certainly seems to be the case, a year or two after the Supreme Court's blockbuster decision, that a measure of clarity and simplicity has been achieved. *Vavilov* is much clearer and more workable than what preceded it.

Setting the standard of review has been straightforward. The keys to unlock the "appeals" and "legislated standard of review" doors are generally easy to identify. Similarly, it will usually be obvious whether a particular question can squeeze through one of the narrow rule-of-law doors leading to correctness review. Of course, some contextual analysis might be hidden from sight as judges play the "classification game" of characterizing different issues as extricable questions of law, mixed questions, or questions of fact, perhaps being influenced in this exercise by considerations of the relative expertise of courts and administrative decision makers. Nonetheless, for now, the formalist approach set out in *Vavilov* has achieved simplicity and clarity. Deference has certainly been reduced, however, especially where there is a statutory appeal on a question of law or jurisdiction, giving force to Justices Abella and Karakatsanis's charge that *Vavilov* is a eulogy for deference.

Applying reasonableness review has also been generally straightforward. *Vavilov* sets out a detailed framework for determining whether a decision was reasonable. The approach is deferential – thereby offsetting the decreased deference where statutory appeals have been provided for – but requires more of administrative decision makers than was expected of them during the *Dunsmuir* decade. Case law suggests that the bar has been meaningfully raised due to the emphasis on the thoroughly substantive considerations of justification, demonstrated expertise, responsiveness, and contemporaneity. So far, the tensions in *Vavilov* have not caused serious difficulties in practice. Life is much simpler and clearer than it was.

Finally, the framework for the exercise of remedial discretion has generally operated in a way respectful of the autonomy of administrative decision makers, as one would expect given the more dynamic conception of reasonableness review set out in *Vavilov*.

All told, the story of the first few years of the *Vavilov* framework is a positive one, which is cause for hope. Even if, in some regard, *Vavilov* papers over fundamental fault lines in Canadian law, the cracks remain hidden from view for now. The compromise between form and substance, deference and nondeference, and reason and authority has held so far.

6

Unresolved Issues after *Vavilov*

AS WE HAVE SEEN in previous chapters, the underlying concern of the Supreme Court of Canada in *Vavilov* was the complexity that existed in terms of selecting the standard of review (correctness or reasonableness) and the lack of clarity on how to apply the reasonableness standard. The majority in *Vavilov* set out to simplify the selection of the standard of review and clarify the application of the reasonableness standard. The goal of *Vavilov* was therefore to simplify and to clarify,[1] which was achieved by way of a compromise between judges who see the administrative law world very differently.

The lesson for those applying the *Vavilov* framework is that it privileges neither form over substance nor deference over nondeference nor authority over reason, but instead requires a "balancing act."[2] None of us will have everything we want; we shall have to compromise. Second, *Vavilov* is an exercise in simplification and clarification. In applying the framework and addressing unresolved issues, we should choose simple solutions over more complex ones, and we should avoid applying glosses to the *Vavilov* framework that are theoretically appealing but might give rise to future uncertainty and further litigation. Keeping these two points in mind is the best way to ensure that the *Vavilov* framework is as workable and durable as its creators intended.

In terms of workability and durability, there are several lingering questions. The analysis in *Vavilov* was wide-ranging, but not quite comprehensive for several reasons:

1 The implications of *Vavilov* for the standard of review of questions of procedural fairness were not spelled out.

One can forgive the judges for not addressing these questions, as they were neither raised nor argued before the court. On two other issues, however, forgiveness is less appropriate:

2 Although the point was argued (and has been the subject of intense debate by courts and commentators), the majority declined to even consider the approach set out in *Doré v Barreau du Québec* to judicial review of administrative decisions infringing Charter rights. It is necessary, therefore, to tease out what *Vavilov* portends for *Doré*.
3 The constitutional foundations of judicial review are left obscure by *Vavilov*. It is not clear what (if anything) the core constitutional minimum of judicial review is, and how far statutes may go in restricting judicial oversight, a point of pressing concern to any legislator or drafter who wishes to create a workable relationship between public administration and the courts.

Briefly, my responses to these lingering questions – crafted with clarity and simplicity in mind – are as follows:

1 Procedural fairness is not included in the *Vavilov* framework but has its own bespoke set of principles.[3]
2 *Doré* is safe for now, absent a full-scale assault on its premises (which could only, realistically, be conducted by the Supreme Court).
3 The core constitutional minimum of judicial review includes reasonableness review, for it ensures the reasoned decision-making that majority judges assured us in *Vavilov* is the wellspring of legitimate exercises of public power.

THE STANDARD OF REVIEW ON QUESTIONS
OF PROCEDURAL FAIRNESS

Several years ago, there was lively debate about the standard of review of questions of procedural fairness.[4] For one thing, the *Dunsmuir* framework was general in nature, presumptively covering the whole field of judicial review of administrative action. In a large number of cases, procedural fairness issues would have fallen into *Dunsmuir*'s reasonableness categories, as some astute appellate judges noted.[5] For another, the Supreme Court's enigmatic pronouncements on procedural fairness suggested not only that procedural fairness had to be addressed as part of the "standard of review" framework but that a measure of "deference" would be appropriate in addressing such questions.[6] Prior to *Vavilov*, there was a divergence of views among lower courts on the standard of review applicable to matters of procedural fairness: some courts applied correctness review;[7] others applied correctness review with some deference;[8] reasonableness review had adherents at least in some circumstances;[9] and some suggested that standard of review was irrelevant as all that mattered was an overall assessment of fairness.[10]

Yet the debate largely petered out. By the time of *Vavilov*, most courts had accepted that issues of procedural fairness are free-standing, to be addressed using the factors set out in *Baker v Canada (Citizenship and Immigration)*;[11] this was sometimes dressed up as "correctness" review, sometimes as an "overall assessment of fairness." There was, nonetheless, some disagreement. As Justice David Stratas of the Federal Court of Appeal noted in *Vavilov v Canada (Citizenship and Immigration)*, the proper approach to procedural fairness was "in dispute" in that court, with a "number of different approaches" competing for primacy.[12] And in Quebec,[13] many first-instance judges continued to defer on procedural issues relating to matters within an administrative decision maker's specialized domain.

In *Vavilov*, the majority summarily put the debate and disagreement to rest.[14] First, the *Vavilov* framework applies "[w]here a court reviews the *merits* of an administrative decision" but not to "a review related to a breach of natural justice and/or the duty of procedural fairness."[15]

Second, where procedure but not merits are at issue, "the specific procedural requirements that the duty [of procedural fairness] imposes are determined with reference to all of the circumstances" consistent with the factors set out in the *Baker* case:[16]

- the nature of the decision being made and the process followed in making it
- the nature of the statutory scheme and the terms of the statute pursuant to which the body operates
- the importance of the decision to the individual or individuals affected
- the legitimate expectations of the person challenging the decision
- the choices of procedure made by the agency itself, particularly when the statute leaves to the decision maker the ability to choose its own procedures, or when the agency has an expertise in determining what procedures are appropriate in the circumstances.[17]

Procedural fairness sits outside the *Vavilov* framework, with its own bespoke set of principles, "fairness" the guiding light regardless of whether a procedural defect is challenged by way of appeal or judicial review. Some deference is built into this framework (a point I will return to below), but presumably we are not to mistake respect for a decision maker's procedural choices (the fifth *Baker* factor) with reasonableness review. And there is no reason to mistake this approach for correctness review,[18] as what matters is the fairness of the process followed, not whether it was the best possible process in the circumstances.[19]

That would seem to be that. In the interests of simplification and clarification, there is much to be said for creating a clear line between matters of procedure, subject to *Baker,* and matters of substance, subject to *Vavilov.* Of course, difficult questions of classification will arise. The line between merits and procedure is blurry: for instance, a "decision based on a deficient investigation can be characterized as one that is not substantively acceptable or defensible because it is based on incomplete information, thereby triggering the standard of review for substantive defects."[20] To take a post-*Vavilov* example, in *Hildebrand v Penticton (City),*[21] Justice Gary Weatherill of the British Columbia Supreme Court applied the *Vavilov* framework to a decision not to grant an adjournment. It is debatable whether this was a matter going to the merits of the underlying decision, to which *Vavilov* clearly applies, or related to procedure, in which case *Vavilov* would not apply.

Although there is no easy answer to this question of classification, one analytical shortcut is provided by the presence or absence of reasons. This distinction is functional, not metaphysical; it does not explain what are "merits" and what is "procedure" (and the history of judicial review suggests that any such explanation will prove elusive). It aims to simplify and to clarify, not to obfuscate.

Where reasons have been given for a particular difficult-to-classify decision, *Vavilovian* reasonableness review can be employed: reviewing courts can examine the rationality and logic of the reasons in light of the relevant factual and legal constraints. Moreover, if a decision maker has provided reasons on a particular point, this fact suggests that the point was important and therefore relates to the merits of the matter before the decision maker.

Where no reasons have been given for a particular difficult-to-classify decision, the reviewing exercise will invariably focus on the outcome.[22] Here, the *Baker* factors can be applied. Indeed, it is hard to see how else a reviewing court could determine whether the procedures at issue were fair. Without reasons to review, the *Baker* factors will have to be applied. In applying these factors, some deference will be due to the decision maker's choice of procedures, but the reviewing court will retain the final word on the overall fairness of the process.

Put simply, my suggestion is that the merits/procedure distinction should track the availability of reasons: where reasons have been provided in an attempt to justify a particular difficult-to-classify decision, the reasons can be reviewed for reasonableness; where no reasons have been provided, the *Baker* factors would govern. To my mind, this is an attractive solution to what might otherwise be an intractable problem.

While this is a helpful analytical shortcut in difficult cases, the mere presence of reasons will not necessarily transform an issue of procedural fairness into an issue of substance.[23] Would deference nonetheless be appropriate in some circumstances where a decision that is clearly procedural in nature has been challenged as a breach of the duty of fairness?

I have two observations. First, in situations where a reviewing court directly assesses the impact on fairness of procedural choices made by an administrative decision maker, deference will be appropriate based on the decision maker's expertise, perhaps even "considerable deference."[24] Second, in some situations, an administrative decision maker will have given reasons on a procedural fairness issue. Here, a "margin of deference" will be appropriate where the expertise of the decision maker is engaged.[25] There is nothing especially controversial about this idea, which has its roots in the Supreme Court's decision in *Bibeault v McCaffrey*.[26] As Professor David Mullan commented at the time – all the way back in the mid-1980s – deference may be owed to an administrative decision maker on a procedural fairness point, depending on "the nature of the decision maker, including its capacities for making procedural judgments (particularly in comparison with the courts' own expertise in such matters) and the seriousness with which it has dealt with the procedural question under review."[27] As such, where a decision maker is well placed to opine on a procedural fairness issue, and has given reasons to support its opinion, it is entitled to a "margin of deference" from the courts.[28]

JUDICIAL REVIEW
FOR CHARTER COMPLIANCE

In *Doré v Barreau du Québec*,[29] the Supreme Court held that alleged infringements of Charter rights by administrative decision makers should be reviewed on the deferential reasonableness standard. What matters is not whether the decision survives the rigours of the proportionality test set out in *R v Oakes*[30] but whether it represents an appropriate balance between Charter values and the decision maker's statutory objectives. In *Vavilov*, the continued survival of *Doré* was argued but the court declined to take a position, merely noting that a "reconsideration of that approach is not germane to the issues in this appeal."[31]

I criticized *Doré* at the time it was decided,[32] and although I recognize that *Doré* provides valuable guidance to administrative decision makers (especially on the front lines),[33] I continue to think that the *Doré* approach to judicial review is insufficiently protective of Charter rights.[34] It is true that more recent applications of *Doré* have hewed quite closely (in substance if not in rhetoric) to the *Oakes* test,[35] but this simply provides further ammunition for those who would return to the pre-*Doré* position: the law as stated by the Supreme Court should be in line with the law as applied by the court. In the meantime, especially on lower courts, there is a risk that *Doré* will lead to under-protection of fundamental rights.[36]

Appreciated, however, in the light of the consensus achieved in *Vavilov*, the question is not whether *Doré* is good, bad, or indifferent as a matter of first principles but whether it is compatible with *Vavilov*. I am not at all persuaded by the argument that the decision in *Vavilov* kicks the conceptual legs from under *Doré*.[37] Mark Mancini argues that, one, the demise of expertise in *Vavilov* and, two, *Vavilov's* relatively formalist, Diceyan approach to reasonableness review mean that *Vavilov* and *Doré* are in serious tension:

> On one understanding, *Vavilov* tends to revert to a Diceyan understanding of administrative law, under which courts reserve to themselves the final say on certain issues. It also shows a focus on justification, as a doctrinal requirement in most cases. However, *Doré* is rooted in a more functionalist understanding of administrative law, under which expertise is taken as a given and administrators are seen as competent to contribute to the content of the law.

By contrast, I would say that *Doré* emerges strengthened from *Vavilov*, not weakened.

First, the excision of expertise from the process of selecting the standard of review means that the presumption of reasonableness review certainly applies to Charter issues. In *Vavilov*, the majority made a distinction between judicial review of the "merits" of an administrative decision and issues of "procedural fairness" or "natural justice."[38] On *anything* to do with the merits of an administrative decision, the *Vavilov* framework applies and, in that framework, reasonableness is the presumptive standard.[39] Resort to expertise and other substantive or contextual considerations is simply unnecessary. Reasonableness review is the starting point whether or not the decision maker has any relevant expertise.[40] Inasmuch as expertise was a conceptual basis for deference in *Doré*, its removal is irrelevant, as it has simply been replaced by another conceptual basis – institutional design choice – which is at least equally solid.

In fact, the conceptual framework of *Vavilov* supports the continued application of *Doré*. Exceptions to the presumption of reasonableness review can be based only on institutional design or the rule of law.[41] But the rule of law, as defined in *Vavilov*, is engaged only where a "final and determinate" judicial interpretation is necessary to ensure "consistency."[42] This rule-of-law exception applies very narrowly, to constitutional questions, questions of central importance to the legal system, and questions of overlapping jurisdiction.

What unites these circumstances conceptually is the need for judicially imposed uniformity. Professional privilege is an example of a question of central importance to the legal system: if the scope of privilege were to vary depending on whether it was invoked in professional disciplinary proceedings or access to information proceedings, professional privilege would be undermined; a uniform approach is necessary.[43] Questions of overlapping jurisdiction, similarly, require judicially imposed "right answers": problems would quickly result were Tribunal A and Tribunal B both to claim jurisdiction over the same subject matter.

As to constitutional questions, the same logic suggests facial challenges to the constitutionality of legislation should be given a uniform answer – for the constitutionality of a statute should not depend on whether the statute is relied on in front of Tribunal A or Tribunal B – and, accordingly, reviewed on a correctness standard.[44] It is also arguable (and, I think, consistent with the jurisprudence) for questions relating to the scope of Charter rights to be dealt with on a correctness standard. There is nothing novel in treating threshold questions of constitutionality as requiring correctness review: see, for instance, on the scope of the duty to consult, *Rio Tinto Alcan Inc v Carrier Sekani Tribal Council,*[45] and on the scope of a *Charter* right (here, section 2(a)), *Ktunaxa Nation v British Columbia (Forests, Lands and Natural Resource Operations).*[46] Perhaps it will soon be made clear that these threshold questions fall into one of the correctness categories: they are, after all, situations in which the courts ought to provide a final, definitive answer, as the application of the Constitution or the scope of Charter rights should not vary between different regulatory regimes.

The discussion in *Doré,* however, is oriented toward the question of the proportionality of individualized exercises of discretion that infringe the Charter. Here, it seems to me, answers can legitimately vary between different regulatory regimes: for example, what is a proportionate restraint on freedom of expression in the workplace may not be proportionate in a municipal election campaign.[47] I can see how professional privilege would be undermined by variations in approach in different regulatory regimes; I can see how incoherence might result from different approaches to jurisdictional overlaps; and I can see how the constitutionality of a statute, or the scope of a Charter right, must be the same across the board. Correctness review in such instances rests solidly on the narrow rule-of-law basis established in *Vavilov.* With regret, however, I cannot see why the presence of a Charter right *requires* uniform answers to be furnished by judges with respect to decisions made in different settings by different decision makers.

Indeed, I would observe in this regard that the application of a proportionality test to individualized decisions would be no guarantor of uniformity. Proportionality review is not correctness review.[48] A superior court determination of whether there were alternative means of achieving the same regulatory objective and whether an appropriate balance was struck in a given case might be very different in, say, the legal-professional context than in the context of a health care professional. Put another way, the degree of deference built into the proportionality test undermines any argument that proportionality must be applied by superior court judges to all alleged Charter violations by administrative decision makers in order to achieve uniformity.

I accept Mancini's point that the scope/application distinction may not be extremely robust, but the question for present purposes is not the robustness of the distinction but whether *Doré* and *Vavilov* are compatible. Given the replacement of expertise as the conceptual basis for deference with an across-the-board presumption of reasonableness review and the narrowness of *Vavilov*'s rule-of-law exception, I do not think there is any incompatibility between *Doré* and *Vavilov*.

I also do not think that *Vavilovian* reasonableness review can fairly be described as formalist or Diceyan. As I have suggested, *Vavilov* is an example of the "culture of justification" in administrative law.[49] There is nothing formalist about the detailed articulation of reasonableness in *Vavilov*. Indeed, the repeated references to the "demonstrated expertise" of administrative decision makers strike an unmistakably functionalist tone.[50] Expertise might now be irrelevant to selecting the standard of review, but it is very relevant to surviving the standard of review.

It is true that there are tensions in the majority's articulation of reasonableness review.[51] *Some* components of *Vavilovian* reasonableness review can fairly be described as formalist or Diceyan – the emphasis on the importance of the governing statutory scheme, for example. But reasonableness review post-*Vavilov* is to begin with the reasons provided by the administrative decision maker, even where the reasons touch on jurisdictional issues.[52] There is nothing formalist or Diceyan about this. Read fairly, *Vavilovian* reasonableness review has both formal and functional, Diceyan and non-Diceyan components.

The discussion of the principles of statutory interpretation is perhaps the best example. On the one hand, administrative decision makers are to apply the principles as courts would.[53] On the other hand, a "formalistic" statutory interpretation exercise is not required in every case.[54] The majority in *Vavilov* does not go as far as I would advocate,[55] but I find it very doubtful that Dicey would have rejoiced at the idea that judicial review would begin not with the judge's view of the best reading of a statute but with the reasons provided by the administrative decision maker "applying its particular insight into the statutory scheme at issue."[56]

At the core of reasonableness review in *Doré* was "balancing *Charter* values against broader objectives,"[57] with courts obliged to uphold an appropriate balance struck by the decision maker.[58] This is just as possible post-*Vavilov* as it was before. Administrative decision makers can continue to contribute to our collective understanding of the Charter in its application to particular regulatory settings. The thick conception of reasonableness review developed in *Vavilov* will, in addition, ensure meaningful judicial oversight of any alleged Charter infringements, for in assessing the reasonableness of decisions touching on the Charter, reviewing courts will determine whether the decision was justified with respect to the legal and factual constraints on the decision maker, particularly whether the decision adequately responds to the stakes for and submissions of the parties.[59] Where the Charter is in play, the burden of justification will be a heavy one, with administrative decision makers required to demonstrate that they gave serious consideration to the relevant Charter implications, justifying the balance struck in light of the effect on the individual and the availability of alternative means of achieving the same objective.[60]

In sum, I have long thought that *Doré* was a misstep in the Canadian law of judicial review of administrative action, but a post-*Vavilov* correction is not at all inevitable. Those who wish to see the back of *Doré* will have to attack it directly and hope their attacks resonate with a majority of the Supreme Court.

THE CONSTITUTIONAL FOUNDATIONS OF *VAVILOV*

In *Dunsmuir v New Brunswick,* Justices Michel Bastarache and Louis LeBel framed their rearticulation of the standard of review analysis by reference to the constitutional foundations of judicial review.[61] In their view, the law of judicial review seeks "to address an underlying tension between the rule of law and the foundational democratic principle."[62] On the one hand, the rule of law imposes on courts a "constitutional duty to ensure that public authorities do not overreach their lawful powers."[63] On the other hand, judicial review has "an important constitutional function in maintaining legislative supremacy,"[64] and in fashioning the law of judicial review, the courts must avoid "undue interference with the discharge of administrative functions in respect of the matters delegated to administrative bodies by Parliament and legislatures."[65] But undue interference could never mean abstinence, as "judicial review is constitutionally guaranteed in Canada, particularly with regard to the definition and enforcement of jurisdictional limits."[66]

By contrast, *Vavilov* is pitched at the level of practice, not constitutional theory. The court was most concerned by criticism from the judiciary, the academy, litigants, and civil society organizations, and with critiques going "to the core of the coherence of our administrative law jurisprudence and to the practical implications of this lack of coherence."[67] The majority's efforts were designed to respond to these critiques. The constitutional foundations of judicial review did not warrant a mention; the Constitution barely figured. The constitutional basis of *Vavilov* is obscure.

This opacity is problematic. At least since *Crevier v Attorney General of Quebec,*[68] the constitutional basis of judicial review in Canadian administrative law has been taken to be the judicature provisions of the *Constitution Act, 1867,* particularly section 96. A great oak has sprouted from this acorn: section 96 simply provides that the federal government shall appoint superior court judges, but judicial exegesis, first by the Privy Council and subsequently by the Supreme Court, means that its branches cast an imposing shade over encroachments on the supervisory powers of the superior courts. Most importantly, as Chief Justice Bora Laskin explained in *Crevier,* "[i]t cannot be left to a provincial statutory tribunal, in the face of s. 96, to determine the limits of its own jurisdiction without appeal or review."[69] Ensuring that administrative decision makers stay within their jurisdiction is, then, a core task of the superior courts; judicial review is how they discharge that task. As Justice Thomas Cromwell observed in his dissenting reasons in the Supreme Court's *Alberta Teachers'* case, "this constitutional guarantee does not merely assure judicial review for reasonableness; it guarantees jurisdictional review on the correctness standard."[70]

166 | A Culture of Justification

The difficulty presented by *Vavilov* is that in the course of the majority's simplification exercise, it whittled the remaining correctness categories down to almost nothing and eliminated jurisdictional error as a distinct correctness category altogether. The narrow rule-of-law basis for correctness review means that the starting point of reasonableness review will typically also be the end point as far as selecting the standard of review is concerned. There is no category of jurisdictional error that allows a reviewing court to police, on a correctness basis, what Laskin described as the "limits" of an administrative decision maker's jurisdiction.[71]

The difficulty thereby presented can be appreciated by reference to the analysis of Justice Mary Gleason of the Federal Court of Appeal in *Canada (Attorney General) v Public Service Alliance of Canada*, a pre-*Vavilov* case.[72] At issue here was sub-section 34(1) of the *Federal Public Sector Labour Relations and Employment Board Act*.[73] Pursuant to this provision, the grounds of review of the board are limited to jurisdictional error, breach of natural justice, and bad faith. The legislation specifically excludes the grounds of review of legal error, factual error, or acting contrary to law. Gleason refused to accept that the exclusion was effective. Giving effect to the exclusion "runs afoul of the rule of law concerns that provide the constitutional underpinning for judicial review of administrative action by the independent judicial branch," because "the scope of jurisdictional issues that arise in administrative law cases is exceedingly limited, if such issues may still even be said to exist at all."[74] Post-*Vavilov,* jurisdictional issues indeed no longer "exist at all." As Gleason explained, the result would be that decisions of the board would be "largely unreviewable," but, given the constitutional basis of judicial review in Canadian law, "[t]his cannot be."[75] Rather, the exclusion of several grounds of review indicated that decisions of the board should be reviewed deferentially.[76]

Let me put the difficulty in stark terms. There is nothing, on the face of *Vavilov,* to prevent a legislature from eliminating reasonableness review. As the majority put it, "where the legislature has indicated the applicable standard of review, courts are bound to respect that designation, within the limits imposed by the rule of law."[77] But the "rule of law" here means only that limited class of cases in which correctness review applies to allow the courts to furnish a final, definitive answer to a question in the interests of uniformity. As long as the courts are able to review constitutional questions, questions of central importance to the legal system, or questions of overlapping jurisdiction for correctness, nothing seems to stand in the way of legislation to eliminate reasonableness review.

This is not merely a theoretical difficulty. There are a couple of ways in which reasonableness review could be eliminated, directly or indirectly. In Alberta, section 539 of the *Municipal Government Act* provides: "No bylaw or resolution may be challenged on the ground that it is unreasonable."[78] Meanwhile, in various provincial statutes[79] and, most famously, British Columbia, patent unreasonableness has been prescribed as the standard of review of some types of administrative action.[80] Indirectly, reasonableness review could be ousted by providing for a limited right of appeal. For example, the Federal Court of Appeal has interpreted various provisions relating to statutory appeals on issues of "law or jurisdiction" as excluding the consideration of factual matters.[81] Where an appellate court whose jurisdiction is circumscribed in this way refuses to grant leave or finds that a matter raised by a party is outside the scope of the appeal clause, reasonableness review is unavailable. This would be a simple solution and would provide significant clarity. Here, however, I would invoke Einstein: everything should be made as simple as possible, but no simpler.

Appearances, moreover, may be deceptive. On the face of it, *Vavilov* would permit legislative ouster of reasonableness review – but only on the face of it. Indeed, *Hamlet* springs to mind: "God hath given you one face, and you make yourself another."[82]

First, in the same paragraph that eliminated jurisdictional error as a category of correctness review, one finds the following assertion: "A proper application of the reasonableness standard will enable courts to fulfill their *constitutional duty* to ensure that administrative bodies have acted within the scope of their lawful authority."[83] The language of constitutional duty is the language of *Crevier* and *Dunsmuir*. It suggests that reasonableness review *cannot*, in fact, be ousted, for its elimination may prevent courts from fulfilling their constitutional duty.

Second, although the point is not expressed in constitutional terms, the majority was very clear that it was directing administrative decision makers to henceforth "adopt a culture of justification and demonstrate that their exercise of delegated public power can be 'justified to citizens in terms of rationality and fairness.'"[84] If reasonableness review has been eliminated, administrative decision makers need never demonstrate that their exercise of public power can be justified in terms of rationality and fairness. This would knock the legs out from under a central pillar of the architecture of *Vavilov*.

The result, I submit, is that *Vavilov* establishes a core constitutional minimum of reasonableness review. With respect, the insistence that correctness review – and only correctness review – must be constitutionally entrenched is, and has been, misplaced. Julius Grey put the point with admirable clarity in the mid-1980s:

> What *Crevier* does entrench is *some* degree of review. The courts will not interfere at the same moment on all issues or against all tribunals. However, they now clearly possess a constitutional right to step in when the bounds of tolerance are exceeded by any decision maker. Clearly, the precise location of the bounds of tolerance is left to the court and that is quite consistent with the general trends in modern administrative law.[85]

In short, the "bounds of tolerance" are supplied in *Vavilov* by reasonableness review. Inasmuch as constitutional questions, questions of central importance to the legal system, and questions of overlapping jurisdiction have a "constitutional dimension,"[86] correctness review is also constitutionally entrenched.[87]

Indeed, this description of the constitutional foundations of *Vavilov* provides an explanation for an otherwise mysterious passage in the majority reasons. Having established institutional design as a key, grounding concept in the selection of the standard of review, the majority considered limited rights of appeal – such as those restricted to questions of law or jurisdiction – and observed: "[T]he existence of a circumscribed right of appeal in a statutory scheme does not on its own preclude applications for judicial review of decisions, or of aspects of decisions, to which the appeal mechanism does not apply, or by individuals who have no right of appeal."[88] If respect for institutional design choices is so important, why can unappealable aspects of decisions nonetheless be judicially reviewed? The answer is that reasonableness review is constitutionally entrenched. A limitation of a right of appeal cannot, constitutionally, effect the elimination of reasonableness review of aspects of a decision.

How, then, should courts address direct and indirect limitations on reasonableness review post-*Vavilov*? Consider first direct limitations, that is, those imposed by eliminating grounds of review or specifying a deferential ground of review. Here, the legislative language can be taken as an indication that the decision maker should benefit from a wider margin of appreciation. As was the case with privative clauses prior to *Vavilov*, they would not be enforced to the letter, but their spirit would be respected. *Vavilovian* reasonableness review is capacious enough to accommodate this solution. In *Vavilov*, the majority recognized that "the language chosen by the legislature in describing the limits and contours of the decision maker's authority" may differ from case to case, sometimes allowing "greater flexibility," sometimes "tightly constraining the decision maker."[89] Where a ground of review has been eliminated, or patent unreasonableness specified as the standard of review, these statutory provisions can be taken as "language chosen by the legislature" to give "greater flexibility" to the decision maker. In this way, reasonableness review is preserved and the constitutionally entrenched core minimum of judicial review safeguarded.[90] This is a fairly simple solution, which takes advantage of the thick conception of reasonableness review set out in *Vavilov*, and provides crystalline clarity about the scope of judicial review.

The second question, of indirect limitations, is slightly more complex. Where an appeal is limited to questions of law or jurisdiction, it is arguable that any issue relating to the "constitutional duty" to ensure that administrative decision makers remain within the boundaries of their authority will fall within the appeal clause. Historically, this was certainly the case, as such clauses respected the constitutional boundaries set out in *Crevier*. However, the core constitutional minimum I have ascribed to reasonableness review includes matters that go beyond questions of law or jurisdiction. For example, the harsh consequences a decision visits upon an individual as a matter of fact – perhaps leaving such an individual homeless[91] – would probably not fall within a limited appeal clause; to exclude any such issues would be problematic, as it would limit the courts' ability to police the boundaries of administrative decision makers' authority and to ensure that exercises of state power are publicly justified. Similarly, the responsiveness of a decision to the arguments of the parties and evidence presented is a key feature of *Vavilovian* reasonableness review, but again would not necessarily come within the scope of a limited appeal clause. The contemporaneity requirement might also be in play in some cases, as on appeal a decision maker may seek to defend its position by relying on documents and other material not referenced in its decision. On a statutory appeal, the court's analysis will be of the correctness of the outcome,[92] whereas on reasonableness review, the question for the court will be whether the reasons adequately justify the outcome.[93]

These considerations help to explain why the majority in *Vavilov* refused to accept that a limited appeal clause could oust judicial review of matters not falling within the clause. Doing so would be unconstitutional.[94]

This has significant practical consequences, but the resulting inconveniences can be addressed relatively straightforwardly. Where a question of law or jurisdiction is appealable only with leave of the appellate court and leave is refused, the appellant should be able to make an application for judicial review; where an appeal is provided for on a question of law or a question of law or jurisdiction, an appellant should also be able to make an application for judicial review of matters falling outside of the appeal clause. Indeed, it might be wise to make the application for judicial review and an appeal (or application for leave to appeal) simultaneously, with the judicial review stayed pending the disposition of the appeal (if leave is granted). Where the appeal and judicial review can be made to the same court, the files can be consolidated pursuant to the relevant procedural rules. Where the appeal is to a court of appeal but judicial review jurisdiction resides in a superior court, consolidation is obviously not an option. Instead, consistent with the principle that an applicant for judicial review should exhaust alternative remedies (most obviously, a right of appeal),[95] the appeal should be considered first of all, with the judicial review application stayed in the interim. Inasmuch as stays lie within the discretion of the judge seized of the matter, the discretion should be exercised largely and liberally: as long as the applicant has made an application for judicial review in a timely manner, stays pending the disposition of the parallel appeal should be readily granted.

This, I think, is the simplest possible set of solutions, perhaps not the one that I or anyone else would have woven from whole cloth, but the best available design from the fabric provided by *Vavilov*. It will require some compromises, perhaps, but *Vavilov* was all about compromise.[96]

There is one final point to make about the constitutional foundations of judicial review post-*Vavilov*. It concerns the relationship between *Vavilovian* reasonableness review and the standard of palpable and overriding error applicable on statutory appeals to questions of fact and mixed law and fact. If *Vavilovian* reasonableness review is constitutionally entrenched, should palpable and overriding error at least match it? My view is that palpable and overriding error is a more deferential standard than *Vavilovian* reasonableness review, and therefore may not always rise to the level of the core constitutional minimum. I would hesitate to say that this means that the provision of a statutory appeal and corresponding application of the *Housen v Nikolaisen* framework are unconstitutional. This conclusion is implausible. I would say, however, that the mismatch between palpable and overriding error and *Vavilovian* reasonableness review is likely to prompt arguments that the standards should converge in administrative law matters. As I have written elsewhere, "if the palpable and overriding error standard on appeal is less generous to appellants than reasonableness review would be, there will inevitably be pressure to expand the scope of the palpable and overriding error standard."[97] If these arguments also have a constitutional foundation, they will prove difficult to resist.

CONCLUSION

Vavilov is a landmark decision in Canadian law. As far as administrative law is concerned, it is the "big bang." It left some issues unresolved but, as I have sought to demonstrate, there is enough in the letter and spirit of the decision to enable us to address them. In simplifying the selection of the standard of review and in clarifying the content of the reasonableness standard, the majority in *Vavilov* provided a framework that can be adapted to resolve the outstanding questions the majority left open: the standard of review for procedural fairness issues, the continued health (or otherwise) of *Doré*, and the constitutional foundations of judicial review. Taking the search for simplicity and the maintenance of consensus as my guides, I have navigated these unresolved issues, suggesting solutions that are as simple as possible though not necessarily those I or anyone else would have developed starting from first principles.

CONCLUSION

THE TALE I HAVE told in this book is about substantive review, the law of reasonableness, and deference. For decades, Canadian courts have wrestled with complex concepts – deference, jurisdiction, legislative intent – in this difficult area, with judges struggling to keep a steady footing around fault lines between form and substance, deference and nondeference, and reason and authority.

I introduced these fault lines and the complexity of administrative law in Chapter 1. Both are useful navigational guides for the deep dives in Chapters 2 and 3 into the recent history of substantive review in Canada. Every ten years or so, the Supreme Court would attempt a paradigm shift or a distillation of settled principles: in 1979, with *New Brunswick Liquor;* in 1988, with *Bibeault;* in 1998, with *Pushpanathan;* in 2008, with *Dunsmuir;* and in 2019, with, of course, *Vavilov.* The sheer variety of administrative decision makers, the fact that administrative law is a body of general principles applicable to innumerable areas of substantive law, the inherent complexity of central concepts, and judicial disagreement about whether Canadian law should be more formal or substantive, deferential or nondeferential, and based on authority or reason caused these regular overhauls of the framework for substantive review in administrative law.

From 1979 to 2008, the Supreme Court of Canada veered back and forth between these fault lines. The *Dunsmuir* decision in 2008 was intended to bring certainty, simplicity, and stability to Canadian administrative law. In this, however, *Dunsmuir* was ultimately a failure. In the 2010s, the *Dunsmuir* framework was subject to constant tinkering and broke down under the weight of its internal contradictions and ad hoc additions. The collapse of the *Dunsmuir* framework set the scene for the judges to attempt, in *Vavilov,* to accomplish what *Dunsmuir* could not, and create a certain, simple, and stable administrative law framework.

What may set *Vavilov* apart from previous efforts to resolve Canada's substantive review conundrum is the fact that it memorializes a careful compromise between judges who hold different views of administrative law. In selecting the standard of review, a formal, nondeferential approach is to be followed, based more on authority than on reason. But in applying the reasonableness standard, judges must be substantive rather than formal, deferential rather than nondeferential, and uphold decisions only if they are based on reason, not because of the authoritative bona fides of the decision maker. There are nuances, of course, and in both selecting and applying the standard of review, there are points at which the *Vavilov* framework is uneasily poised relative to the form/substance, deference/nondeference, and reason/authority fault lines. Nonetheless, *Vavilov* is, broadly speaking, a compromise that seeks to achieve an overlapping consensus between judges who are normally divided along these fault lines.

A discussion of the first two applications of the framework, in *Vavilov* and the companion cases about the Super Bowl, helps to bring out the compromise.

Recall that the issue in *Vavilov* turned on paragraph 3(2)(a) of the *Citizenship Act.*[1] Normally those born in Canada are entitled to Canadian citizenship, but paragraph 3(2)(a) makes an exception for the children of "a diplomatic or consular officer or other representative or employee in Canada of a foreign government." Alexander Vavilov's parents were not diplomatic or consular officers. Were they "other representative[s] or employee[s] in Canada of a foreign government"? The analyst working for the Registrar of Canadian Citizenship concluded that they were. The Registrar adopted this analysis and, as a result, Vavilov could not be recognized as a Canadian citizen.[2]

The majority of the Supreme Court (whose analysis did not differ all that much from the analysis of Justices Rosalie Abella and Andromache

Karakatsanis in their concurring reasons) found that the analyst's interpretation was unreasonable. Starting with the analyst's reasons, the majority picked them apart, concluding that they could not stand.

First, a closely related provision of the *Citizenship Act* suggested that the people referred to in paragraph 3(2)(a) are those who benefit from diplomatic privileges and immunities. Indeed, the closely related provision – paragraph 3(2)(c) – would make little sense if those mentioned in paragraph 3(2)(a) did not have diplomatic privileges and immunities. But the analyst did not account for the "tension" created by her interpretation.[3]

Second, Vavilov had argued to the analyst that she should take into consideration the fact that these provisions of the *Citizenship Act* were designed to give effect to Canada's international obligations, as recognized by the parliamentarians who debated and adopted the provisions. Yet, there was no attempt to grapple with this fact: "In the face of compelling submissions that the underlying rationale ... was consistent with established principles of international law, the analyst and the Registrar chose a different interpretation without offering any reasoned explanation for doing so."[4]

Third, the analyst dismissed as irrelevant case law submitted by Vavilov on the meaning of paragraph 3(2)(a). Strictly speaking, these cases did not cover Vavilov's circumstances, but they contained "persuasive and comprehensive legal reasoning" with which the analyst should have grappled.[5]

Finally, the analyst failed to consider the possible consequences of her interpretation. The problem was that her logic would cover many other cases, not just those involving spies, as it would be "equally applicable to a number of other scenarios, including that of a child of a non-citizen worker employed by an embassy as a gardener or cook, or of a child of a business traveller who represents a foreign government-owned corporation."[6] Harsh consequences would befall people in these categories by virtue of the analyst's interpretation, yet there was no attempt to consider them, or whether, in light of such consequences, Parliament's intention in section 3(2)(a) was truly to exclude people like Vavilov from citizenship.[7]

For these reasons, taken together, the Registrar's decision was unreasonable. Notice just how rich the reasonableness analysis was. Compare and contrast, in particular, the judicial review that Vavilov got with the judicial review that Thanh Tam Tran got (described in the Introduction).[8] The Supreme Court's approach was deferential but it was also substantive – considering such matters as Canada's international obligations and the consequences of a particular interpretation of a statutory provision – and ultimately sought to identify a reasoned basis for the exercise of public power.

So much for the substance/deference/reason side of the *Vavilovian* compromise.

Let us turn now to the companion decision in *Bell Canada v Canada (Attorney General).*[9] At issue here was the scope of paragraph 9(1)(h) of the *Broadcasting Act,* which empowers the Canadian Radio-television and Telecommunications Commission (CRTC) to require broadcasters to "carry, on such terms and conditions as the Commission deems appropriate, programming services specified by the Commission." Although this question was wrapped up in Canada's complex "simultaneous substitution regime," the issue was, in the end, quite simple: could the CRTC use this power to compel broadcasters who were already showing a Canadian feed of the event to carry US advertisements during the Super Bowl halftime show?

Despite the complexity of the regulatory regime and the expertise of the CRTC in matters relating to broadcasting, the majority had no difficulty in concluding that the correctness standard should be applied. There is an appeal from decisions of the CRTC on questions of law or jurisdiction, and the issue here was whether the CRTC "lacked" the authority to make a "specific" order: "This raises a question that goes directly to the limits of the CRTC's statutory grant of power, and therefore plainly falls within the scope of the statutory appeal mechanism of s. 31(2)."[10]

The majority took the view that the CRTC's authority "is limited to issuing orders that require television service providers to carry specific channels as part of their service offerings, and attaching terms and conditions to such mandatory carriage orders."[11] The majority began with the text of paragraph 9(1)(h), placing great emphasis on where Parliament had placed commas: "This, in our view, indicates that the *primary* power delegated to the CRTC is to mandate that television service providers carry specific programming services as part of their cable or satellite offerings, and that the *secondary* power relates to the imposition of terms and conditions on such mandatory carriage orders."[12] This "plain meaning"[13] of the statutory language was supported by the surrounding context. Elsewhere in sub-section 9(1), the CRTC was granted specific compulsory powers, which "weighs against reading s. 9(1)(h) as conferring a *general* power to impose terms and conditions on any carriage of programming services."[14] And a "narrow reading"[15] of paragraph 9(1)(h) was consistent with Parliament's overall purpose in adopting the provision, namely, to enable the CRTC to compel the broadcast of television services (not specific programs) that assist the commission in achieving its statutory objectives; this was in line with how the CRTC had historically used paragraph 9(1)(h).[16]

This analysis – as Justices Abella and Karakatsanis noted in dissent – was much more formalistic, nondeferential, and authority-driven than the analysis in *Vavilov.*[17] The CRTC's own reasons for concluding that it had the authority in question did not warrant a mention: there is not a hint of deference in the majority's reasons. Substantive considerations, such as expertise, were left to one side: it was for the court to determine the weight to be given to various contextual factors, such as the CRTC's past practice. The analysis is based on the authoritativeness of Parliament. The legislature had spoken once, with the appeal clause; twice, with the limits on the CRTC's jurisdiction – and there was nothing for the Supreme Court to do but confirm that Parliament meant what (in the majority's view) it said.

This is the *Vavilovian* compromise in action. A formal, nondeferential, and authority-based approach to selecting the standard of review and adjudicating on statutory appeals; a substantive, deferential, and reasoned approach to applying the reasonableness standard. It is not a particularly principled compromise, but it might nonetheless work. As an Irish prime minister who in a previous life had been a professor of economics was once heard to ask: "It works in practice, but will it work in theory?" Maybe not, but maybe it does not matter.

Whatever one's personal views about where administrative law should be placed in relation to the form/substance, deference/nondeference, and reason/authority fault lines, it is clear that with *Vavilov*, the Supreme Court of Canada may have achieved what many observers thought would be impossible, namely, developing a stable general framework for Canadian administrative law. In short, it might have turned the law of substantive review into something closer to the law of procedural fairness.

Since the Supreme Court's decision in *Nicholson v Haldimand-Norfolk Regional Police Commissioners*,[18] it has been accepted that the requirements of procedural fairness are to be assessed by reference to a variety of contextual considerations. There is a general duty of fairness, which applies to all statutory schemes:[19]

> The duty of fairness is not a "one-size-fits-all" doctrine. Some of the elements to be considered were set out in a non-exhaustive list in [*Baker v Canada (Minister of Citizenship and Immigration)*, [1999] 2 SCR 817] to include (i) "the nature of the decision being made and the process followed in making it" (para. 23); (ii) "the nature of the statutory scheme and the 'terms of the statute pursuant to which the body operates'" (para. 24); (iii) "the importance of the decision to the individual or individuals affected" (para. 25); (iv) "the legitimate expectations of the person challenging the decision" (para. 26); and (v) "the choices of procedure made by the agency itself, particularly when the statute leaves to the decision maker the ability to choose its own procedures, or when the agency has an expertise in determining what procedures are appropriate in the circumstances" (para. 27).[20]

Over the years, procedural fairness has remained settled, while the concept of reasonableness has been anything but. Procedural fairness can be difficult to apply in practice; nonetheless, the same framework has been applied for decades. One important consideration is that most administrative law cases adjudicated by the courts (especially those that reach the Supreme Court of Canada) involve issues relating to specific areas of law: the judges must always apply the general principles of administrative law to a specific problem – it is much rarer for the procedures used to resolve a specific problem to be contested. Volume, then, is an important difference.

In addition, however, the fault lines are much less visible with respect to procedural fairness. In terms of deference/nondeference, both sides of the fault line have been provided for: the courts have the final word on whether the requirements of procedural fairness have been satisfied in a given case, but they are to give some deference to the procedural choices made by the decision maker. As for form and substance, the question has simply been resolved in favour of substance, which has the additional advantage of better accommodating the complexity of the modern administrative state, with its variety of decision makers, decisions, and specific areas of law.[21] Finally, judges who prefer reason and those who prefer authority are both accommodated: the courts retain the ultimate authority on matters of procedure, but the contextual considerations also allow judges to make a reasoned case for why a particular procedure did or did not meet the requirements of procedural fairness. The downside, of course, is that there is less certainty about what will be sufficient to meet the demands of the duty of fairness in any given case.[22] But while this downside may be worth worrying about in the procedural fairness context, it is less of a concern when it comes to substantive review, given the uncertainty that has reigned for many years about the best way to select the standard of review and apply the reasonableness standard.

What is next for Canadian administrative law? As discussed in Chapter 6, there are some lingering issues that will need to be resolved. And, as noted in Chapter 4, some aspects of *Vavilov* are in tension with each other. In resolving lingering questions and applying the *Vavilov* framework, judges will have to remain sensitive to the underlying rationales of the framework. *Vavilov* is a delicate compromise. As such, anyone using the *Vavilov* framework has to accept that an honest application of the framework is occasionally going to lead them to take a position that, left to their own devices, they would not adopt. As long as Canada's legal community appreciates this fact, the *Vavilov* framework promises to be a durable solution to what previously seemed to be a perennial problem. In the summer of 2022, the Supreme Court decided two administrative law cases and in doing so departed from the *Vavilov* framework in subtle but potentially important ways.[23] Only time will tell, however, whether these cases will prove mostly of historical interest or, more ominously, precursors of modifications to the *Vavilov* framework, modifications capable of destabilizing the careful compromise reached in that decision.

There is one last question to pose: How much does *Vavilov* really matter? This is an evergreen question for administrative lawyers. When matters are debated on judicial review in the courtroom, they are debated away from the front lines of administrative decision-making. Hardly any of the hundreds of thousands of administrative decisions made in Canada every year are ever judicially reviewed. A lot of procedurally unfair and substantively unreasonable decisions are never challenged in court. Many administrative decision-making institutions are understaffed, underfunded, and subject to the whims of the government of the day when it comes to appointments (often partisan rather than merit-based) and funding (often inadequate). Some cynical observers might therefore think that counting angels on the standard of review pinhead is a distraction from the need to ensure that *good* decisions are made in the first place.[24]

To be fair, however, the Supreme Court was alive to this difficulty in *Vavilov*. The majority commented that administrative decision makers' "exercise of delegated public power [must] be 'justified to citizens in terms of rationality and fairness.'"[25] The judges sent a message about the need for the reasoned exercise of public power. It is up to Canada's administrative decision makers – all of them – to take that message seriously. By reducing the confusion about administrative law, the Supreme Court of Canada has made it easier to focus on the things that really matter for Canadians.[26]

Notes

INTRODUCTION

1 2019 SCC 65 [*Vavilov*].

2 2015 FCA 237 [*Tran*].

3 *Ibid* at para 42.

4 *Ibid* at para 44.

5 *Ibid* at paras 60, 87.

6 *Ibid* at para 87.

7 Federal Court of Appeal, 2017 FCA 249; Supreme Court, 2019 SCC 66.

8 The following paragraphs draw on Paul Daly, "The Supreme Court of Canada's Administrative Law Trilogy" (2020) *Public Law* 408.

9 *Citizenship Act*, RSC 1985, c C-29, s 3(1)(a) [*Citizenship Act*].

10 *Ibid*, s 3(2)(a) [emphasis added].

11 Summarized by Bell J in the Federal Court, 2015 FC 960 at paras 7–12.

12 For the story of how the case of David Dunsmuir, a municipal clerk and part-time Elvis Presley impersonator, made it to Ottawa and shaped a decade of Canadian administrative law jurisprudence, see Clarence Bennett, "David Dunsmuir – an Unlikely Administrative Law Celebrity" in Paul Daly and Léonid Sirota, eds, *The Dunsmuir Decade/Les 10 ans de Dunsmuir: Special Issue of Canadian Journal of Administrative Law and Practice* (Toronto: Carswell, 2018).

13 David Stratas, "The Canadian Law of Judicial Review: A Plea for Doctrinal Coherence and Consistency" (2016) 42:1 Queen's LJ 27 at 29.

14 See generally Paul Daly and Léonid Sirota, eds, *The Dunsmuir Decade/Les 10 ans de Dunsmuir: Special Issue of Canadian Journal of Administrative Law and Practice* (Toronto: Carswell, 2018). This special issue emerged from a blog symposium. The original versions of all the contributions can be accessed from the links at <https://www.administrativelawmatters.com/blog/2018/05/11/revisiting-dunsmuir-food-for-thought/>.

15 Sean Fine, "Supreme Court Ruling Could Quell Chaos around Canadian Administrative Law," *Globe and Mail* (18 December 2019).

16 [1979] 2 SCR 227, 97 DLR (3d) 417.

17 *Canada (Citizenship and Immigration) v Khosa*, 2009 SCC 12 at para 28.

18 *Baker v Canada (Minister of Citizenship and Immigration)*, [1999] 2 SCR 817 at paras 53–56, 174 DLR (4th) 193 [*Baker*].

19 See especially *Canada (Director of Investigation and Research) v Southam Inc*, [1997] 1 SCR 748, 144 DLR (4th) 1.

20 See especially *Mouvement laïque québécois v Saguenay (City)*, 2015 SCC 16; *Edmonton (City) v Edmonton East (Capilano) Shopping Centres Ltd*, 2016 SCC 47. One appellate judge refused point-blank (albeit in dissent) to apply the *Edmonton East* decision, as it "spurns well-established norms of statutory interpretation": *Nova Scotia (Attorney General) v S&D Smith Central Supplies Limited*, 2019 NSCA 22 at para 278, Beveridge JA.

21 Since the decision in *Baker, supra* note 18, reasons for decision in Canadian law are primarily addressed as part of the law of substantive review. Only a complete failure to give reasons will amount to a breach of procedural fairness.

22 Matthew Lewans, "Deference and Reasonableness since *Dunsmuir*" (2012) 38:1 Queen's LJ 59 at 92, 94–95.

23 See generally Paul Daly, "The Signal and the Noise in Administrative Law" (2017) 68 UNBLJ 68.

24 An excellent example is *Canada (Canadian Human Rights Commission) v Canada (Attorney General)*, 2018 SCC 31, where the majority reasons of Gascon J embrace deference while the concurring reasons of Côté and Rowe JJ reject it.

25 *Vavilov, supra* note 1 at para 10.

26 *Ibid* at para 11.

27 *Bell Canada v Canada (Attorney General)*, 2019 SCC 66 at para 44 [*Bell*].

28 *Vavilov, supra* note 1 at para 194.

29 *Vavilov, supra* note 1 at para 14.

CHAPTER 1: WHY IS ADMINISTRATIVE LAW SO COMPLICATED?

1 See also Cristie Ford, "What People Want, What They Get, and the Administrative State" in Colleen Flood and Paul Daly, eds, *Administrative Law in Context*, 4th ed (Toronto: Emond Montgomery, 2021).

2 *R v Titchmarsh* (1914), 22 DLR 272 at 277–78, 24 CCC 38 (ONCA).

3 *R v Northumberland Compensation Appeal Tribunal, ex parte Shaw*, [1952] 1 KB 338 (CA) at 338, 357.

4 As Coke CJ explained in *Bagge's Case*, [1615] 11 Co Rep 93b at 98:

> And in this case it was resolved, that to this Court of King's Bench belongs authority, not only to correct errors in judicial proceedings, but

other errors and misdemeanors extra-judicial, tending to the breach of peace, or oppression of subjects, or to the raising of faction, controversy, debate or any manner of misgovernment; so that no wrong or injury, neither private nor public, can be done, but that it shall be here reformed or punished by due course of law.

5 (1700) 91 ER 179, (1700) 1 Salkeld 200.

6 *R v Electricity Commissioners, ex parte London Electricity Joint Committee Co (1920) Ltd,* [1924] 1 KB 171 (CA) at 204–5, [1923] 7 WLUK 128 (Atkin LJ).

7 *R v Criminal Injuries Compensation Board, ex parte Lain,* [1967] 2 QB 864 (HL) at 882 (in relation to *certiorari* specifically, but his comments are generally applicable). See also Law Reform Commission of Canada, "Independent Administrative Agencies" (1980) Working Paper No 25 at 20, online: <http://www.lareau -legal.ca/LRCWP25.pdf>.

8 *Reference re Code of Civil Procedure (Que), art 35,* 2021 SCC 27 at paras 51, 63.

9 *Attorney General of Quebec v Labrecque et al,* [1980] 2 SCR 1057, 125 DLR (3d) 545.

10 Donald Creighton, *The Empire of the St. Lawrence: A Study in Commerce and Politics,* 2d ed (Toronto: University of Toronto Press, 2002) at 220.

11 Robert Stevens, *The English Judges* (Oxford: Hart, 2005) at 19.

12 Gerald Le Dain, "The Twilight of Judicial Control in the Province of Quebec?" (1952) 1:1 McGill LJ 1.

13 H.W.R. Wade, "Crossroads in Administrative Law" (1968) 21:1 Curr Legal Probs 75.

14 *United Australia Ltd v Barclay's Bank Ltd,* [1941] AC 1 at 29, Lord Atkin.

15 See generally Stanley Alexander de Smith, *Judicial Review of Administrative Action* (London: Stevens and Sons, 1959); Paul Daly, "The Ages of Administrative Law" (9 June 2022) University of Ottawa Working Paper No 2022–16.

16 The following paragraphs draw heavily on "*Vavilov* and the Culture of Justification in Contemporary Administrative Law" (2020) 100 Sup Ct L Rev (2d) 279.

17 For a different perspective, see T.T. Arvind and Lindsay Stirton, "The Curious Origins of Judicial Review" (2017) 133 Law Q Rev 91.

18 John Bell, "Comparative Administrative Law" in Mathias Reimann and Reinhard Zimmermann, eds, *The Oxford Handbook of Comparative Law* (Oxford: Oxford University Press, 2006) 1259 at 1285.

19 [1964] AC 40.

20 [1969] 2 AC 147.

21 [1968] AC 997.

22 See, e.g., *R v Inland Revenue Commissioners, ex parte National Federation of Self-Employed and Small Businesses Ltd,* [1982] AC 617 at 657, Lord Roskill.

23 *Council of Civil Service Unions v Minister for the Civil Service,* [1985] AC 374 at 407.

24 "Rethinking Judicial Review: A Slightly Dicey Business" (1979) 17:1 Osgoode Hall LJ 1.

25 "Judicial Review in Canada: How Much Do We Need It?" (1974) 26:3 Admin L Rev 337.

26 David Mullan, "Fairness: The New Natural Justice" (1975) 25:3 UTLJ 281.

27 "The Slippery Slope of Judicial Intervention: The Supreme Court and Canadian Labour Relations 1950–1970" (1971) 9:1 Osgoode Hall LJ 1.

28 See, e.g., David Mullan, "Reform of Administrative Law Remedies: Method or Madness?" (1975) 6:3 Fed L Rev 340; John Evans, "Judicial Review in Ontario – Recent Developments in the Remedies – Some Problems of Pouring Old Wine into New Bottles" (1977) 55 Can Bar Rev 148.

29 [1979] 1 SCR 311.

30 *R v Electricity Commissioners, ex parte London Electricity Joint Committee Company (1920) Ltd,* [1924] 1 KB 171.

31 *Martineau v Matsqui Institution Disciplinary Board (No. 2),* [1980] 1 SCR 602 at 623, 106 DLR (3d) 385 [*Martineau*], Dickson J dissenting, but in terms that were later adopted in *Cardinal v Director of Kent Institution,* [1985] 2 SCR 643, 24 DLR (4th) 44. See, e.g., *Irvine v Canada (Restrictive Trade Practices Commission),* [1987] 1 SCR 181, 41 DLR (4th) 429, applying procedural fairness to a nonjudicial regulatory investigation that concerned privileges, not rights.

32 Mullan, *supra* note 26 at 315.

33 See generally Robert Thomas, "From 'Adversarial v. Inquisitorial' to 'Active, Enabling, and Investigative': Developments in UK Administrative Tribunals" and Lorne Sossin and Sarah Green, "Administrative Justice and Innovation: Beyond the Adversarial/Inquisitorial Dichotomy" in Laverne Jacobs and Sasha Baglay, eds, *The Nature of Inquisitorial Processes in Administrative Regimes* (London: Routledge, 2016).

34 Zach Richards, *Responsive Legality: The New Administrative Justice* (Abingdon, UK: Routledge, 2019).

35 *Baker v Canada (Minister of Citizenship and Immigration),* [1999] 2 SCR 817 at para 25, 174 DLR (4th) 193.

36 See generally Paul Daly, "Substantive Review in the Common Law World: *AAA v. Minister for Justice* in Comparative Perspective" (2019) 1 Ir Sup Ct Rev 105; Dean Knight, *Vigilance and Restraint in the Common Law of Judicial Review* (Cambridge: Cambridge University Press, 2018).

37 The apotheosis of this approach was *Pushpanathan v Canada (Minister of Citizenship and Immigration),* [1998] 1 SCR 982, 160 DLR (4th) 193.

38 [1985] 1 SCR 441, 18 DLR (4th) 481.

39 *Dunsmuir v New Brunswick,* 2008 SCC 9 at para 28.

40 *Crevier v AG (Québec),* [1981] 2 SCR 220, 127 DLR (3d) 1.

41 Paul Daly, "Royal Treatment: The Special Status of the Crown in Administrative Law" (2017) 22:1 Rev Const Stud 81.

42 *Hupacasath First Nation v Canada (Foreign Affairs and International Trade Canada),* 2015 FCA 4 at para 67.

43 See generally the discussion in *Air Canada v Toronto Port Authority,* 2011 FCA 347. *Cf Highwood Congregation of Jehovah's Witnesses (Judicial Committee) v Wall,* 2018 SCC 26, [2018] 1 SCR 750. See Derek McKee, "The Boundaries of Judicial Review since *Highwood Congregation of Jehovah's Witnesses v Wall*" (2021) 47 Queen's LJ 112.

44 See generally *Canada (Attorney General) v Downtown Eastside Sex Workers United Against Violence Society,* 2012 SCC 45.

45 See Mary Liston, "Transubstantiation in Canadian Public Law: Processing Substance and Instantiating Process" in John Bell et al., eds, *Public Law Adjudication in Common Law Systems: Process and Substance* (Oxford: Hart, 2016) 213 at 226–30.

46 *Clyde River (Hamlet) v Petroleum GeoServices Inc,* 2017 SCC 40; *Chippewas of the Thames First Nation v Enbridge Pipelines Inc,* 2017 SCC 41.

47 *Coldwater First Nation v Canada (Attorney General),* 2020 FCA 34 at para 40.

48 Lauren Wihak, "The Withering of Correctness Review" in Paul Daly and Leonid Sirota, eds, *A Decade of Dunsmuir/Les 10 ans de Dunsmuir* (Toronto: Carswell, 2018) 89 at 93.

49 On the general range of administrative decision makers, the discussion in Gilles Pépin, *Les tribunaux administratifs et la Constitution: Étude des articles 96 à 101 de l'A.A.N.B.* (Montreal: Les Presses de l'Université de Montréal, 1969) at 48–69 remains instructive.

50 2003 SCC 58 at para 31. The following paragraphs draw on "The Language of Administrative Law" (2016) 94 Can Bar Rev 519.

51 *Ibid.*

52 *Martineau, supra* note 31 at 628–29, Dickson J dissenting. See also *Apotex Inc v Canada (Attorney General),* [2000] 4 FC 264 at para 104, 188 DLR (4th) 145, Evans JA referring to "the spectrum of powers ranging from the legislative, through the administrative, to the judicial."

53 I have in mind here government departments headed by a politician who is accountable to a legislature (and perhaps also, as a modern addition to the

convention of responsible government, to the public at large) and in whose name departmental officials may act.

54 I have in mind here the various bodies established by the state to achieve commercial goals; these commercial bodies are relatively rarely subject to judicial review, but they are subject to governmental control.

55 I have in mind here bodies charged with regulating complex aspects of society and the economy. Central banks, telecommunications regulators, and competition regulators would fall under this rubric.

56 I have in mind here administrative tribunals that the legislature has established to settle disputes, usually between an administrative body and an individual. Often these tribunals complement the work of social and economic regulators. In some of its functions, for instance, a telecommunications regulator will act quasi-judicially, but in others it will act as a developer of general rules of policy for its regulatory sector.

57 Ron Ellis, *Unjust by Design: Canada's Administrative Justice System* (Vancouver: UBC Press, 2013), inveighs most effectively against political interference, largely unremarked by the wider public, with judicial tribunals.

58 For a particularly vivid illustration of this point, see Martin Shapiro, *Who Guards the Guardians? Judicial Control of Administration* (Athens: University of Georgia Press, 1988) at 112:

> Imagine our outrage if, at the end of a court trial, the president of the United States called up the judge and told her how he wanted the case to come out. Let us suppose an agency has held a rule-making proceeding that involved hundreds of hours of testimony and thousands of pages of written submissions. It has listened at length to every interested group and heard the rebuttal of each group to the testimony of every other. It has compiled a thousand-page-long rule-making record. It has then composed a statement showing that it has acted synoptically to consider every significant issue and arrive at the best possible decision. Those who have been watching and participating in such a process are going to be equally outraged if, just before the agency publishes its final rule, the president calls to tell the agency what rule it should adopt.

59 [1959] SCR 271, 17 DLR (2d) 449.

60 See, e.g., *Canadian National Railway Company v Canada (Transportation Agency)*, 2021 FCA 173.

61 *Canadian Pacific v Canadian Transport Commission*, [1985] 2 FC 136 at 148, *per* McGuigan JA.

62 *Toronto Star v AG Ontario*, 2018 ONSC 2586; *Bell Canada v Canada (Environment and Climate Change)*, 2021 EPTC 3.

63 *R (Agyarko) v Secretary of State for the Home Department* (2017) 1 WLR 823 at para 71, Lord Reed.

64 See also Michael Taggart, "Deference, Proportionality, *Wednesbury*" (2008) NZLR 423 at 463–64.

65 See also Martine Valois, "Si l'histoire de la norme m'était contée: Évolution et circonvolutions du principe de déférence au Canada" in Daly and Sirota, *supra* note 48, 19.

66 X need not be singular. There could be a set of such preconditions. I refer to X for ease of exposition.

67 See *Bell v Ontario Human Rights Commission,* [1971] SCR 756, 18 DLR (3d) 1. See also *R v London Rent Tribunal, ex parte Honig,* [1951] 1 KB 641; *R(A) v London Borough of Croydon,* [2009] UKSC 8.

68 *Union des employés de service, local 298 v Bibeault,* [1988] 2 SCR 1048 at 1086, 95 NR 161, Beetz J.

69 S.A. de Smith et al., *Judicial Review of Administrative Action,* 5th ed (London: Sweet and Maxwell, 1995) at 255. See similarly Louis Jaffe, "Judicial Review: Constitutional and Jurisdictional Fact" (1957) 70:6 Harv L Rev 953 at 959.

70 Paul Craig, "Jurisdiction, Judicial Control, and Agency Autonomy" in Ian Loveland, ed, *A Special Relationship? American Influences on Public Law in the United Kingdom* (Oxford: Clarendon, 1995) 173 at 177.

71 Paul Craig, *Administrative Law,* 6th ed (London: Sweet and Maxwell, 2008) at 441. See similarly William Wade, "Constitutional and Administrative Aspects of the *Anisminic* Case" (1969) 85 LQR 198 at 210–11.

72 Gary Lawson and Guy Seidman, *Deference: The Legal Concept and the Legal Practice* (New York: Oxford University Press, 2020). See also Dean Knight, "Locating *Dunsmuir*'s Meta-Structure within Anglo-Commonwealth Traditions" in Daly and Sirota, *supra* note 48, 191.

73 Lawson and Seidman, *supra* note 72 at 75.

74 *Ibid* at 77.

75 See also David Stratas, "A Decade of *Dunsmuir:* Please No More" in Daly and Sirota, *supra* note 48, 7 at 8: "In this area of law, individual judges at all levels of court – for the best of motives – have been decreeing rules and outcomes based on their own personal notions of the proper role of the judicial branch vis-à-vis administrative decision makers." And this can create a feedback loop, as law students and lawyers learn to hit judges' emotional buttons rather than to ground arguments in doctrinal rules: "[I]t was better, I concluded, to teach [administrative law] as an exercise in advocacy; ends-motivated analyses designed to serve the interests of clients" (Craig Forcese, "Teaching Canada's Administrative Law Standard of Review" in Daly and Sirota, *supra* note 48, 159 at 160).

76 The following paragraphs draw on Paul Daly, "Canadian Labour Law after *Vavilov*" (2021) 23 Can J Lab & Emp L 103.

77 *National Corn Growers Association v Canada (Import Tribunal)*, [1990] 2 SCR 1324 at 1333, 74 DLR (4th) 449, Wilson J.

78 "[A] rational basis for a holding of law means that a *reasonableness* test rather than a *rightness* test of administrative determination is applied." Hudson N. Janisch, "Towards a More General Theory of Judicial Review in Administrative Law" (1989) 53:2 Sask L Rev 327 at 336.

79 *Canadian Union of Public Employees v New Brunswick Liquor Corporation*, [1979] 2 SCR 227 at 237, 97 DLR (3d) 417.

80 See, e.g., H. Wade MacLauchlan, "Judicial Review of Administrative Interpretations of Law: How Much Formalism Can We Reasonably Bear?" (1986) 36:4 UTLJ 343 at 367. And perhaps also the current of legal practice that emphasizes the primacy of lawyerly tools of analysis in the search for the best answers to legal questions (Luc Tremblay, "La norme de retenue judiciaire et les "erreurs de droit" en droit administratif: Une erreur de droit? Au-delà du fondationalisme et du scepticisme" (1996) 52 R du B 141) and the differing perspectives that judges and administrators bring to bear on the task of interpreting statutes (Roderick A. Macdonald, "On the Administration of Statutes" (1987) 12:3 Queen's LJ 488 at 494–504).

81 See Paul Daly, *A Theory of Deference in Administrative Law: Basis, Application and Scope* (Cambridge: Cambridge University Press, 2012).

82 See also Martin Olszynski, "*Dunsmuir* Is Dead – Long Live *Dunsmuir*! An Argument for a Presumption of Correctness" in Daly and Sirota, *supra* note 48, 99.

83 See generally David Dyzenhaus, "Constituting the Rule of Law: Fundamental Values in Administrative Law" (2002) 27:2 Queens LJ 445; Paul Daly, "The Unfortunate Triumph of Form over Substance in Canadian Administrative Law" (2012) 50:2 Osgoode Hall LJ 317.

84 See also the distinction between form and substance suggested by Patrick Atiyah and Robert Summers, *Form and Substance in Anglo-American Law* (Oxford: Clarendon, 1987). A substantive reason "may be defined as a moral, economic, political, institutional or other social consideration" (at 5–6), whereas a formal reason "is a legally authoritative reason on which judges and others are empowered or required to base a decision or action, and such a reason usually excludes from consideration, overrides, or at least reduces the weight of, any countervailing substantive reasoning arising at the point of decision or action" (at 2).

85 *Supra* note 79. See also John M. Evans and Trevor Knight, "Cory on Administrative Law" in Patrick J. Monahan and Sandra A. Forbes, eds, *Peter Cory at the Supreme Court of Canada: 1989–1999* (Winnipeg: Canadian Legal History Project, 2001) 71.

86 See also Mary Liston, "Deference as Respect: Lost in Translation?" in Daly and Sirota, *supra* note 48, 47.

87 "The Politics of Deference: Judicial Review and Democracy" in Michael Taggart, ed, *The Province of Administrative Law* (Oxford: Hart, 1997) 279.

88 See further Paul Daly, "The Autonomy of Administration," UTLJ (forthcoming).

CHAPTER 2:
A DEEP DIVE INTO JUDICIAL REVIEW

Acknowledgments: In this chapter, I reproduce extensive extracts from my essay "The Struggle for Deference in Canada" in Mark Elliott and Hanna Wilberg, eds, *The Scope and Intensity of Substantive Review: Traversing Taggart's Rainbow* (Oxford: Hart Publishing, 2015) 297. The analysis in the section "Neither Pragmatic nor Functional" is, however, mostly new material.

1 Peter W. Hogg, "The Supreme Court of Canada and Administrative Law, 1949–1971" (1973) 11:2 Osgoode Hall LJ 187 at 222.

2 *R v Inland Revenue Commissioners, ex parte National Federation of Self-Employed and Small Businesses,* [1982] AC 617 at 649.

3 Gerald E. Le Dain, "The Twilight of Judicial Control in the Province of Quebec?" (1952) 1 McGill LJ 1.

4 *R v Nat Bell Liquors,* [1922] 2 AC 128 at 151–52, Lord Sumner.

5 See, e.g., *Toronto Newspaper Guild v Globe Printing,* [1953] 2 SCR 18, [1953] 3 DLR 561 (decision of the Ontario Labour Relations Board quashed for failure to take into account a relevant factor, i.e., whether individuals had resigned from a union between the application for certification and the certification hearing); *Labour Relations Board v Canada Safeway Ltd,* [1953] 2 SCR 46, [1953] 3 DLR 641 (decision of the British Columbia Labour Relations Board upheld because it was correct (at 50), Kerwin J, but compare 54–55, Rand J, upholding the board because "its judgment can be said to be consonant with a rational appreciation of the situation presented"); *The Queen v Leong Ba Chai,* [1954] SCR 10, [1954] 1 DLR 401 (writ of *mandamus* issued against a refusal to admit to Canada a child born out of wedlock because the child was in fact legitimate under the law of the child's place of birth). There was also a series of cases in the 1950s in which exercises of discretion were struck down for improperly interfering with individuals' rights of religion and freedom of association. See, e.g., *Smith and Rhuland Ltd v The Queen,* [1953] 2 SCR 95, [1953] 3 DLR 690 (refusal to certify a bargaining group because an official was a communist was an invalid exercise of discretion). In another line of cases, however, exercises of discretion that were characterized as "administrative" were beyond review as long as exercised in accordance with statutory requirements. See, e.g., *Calgary Power Ltd and Halmrast v Copithorne,* [1959] SCR 24, 16 DLR (2d) 241; *Moore v Minister of Manpower and Immigration,* [1968] SCR 839, 69 DLR (2d) 273.

6 John W. Willis, "Administrative Law and the British North America Act" (1939) 53:2 Harv L Rev 251 at 262. There are of course echoes here of Lord Hewart, *The New Despotism* (London: Benn, 1929).

7 [1964] SCR 497, 44 DLR (2d) 407.

8 Le Dain, *supra* note 3 at 5.

9 [1964] SCR 342, 45 DLR (2d) 730 [*Burlington Mills* cited to SCR].

10 *Ibid* at 346.

11 [1970] SCR 425, 11 DLR (3d) 336.

12 John M. Evans et al., *Administrative Law: Cases, Text and Materials*, 3d ed (Toronto: Emond Montgomery, 1989) at 565.

13 *Labour Relations Act*, RSO 1960, c 202, s 7(3).

14 [1970] SCR 425 at 435.

15 [1971] SCR 756.

16 Paul C. Weiler, "The 'Slippery Slope' of Judicial Intervention: The Supreme Court and Canadian Labour Relations 1950–1970" (1971) 9 Osgoode Hall LJ 1 at 9.

17 Hogg, *supra* note 1 at 205. See, similarly, Weiler, *supra* note 16 at 79.

18 Hogg, *supra* note 1 at 205.

19 *National Corn Growers Association v Canada (Import Tribunal)*, [1990] 2 SCR 1324 at 1335, 74 DLR (4th) 449. See Philip Bryden, "Justice Wilson's Administrative Law Legacy: The National Corn Growers Decision and Judicial Review of Administrative Decision-Making" (2008) 41 Sup Ct L Rev (2d) 225.

20 [1953] 2 SCR 18 at 30, [1953] 3 DLR 56 [emphasis added]. See also *Labour Relations Board v Canada Safeway Ltd*, [1953] 2 SCR 46 at 54–55, [1953] 3 DLR 641, where Rand J upheld the decision of the board because "its judgment can be said to be consonant with a *rational appreciation* of the situation presented" [emphasis added]. Again, the reference to "rational appreciation" suggests that the decision maker might have a margin of appreciation with respect to its interpretation and application of some statutory provisions.

21 [1975] 1 SCR 382, 41 DLR (3d) 6.

22 [1975] 1 SCR 382 at 388–89, 41 DLR (3d) 6.

23 [1979] 2 SCR 227, 97 DLR (3d) 417 [*New Brunswick Liquor* cited to SCR].

24 *Public Service Labour Relations Act*, RSNB 1973, c P-25, s 19.

25 *New Brunswick Liquor, supra* note 23 at 230.

26 (1978) 21 NBR (2d) 441 at para 20, 1978 CanLII 2696 (NBCA).

27 *New Brunswick Liquor, supra* note 23 at 233.

28 David Dyzenhaus, "The Politics of Deference: Judicial Review and Democracy" in Michael Taggart, ed, *The Province of Administrative Law* (Oxford: Hart, 1997) 279 at 290.

29 *New Brunswick Liquor, supra* note 23 at 235–36.

30 *Ibid* at 237.

31 *Ibid* at 242.

32 Brian A. Langille, "Judicial Review, Judicial Revisionism and Judicial Responsibility" (1986) 17:1–2 RGD 169 at 193. This message was underscored by a trilogy of labour relations decisions in which the new "patent unreasonableness" test was applied to the decision under review: *Volvo Canada Ltd v UAW, Local 720,* [1980] 1 SCR 178, 99 DLR (3d) 193; *Douglas Aircraft Co of Canada v McConnell,* [1980] 1 SCR 245, 99 DLR (3d) 385; *Alberta Union of Provincial Employees, Branch 63 v Board of Governors of Olds College,* [1982] 1 SCR 923, 136 DLR (3d) 1.

33 John M. Evans, "Developments in Administrative Law: The 1984–85 Term" (1986) 8 Sup Ct L Rev (2d) 1 at 27.

34 [1984] 2 SCR 412, 14 DLR (4th) 457 [*Syndicat* cited to SCR].

35 *Ibid* at 422.

36 *Ibid* at 425.

37 *Ibid* at 421. Beetz J distinguished this from the "initial jurisdiction" of the administrative decision maker, established at the outset of the inquiry (*ibid*); he also referred to jurisdiction-conferring provisions at 424.

38 *Ibid* at 432.

39 A leading commentator suggested shortly after this decision that the Supreme Court of Canada was full of "contempt ... for its own recent pronouncements": "Thus, by resurrecting the false god of 'jurisdiction' in the form of the new distinction between sections which confer jurisdiction and those which do not, the Court has rewritten history and redrawn the map of judicial review" (Langille, *supra* note 32 at 198). Another wrote that the decision was an "unpleasant surprise" (Evans, *supra* note 33 at 26).

40 [1988] 2 SCR 1048, 35 Admin LR 153 [*Bibeault* cited to SCR].

41 *Ibid* at 1086.

42 *Ibid* at 1087.

43 *Ibid* at 1088.

44 *Ibid.*

45 *Ibid* at 1097.

46 *Ibid* at 1098.

47 See, e.g., Sheila Wildeman, "Pas de Deux: Deference and Non-Deference in Action" in Lorne Sossin and Colleen Flood, eds, *Administrative Law in Context,* 2d ed (Toronto: Emond Montgomery, 2013) 323 at 334–35.

48 See, e.g., Claire L'Heureux-Dubé, "L'arrêt *Bibeault:* Une ancre dans une mer agitée" (1994) 28:2–3 RJT 731.

49 As La Forest J made clear in *Canadian Association of Industrial, Mechanical and Allied Workers, Local 14 v Paccar of Canada Ltd,* [1989] 2 SCR 983 at 1003, 62 DLR (4th) 437, the relevant question was the "legislative intention" whether to vest a decision in the decision maker or the reviewing court.

50 [1998] 1 SCR 982, 160 DLR (4th) 193 [*Pushpanathan* cited to SCR]. In my view, *Pushpanathan* represents the logical conclusion of the pragmatic and functional analysis because it sidelines the concept of jurisdictional error as completely as possible. Two other very significant cases deserve mention. In *Domtar Inc v Quebec (Commission d'appel en matière de lésions professionnelles)*, [1993] 2 SCR 756, 105 DLR (4th) 385, the court stated that a conflict between two tribunals on the appropriate interpretation of a statutory provision is not an independent basis for judicial review. Both interpretations could coexist, as long as both were reasonable. Less dramatically, in *British Columbia Telephone Co v Shaw Cable Systems (BC) Ltd*, [1995] 2 SCR 739, 125 DLR (4th) 443, the court performed an analysis of the constitutive legislation of two tribunals that had issued contradictory decisions in order to determine which ought to prevail, rather than undertake an independent analysis of whose claim was stronger.

51 Mark D. Walters, "Jurisdiction, Functionalism, and Constitutionalism in Canadian Administrative Law" in Christopher Forsyth et al., eds, *Effective Judicial Review: A Cornerstone of Good Governance* (Oxford: Oxford University Press, 2010) 300 at 307.

52 As for privative clauses, it soon became clear that truly privative language was not the only means of indicating a legislative intent to vest power in administrative decision makers: "Although their preclusive effect may be less obvious than that of the true privative clause, other forms of clauses purporting to restrict review may also have privative effect": *United Brotherhood of Carpenters and Joiners of America, Local 579 v Bradco Construction*, [1993] 2 SCR 316 at 333, 102 DLR (4th) 402, Sopinka J. See also *Pasiechnyk v Saskatchewan (Workers' Compensation Board)*, [1997] 2 SCR 890 at 905, 149 DLR (4th) 577.

53 It still retained some vitality, in the sense that administrative decision makers had to operate within boundaries set ultimately by reviewing courts, but these boundaries were largely to be marked out by reasonableness.

54 *Pushpanathan*, *supra* note 50 at para 28.

55 Thus, in *McLeod v Egan*, [1975] 1 SCR 517 at 519, 46 DLR (3d) 150, Laskin CJ suggested it would be inappropriate to defer to the interpretation by a labour arbitrator of a "general public enactment."

56 [1993] 1 SCR 554, 100 DLR (4th) 658 [*Mossop* cited to SCR].

57 *Canadian Human Rights Act*, RSC 1985, c H-6, s 3.

58 *Mossop*, *supra* note 56 at 585.

59 *Federal Court Act*, RSC 1985, c F7, s 28.

60 See similarly *Gould v Yukon Order of Pioneers*, [1996] 1 SCR 571, 133 DLR (4th) 449 (whether human rights legislation applied to a fraternal organization that refused to admit women as members); *Quebec (Commission des droits de la personne et des droits de la jeunesse) v Montréal (City)*, 2000 SCC 27 (whether

medical conditions could amount to "handicap[s]" for the purposes of human rights legislation).

61 2008 SCC 9 [*Dunsmuir*].

62 The following paragraphs draw on Paul Daly, *A Theory of Deference in Administrative Law: Basis, Application and Scope* (Cambridge: Cambridge University Press, 2012) at 174–77.

63 *Canada (Attorney General) v Public Service Alliance of Canada*, [1993] 1 SCR 941 at 963–64, 101 DLR (4th) 673.

64 *Law Society of New Brunswick v Ryan*, 2003 SCC 2 at para 52 [*Ryan*].

65 *Canada (Director of Investigation and Research) v Southam Inc*, [1997] 1 SCR 748 at para 56, 144 DLR (4th) 1.

66 *Ryan, supra* note 64 at para 46.

67 *Ibid* at para 55.

68 2003 SCC 63 [*Toronto (City)*].

69 *Ibid* at para 137.

70 *Canadian Association of Industrial, Mechanical and Allied Workers v Paccar of Canada*, [1989] 2 SCR 983 at 1022, 62 DLR (4th) 437.

71 See, e.g., *National Corn Growers Association v Canada (Import Tribunal)*, [1990] 2 SCR 1324 at 1370, 74 DLR (4th) 449: "In some cases, the unreasonableness of a decision may be apparent without detailed examination of the record."

72 *Toronto (City), supra* note 68 at para 143. See also *Voice Construction Ltd v Construction & General Workers' Union, Local 92*, 2004 SCC 23 at paras 40–42; Louis LeBel, "Some Properly Deferential Thoughts on Deference" (2008) 21:1 Can J Admin L & Prac 1.

73 *Miller v Workers' Compensation Commission (Newfoundland)* (1997) 154 Nfld & PEIR 52 at 57–58, 2 Admin LR (3d) 178, LD Barry J (SC).

74 *Mountain Parks Watershed Assn v Chateau Lake Louise Corp*, 2004 FC 1222 at para 11, Rouleau J.

75 In decisions such as *Nanaimo (City) v Rascal Trucking Ltd*, 2000 SCC 13 at paras 29–30; *Regina Police Assn Inc v Regina (City) Board of Police Commissioners*, 2000 SCC 14, [2000] 1 SCR 360 at para 40; *Chieu v Canada (Minister of Citizenship and Immigration)*, 2002 SCC 3 at para 24; and *United Taxi Drivers' Fellowship of Southern Alberta v Calgary (City)*, 2004 SCC 19 at para 5, the pragmatic and functional analysis led to correctness review on questions that the judges also labelled as "jurisdictional."

76 Clarence Bennett, "David Dunsmuir: An Unlikely Administrative Law Celebrity" in Paul Daly and Leonid Sirota, eds, *A Decade of Dunsmuir/Les 10 ans de Dunsmuir* (Toronto: Carswell, 2018) 31 at 32.

77 Norman Siebrasse, "Correctness Standard of Review for Minister's Interpretation of S 5 of the PM(NOC) Regulations" (12 January 2015), *Sufficient*

Description (blog), online: <http://www.sufficientdescription.com/2015/01/
correctness-standard-of-review-for.html>:

> Finally, on a personal note, Dunsmuir was the clerk of the court in
> Fredericton, New Brunswick (the full name of the case is *Dunsmuir v
> New Brunswick*), and my wife and I were married in 2004 at the
> Fredericton City Hall, by David Dunsmuir, about a year before he was
> removed from office. He did a brief Elvis impersonation, which my wife
> particularly enjoyed, but so far as I know he performed competently,
> and we are validly married.

78 Bennett, *supra* note 76 at 33.

79 *Ibid* at 34 [emphasis in original].

80 *Dunsmuir, supra* note 61.

81 *Ibid* at para 1.

82 *Ibid* at para 47.

83 For a critique, see Paul Daly, "The Unfortunate Triumph of Form
over Substance in Canadian Administrative Law" (2012) 50:2 Osgoode Hall LJ
317.

84 *Dunsmuir, supra* note 61 at para 54.

85 *Ibid* at para 52.

86 *Ibid* at para 64.

87 *Ibid* at paras 66–71.

88 *Ibid* at para 53.

89 *Ibid* at para 139 [emphasis in original].

90 *Ibid* at paras 51, 53–54, 57.

91 *Alberta (Information and Privacy Commissioner) v Alberta Teachers' Association*,
2011 SCC 61 at para 92, Cromwell J [*Alberta Teachers' Association*].

92 An example may be *Dr Q v College of Physicians and Surgeons of British
Columbia*, 2003 SCC 19, where in the view of the court three of the standard of
review analysis factors pointed to correctness and only one toward deference. There,
the standard of reasonableness *simpliciter* was available. Post-*Dunsmuir*, the four-factor analysis would at least point toward review on a correctness standard, but this
may not be sufficient to rebut the presumption of deference.

93 See also Mark D. Walters, "Theorizing Administrative Law – Does *Dunsmuir*
Have a Philosophy?" in Daly and Sirota, *supra* note 76, 43 at 45.

94 David J. Mullan, "*Dunsmuir v New Brunswick:* Standard of Review and
Procedural Fairness for Public Servants: Let's Try Again!" (2008) 21:2 Can J Admin
L & Prac 117 at 125.

95 *Dunsmuir, supra* note 61 at paras 47–48.

96 David Stratas, "A Decade of *Dunsmuir:* Please No More" in Daly and
Sirota, *supra* note 76, 7 at 12.

97 *Alberta Teachers' Association, supra* note 92 at para 34; *Rogers Communications Inc v Society of Composers, Authors and Music Publishers of Canada,* 2012 SCC 35 at para 15.

98 *Nolan v Kerry (Canada) Inc,* 2009 SCC 39 (claim of jurisdictional error); *Nor-Man Regional Health Authority Inc v Manitoba Association of Health Care Professionals,* 2011 SCC 59 (question of general law); *Alberta Teachers' Association, supra* note 92 (jurisdictional error); *Communications, Energy and Paperworkers Union of Canada, Local 30 v Irving Pulp & Paper Ltd,* 2013 SCC 34 (question of general law); *McLean v British Columbia (Securities Commission),* 2013 SCC 67 (question of general law). A correctness standard was applied to a jurisdictional issue in *Northrop Grumman Overseas Services Corp v Canada (Attorney General),* 2009 SCC 50 at para 10, but only because previous case law had satisfactorily identified the appropriate standard.

99 See, e.g., John M. Evans, "Triumph of Reasonableness: But How Much Does It Really Matter?" (2014) 27:1 Can J Admin L & Prac 101.

CHAPTER 3: THE *DUNSMUIR* DECADE

1 *Dunsmuir v New Brunswick,* 2008 SCC 9 [*Dunsmuir*].

2 Michel Bastarache, "*Dunsmuir* 10 Years Later" in Paul Daly and Leonid Sirota, eds, *A Decade of Dunsmuir/Les 10 ans de Dunsmuir* (Toronto: Carswell, 2018) 249 at 251.

3 Andrew Green, "The Search for a Simpler Test: *Dunsmuir* and Categories" in Daly and Sirota, *supra* note 2, 55.

4 *Smith v Alliance Pipeline Ltd,* 2011 SCC 7 at para 26.

5 The following paragraphs draw from Paul Daly, "*Dunsmuir's* Flaws Exposed: Recent Decisions on Standard of Review" (2012) 58 McGill LJ 483, and "The Unfortunate Triumph of Form over Substance in Canadian Administrative Law" (2012) 50 Osgoode Hall LJ 317.

6 2011 SCC 61 [*Alberta Teachers'*].

7 *Ibid* at para 98.

8 2009 FCA 309 [*Mowat*].

9 2011 SCC 53 [*Canadian Human Rights Commission*].

10 *Canadian Human Rights Act,* RSC 1985, c H-6, s 53.

11 *Mowat, supra* note 8 at paras 43–44.

12 [1970] SCR 425, 11 DLR (3d) 336.

13 Equally, of course, it could be said to be an interpretation of a home statute. As discussed below, there will often be such conflict between the categories.

14 See, e.g., *Trade Unions Act,* RSC 1985, c T-14, ss 4(1)(a), 6; *Labour Relations Act,* RSNL 1990, c L-1, ss 70(7)(b), 70(8), 128(1); *Labour Relations Code,* RSA 2000, c L-1, ss 29(1), 85(a), 92(3), 151(d), 151(e), 202(1), 203.

15 See Chapter 2.

16 Paul Weiler, "The Slippery Slope of Judicial Intervention: The Supreme Court and Canadian Labour Relations 1950–1970" (1971) 9:1 Osgoode Hall LJ 1 at 2–4.

17 *Canadian Human Rights Commission, supra* note 9.

18 See, e.g., *Kelly v Alberta (Energy Resources Conservation Board)*, 2012 ABCA 19.

19 *Canadian Human Rights Commission, supra* note 9 at para 25.

20 *Ibid.*

21 *Ibid.*

22 *Ibid* at para 26.

23 See similarly *Canada (Attorney General) v Tipple*, 2011 FC 762 at paras 27–35.

24 *Smith v Alliance Pipeline Ltd, supra* note 4 at para 92.

25 See further Evan Fox-Decent and Alexander Pless, "*Dunsmuir* and Jurisdiction" in Daly and Sirota, *supra* note 2, 65.

26 2009 FCA 223.

27 *Ibid* at para 52. See also *Canada (Attorney General) v Public Service Alliance of Canada*, 2011 FCA 257 at para 30.

28 *Alberta Teachers,' supra* note 6.

29 *Ibid* at para 42.

30 *Ibid* at paras 30, 34.

31 *Ibid* at para 42.

32 2018 SCC 31 at paras 34–41 [*Canada (Attorney General)*].

33 2017 SCC 42 [*Guérin*].

34 CQLR, c A-29.

35 *Guérin, supra* note 33 at para 33.

36 *Ibid* at para 49.

37 *Ibid* at para 50.

38 *Ibid* at para 70. See also the thoughtful comments of Justice Donald Rennie in *Bell Canada v 7262591 Canada Ltd.,* 2018 FCA 174 [*Bell Canada*] at paras 41–48.

39 *Ibid* at para 71 [emphasis added].

40 The following paragraphs draw on Paul Daly, "Unreasonable Interpretations of Law" in Joseph Robertson, Peter Gall, and Paul Daly, eds, *Judicial Deference to Administrative Tribunals in Canada: Its History and Future* (Toronto: LexisNexis Canada, 2014) 233.

41 *Personal Information Protection Act,* SA 2003, c P-6.5.

42 Rothstein J pronounced himself "unable to provide a definition" of such a question (*Alberta Teachers,' supra* note 6 at para 42) but twice emphasized that

true jurisdictional questions are "exceptional" (*ibid* at paras 30, 34) and concluded that this was not such an exceptional case. Notably, in *McLean v British Columbia (Securities Commission)*, 2013 SCC 67 at para 25, n 3 [*McLean*], the court cited with approval an American case in which deference was accorded to a decision maker's interpretation of its jurisdiction: *City of Arlington v Federal Communications Commission*, 569 US 290 (2013).

43 *Alberta Teachers,' supra* note 6 at para 32.

44 *Dunsmuir, supra* note 1 at para 54.

45 *Adams Fruit Co Inc v Barrett*, 494 US 638 at 649–50 (1990); *McLeod v Egan*, [1975] 1 SCR 517 at 519, 46 DLR (3d) 150, Laskin CJ.

46 It could also be advanced under the banner of general questions of law of central importance to the legal system, but would not make much headway there either. See the text accompanying notes 22–25.

47 *Bernard v Canada (Attorney General)*, 2012 FCA 92 at para 37, Evans JA, aff'd 2014 SCC 13. See also *Ontario (Community Safety and Correctional Services) v Ontario (Information and Privacy Commissioner)*, 2014 SCC 31 at para 27.

48 See, e.g., *Syndicat canadien des communications, de l'énergie et du papier, section locale 30 c Les Pâtes et Papier Irving, Limitée*, 2011 NBCA 58 at para 5, rev'd *sub nom Communications, Energy and Paperworkers Union of Canada, Local 30 v Irving Pulp & Paper, Ltd*, 2013 SCC 34 [*Irving Paper*].

49 See, e.g., *McLean, supra* note 42.

50 *Alberta (Information and Privacy Commissioner) v University of Calgary,* 2016 SCC 53 at paras 19–27 [*University of Calgary*].

51 *Chagnon v Syndicat de la fonction publique et parapublique du Québec*, 2018 SCC 39 at para 17 [*Chagnon*].

52 *Mouvement laïque québécois v Saguenay (City)*, 2015 SCC 16 at para 49 [*Saguenay*].

53 2012 SCC 12 [*Doré*]. For discussion, see Evan Fox-Decent and Alexander Pless, "The Charter and Administrative Law: Cross-Fertilization in Public Law" in Colleen Flood and Lorne Sossin, eds, *Administrative Law in Context*, 2d ed (Toronto: Emond Montgomery, 2012) 407; Paul Daly, "Prescribing Greater Protection for Rights: Administrative Law and Section 1 of the *Canadian Charter of Rights and Freedoms*" (2014) 65 Sup Ct L Rev (2d) 247.

54 *R v Oakes*, [1986] 1 SCR 103, 26 DLR (4th) 200.

55 *Doré, supra* note 53 at para 57.

56 This may also be the case with respect to federalism principles. See, though the point is not fully discussed, *Martin v Alberta (Workers' Compensation Board)*, 2014 SCC 25 at paras 39–41. For an earlier, similarly inconclusive case, see *Westcoast Energy Inc v Canada (National Energy Board)*, [1998] 1 SCR 322, 156 DLR (4th) 456.

57   *Loyola High School v Quebec (Attorney General)*, 2015 SCC 12 at para 38.

58   *Law Society of British Columbia v Trinity Western University,* 2018 SCC 32 at para 81 [*Trinity Western University*] [emphasis in original].

59   2013 SCC 11 [*Whatcott*].

60   SS 1979, c S-24.1, s 14.

61   *Whatcott, supra* note 59 at para 59. See also *Ktunaxa Nation v British Columbia (Forests, Lands and Natural Resource Operations)*, 2017 SCC 54 at paras 61–75 [*Ktunaxa Nation*].

62   *Whatcott, supra* note 59 at para 168. See also *Ktunaxa Nation, supra* note 61 at paras 76–115.

63   2016 SCC 47 [*Edmonton East*]. See further Joseph T. Robertson, QC, "*Dunsmuir*'s Demise and the Rise of Disguised Correctness Review" in Daly and Sirota, *supra* note 2, 111 at 112–13.

64   *Edmonton East (Capilano) Shopping Centres Limited v Edmonton (City)*, 2015 ABCA 85 at para 40.

65   *Edmonton East, supra* note 63 at para 20.

66   *Ibid* at para 28.

67   *Ibid* at para 35.

68   See, e.g., Mark Mancini, "The Dark Art of Deference: Dubious Assumptions of Expertise on Home Statute Interpretation" in Daly and Sirota, *supra* note 2, 83; Peter Gall, "*Dunsmuir:* Reasonableness and the Rule of Law" in Daly and Sirota, *supra* note 2, 229.

69   *Edmonton East, supra* note 63 at para 70.

70   *Ibid* at para 71 [emphasis in original].

71   *Ibid* at para 89.

72   *Ibid* at para 83.

73   *Ibid* at para 82.

74   *Ibid* at para 73.

75   *Ibid* at paras 75–78.

76   *Ibid* at para 79.

77   *Ibid* at para 80.

78   *Ibid* at para 87.

79   *Ibid* at para 40.

80   *Ibid* at paras 41–61.

81   *Ibid* at para 40 [emphasis in original].

82   *Ibid* at para 44.

83   This section features extensive passages from Paul Daly, "The Scope and Meaning of Reasonableness Review" (2015) 52 Alta L Rev 799.

84   David Dyzenhaus, "The Politics of Deference: Judicial Review and Democracy" in Michael Taggart, ed, *The Province of Administrative Law* (London: Hart, 1997) 279 at 286.

85 2011 SCC 62.

86 *Ibid* at para 13.

87 *Ibid* at para 16. See similarly *Public Service Alliance of Canada v Canada Post Corporation,* 2010 FCA 56 at para 163, Evans JA dissenting ("perfection is not the standard"), rev'd 2011 SCC 57; *Irving Paper, supra* note 48 at para 54 ("The board's decision should be approached as an organic whole, without a line-by-line treasure hunt for error").

88 2013 FC 431 at para 11. See, e.g., *Leahy v Canada (Citizenship and Immigration),* 2012 FCA 227; *Wall v Independent Police Review Director,* 2013 ONSC 3312.

89 See, e.g., David Dyzenhaus, "Constituting the Rule of Law: Fundamental Values in Administrative Law" (2002) 27:2 Queen's LJ 445. See also John M. Evans, "Reflections on *Dunsmuir* of a Recovering Judge" in Daly and Sirota, *supra* note 2, 175 at 181.

90 *Alberta Teachers,' supra* note 6 at para 29.

91 *Ibid* at paras 53–55.

92 *McLean, supra* note 42.

93 *Securities Act,* RSBC 1996, c 418, s 161(6)(d).

94 *Ibid,* s 159.

95 *McLean (Re),* 2010 BCSECCOM 262.

96 *McLean v British Columbia (Securities Commission),* 2011 BCCA 455 at para 30.

97 *McLean, supra* note 42 at para 72.

98 2013 SKCA 79 [*Areva*], leave to appeal dismissed, 2014 CanLII 5971.

99 *Ibid* at para 36. See also para 110 (reasons of Ottenbreit JA).

100 See, e.g., *Re Downing and Graydon* (1978), 92 DLR (3d) 355 at 377, 21 OR (2d) 292, Wilson JA (as she then was) ("it was not the factual basis alone that the appellant was entitled to respond to but also the legal basis of the employment standards officers' decision"), adopted in *Syndicat des employés de production du Québec et de l'Acadie v Canada (Canadian Human Rights Commission),* [1989] 2 SCR 879, 62 DLR (4th) 385.

101 *Alberta Teachers,' supra* note 6 at para 54.

102 *Agraira v Canada (Public Safety and Emergency Preparedness),* [2013] 2 SCR 559.

103 SC 2001, c 27.

104 The minister's reasons were as follows:

> After having reviewed and considered the material and evidence submitted in its entirety as well as specifically considering these issues:
>
> • The applicant offered contradictory and inconsistent accounts of his involvement with the Libyan National Salvation Front (LNSF).

- There is clear evidence that the LNSF is a group that has engaged in terrorism and has used terrorist violence in attempts to overthrow a government.
- There is evidence that LNSF has been aligned at various times with Libyan Islamic opposition groups that have links to Al-Qaeda.
- It is difficult to believe that the applicant, who in interviews with officials indicated at one point that he belonged to a "cell" of the LNSF which operated to recruit and raise funds for LNSF, was unaware of the LNSF's previous activity.

It is not in the national interest to admit individuals who have had sustained contact with known terrorist and/or terrorist-connected organizations. Ministerial relief is denied.

105 There was also an issue as to the applicant's credibility, but this went only to the extent of his involvement with the terrorist organization. It could not have been an independent ground for refusing an application on the basis of "national interest."

106 *Agraira, supra* note 102 at para 62.

107 Section 9.2 of the guidelines (reproduced in an appendix to the judgment) included the following:

the details of the application and any personal or exceptional circumstances to be taken into consideration; this would include:

- details of immigration application
- basis for refugee protection, if applicable
- other grounds of inadmissibility, if applicable
- activities while in Canada
- details of family in Canada or abroad
- any Canadian interest.

108 *Agraira, supra* note 102 at paras 89–90.

109 *Lemus v Canada (Citizenship and Immigration),* 2014 FCA 114 at para 35, Stratas JA. At para 33, Stratas posed but did not answer a series of pertinent questions:

One might well query the idea that reviewing courts are to presume the correctness of administrators' decisions, even in the face of a defect. One might also query whether, in trying to sustain an outcome reached by flawed reasoning, the reviewing court might be coopering up an outcome that the administrator, knowing of its error, might not have itself reached. Finally, whether an outcome should be left in place because of the strength of the record or other considerations has traditionally been something for the remedial stage of the analysis, not an earlier stage.

110 *Catalyst Paper Corp v North Cowichan (District)*, 2012 SCC 2 at para 18.

111 *Irving Paper, supra* note 48.

112 *Irving Pulp & Paper, Limited v Communications, Energy and Paperworkers Union of Canada, Local 30*, 2010 NBQB 294.

113 *Communications Energy and Paperworkers Union of Canada, Local 30 v Irving Pulp & Paper, Limited*, 2011 NBCA 58.

114 *Ibid* at paras 51–52.

115 *Irving Paper, supra* note 48 at para 31.

116 *Ibid* at para 104

117 *Ibid* at para 105.

118 Matthew Lewans, "Deference and Reasonableness since *Dunsmuir*" (2012) 38 Queen's LJ 59.

119 *Irving Paper, supra* note 48 at paras 6, 16, 42, 64, 75.

120 *Canada Post Corp v Public Service Alliance of Canada*, 2011 SCC 57.

121 Eddie Clarke, "*Dunsmuir* and the Hows and Whys of Judicial Review" in Daly and Sirota, *supra* note 2, 119 at 121.

122 *Canada (Public Safety and Emergency Preparedness) v. Tran*, 2015 FCA 237.

123 This section reproduces parts of Paul Daly, "The Signal and the Noise in Administrative Law" (2017) 68 UNBLJ 68.

124 *Tran v Canada (Public Safety and Emergency Preparedness)*, 2017 SCC 50.

125 2014 SCC 68.

126 David J. Mullan, "2015 Developments in Administrative Law Relevant to Energy Law and Regulation" (2016) 4:1 Energy Regulation Quarterly, online: <https://energyregulationquarterly.ca/articles/2016-developments-in-administrative-law-relevant-to-energy-law-and-regulation#sthash.BOCgExgz.dpbs>; David J. Mullan, "The True Legacy of *Dunsmuir* – Disguised Correctness Review?" in Daly and Sirota, *supra* note 2, 107. See, e.g., *Canadian Human Rights Commission, supra* note 9.

127 See the discussion of *Bombardier* accompanying notes 129–31. See *Saguenay, supra* note 52; Paul Daly, "Why Would Jurisdiction Be Concurrent? Another Thought on Mouvement laïque québécois v. Saguenay (City), 2015 SCC 16" (17 April 2015), *Administrative Law Matters* (blog), online: <http://www.administrativelawmatters.com/blog/2015/04/17/why-would-jurisdiction-be-concurrent-another-thought-on-mouvement-laique-quebecois-v-saguenay-city-2015-scc-16/>.

128 See also David Stratas, "A Decade of *Dunsmuir*: Please No More" in Daly and Sirota, *supra* note 2, 7 at 17.

129   *Quebec (Commission des droits de la personne et des droits de la jeunesse) v Bombardier Inc (Bombardier Aerospace Training Center),* 2015 SCC 39 [*Bombardier*].

130   *Ibid* at para 16.

131   *Ibid* at para 101

132   *Canada (Minister of Citizenship and Immigration) v Vavilov,* 2019 SCC 65; *Bell Canada v Canada (Attorney General),* 2019 SCC 66.

133   *Bombardier, supra* note 129 at para 2.

134   *Ibid* at para 55.

135   *Ibid* at para 65, though note that, strictly speaking, this conclusion applies only to Quebec, which has a specific legislative provision about the burden of proof.

136   *Ibid* at paras 67–68.

137   *Ibid* at para 69.

138   *Ibid.*

139   2011 SCC 59 at para 45.

140   *Bombardier, supra* note 129 at para 81.

141   *Ibid* at para 88.

142   *Ibid* at para 84.

143   *Ibid* at para 89.

144   *Ibid.*

145   *Ibid* at para 99.

146   *Canada (Citizenship and Immigration) v Khosa,* 2009 SCC 12 at para 60.

147   *Irving Paper, supra* note 48 at para 54.

148   2015 SCC 61.

149   *Ibid* at para 112.

150   *Cf* Alice Woolley, "Stranger Things – a Defence of *Dunsmuir*" in Daly and Sirota, *supra* note 2, 217.

151   2016 SCC 29 [*Wilson*].

152   See *Commission scolaire de Laval v Syndicat de l'enseignement de la région de Laval,* 2016 SCC 8 at paras 76–78 (where Wagner and Brown JJ agreed with her); *Barreau du Québec v Quebec (Attorney General),* 2017 SCC 56 at paras 52–66; *Canada (Attorney General), supra* note 32 at paras 82–90 (where Rowe J agreed with her); *West Fraser Mills Ltd v British Columbia (Workers' Compensation Appeal Tribunal),* 2018 SCC 22 at paras 62–74 [*West Fraser Mills*] (where Brown J at paras 114–117 and Rowe J at paras 126–27 separately expressed the same view about the applicable standard); *Groia v Law Society of Upper Canada,* 2018 SCC 27 at paras 163–69; and *Chagnon, supra* note 51 at paras 86–88 (where Brown J concurred; here the court was unanimous that the correctness standard applied, as parliamentary privilege was at issue). See also *Canada (Attorney General) v Igloo Vikski Inc,* 2016 SCC 38 at para 58 (applying reasonableness review but noting that the range of reasonable interpretations was quite narrow) and *University*

of Calgary, supra note 50 (writing for the majority of judges, in a case involving solicitor-client privilege).

153 See *Guérin, supra* note 33 (where Brown and Rowe JJ identified a jurisdictional question, a point with which Côté J agreed); *Quebec (Commission des normes, de l'équité, de la santé et de la sécurité du travail) v Caron,* 2018 SCC 3 at para 81 (where Côté J concurred); *West Fraser Mills Ltd v British Columbia (Workers' Compensation Appeal Tribunal), supra* note 2 at paras 126–27; and the other cases in the previous note where Rowe J agreed that correctness was the applicable standard of review.

154 *Trinity Western University, supra* note 58 at para 175, Rowe J, and 302–14, Côté and Brown JJ.

155 David Stratas, "The Canadian Law of Judicial Review: A Plea for Doctrinal Coherence and Consistency" (2016) 42:1 Queen's LJ 27.

156 2016 SCC 47.

157 *Atlantic Mining NS Corp (DDV Gold Limited) v Oakley,* 2019 NSCA 22 at para 13.

158 RSNS 1989, c 156.

159 *Nova Scotia (Attorney General) v S&D Smith Central Supplies Limited,* 2019 NSCA 22 at para 51 [*Smith Central*].

160 *Ibid* at para 250.

161 *Smith Central, supra* note 159 at para 278. See also the compelling criticism developed by Justice Marc Nadon in *Bell Canada, supra* note 38 at paras 175–99.

162 *Wilson, supra* note 151.

163 *Ibid* at para 19.

164 *Ibid* at para 70.

165 *Ibid* at para 78.

166 See especially *Canada (Attorney General), supra* note 32 at paras 108–15, where Brown J expressed disagreement with the majority about the utility of the "true" questions of jurisdiction category and urged recognition of the importance of context for the purpose of performing judicial review.

CHAPTER 4: *VAVILOV'S* BIG BANG

Acknowledgment: This chapter draws heavily on my essays "Big Bang Theory: *Vavilov's* New Framework for Administrative Law" in Paul Daly and Colleen Flood, eds, *Administrative Law in Context,* 4th ed (Toronto: Emond Montgomery, 2021) 327, and "The *Vavilov* Framework and the Future of Canadian Administrative Law" (2020) 33 Can J Admin L & Prac 111.

1 See the discussion in Chapter 1.

2 *Canada (Minister of Citizenship and Immigration) v Vavilov,* 2019 SCC 65 [*Vavilov*].

3 This was not enough for Abella and Karakatsanis JJ, who disagreed with the majority's approach to both issues. In this chapter, I will focus mostly on the majority reasons.

4 *Vavilov, supra* note 2 at para 10.

5 *Ibid* at para 12.

6 In their concurring reasons, Abella and Karakatsanis JJ accepted that it was important to "steady the ship" (*ibid* at para 199) but rejected the course set by the majority. On measuring simplicity and clarity, see Robert Danay, "Did *Dunsmuir* Simplify the Standard of Review?" in Paul Daly and Leonid Sirota, eds, *A Decade of Dunsmuir/Les 10 ans de Dunsmuir* (Toronto: Carswell, 2018) 201.

7 *Vavilov, supra* note 2 at para 47.

8 *Ibid* at para 23.

9 *Ibid* at para 30 [emphasis in original].

10 *Ibid.*

11 To be clear, I do not mean to suggest that there is no substantive basis for relying on institutional design. Lying underneath institutional design is a substantive judgment about the value of relying on legislative intent. Formalism in administrative law, as I defined it in Chapter 1, is about using forms detached from their substance. Every form must be underpinned by substance, somewhere. The point here is that institutional design operates in a formal way, by precluding courts from any consideration of the contextual substantive considerations underpinning it.

12 *Ibid* at paras 34–35. The classic example here is the *Administrative Tribunals Act,* SBC 2004, c 45, which sets out detailed standards of review, including the "patent unreasonableness" standard, which remains in force despite its elimination from the common law of judicial review in *Dunsmuir.* See generally *Speckling v British Columbia (Workers' Compensation Board),* 2005 BCCA 80 at para 33; *Pacific Newspaper Group Inc v Communications, Energy and Paperworkers Union of Canada, Local 2000,* 2014 BCCA 496 at para 48; *Red Chris Development Co v United Steel, Paper and Forestry, Rubber, Manufacturing, Energy, Allied Industrial and Service Workers International Union, Local 1-1937,* 2021 BCCA 152 at paras 30–31. There are other statutory provisions here and there that prescribe a standard of review: see further Paul Daly, "Patent Unreasonableness after *Vavilov*" (2021) 34:2 Can J Admin L & Prac 167.

13 *Housen v Nikolaisen,* 2002 SCC 33 [*Housen*]. On what constitutes an appeal for these purposes, compare *McCarthy v Guest,* 2020 NBQB 150 (a statutory appeal, although the word "review" was used) with *GSR Capital Group Inc v The City of White Rock,* 2020 BCSC 489 at para 69, and *O'Shea/Oceanmount Community Association v Town of Gibsons,* 2020 BCSC 698 at para 51 (a mechanism to get a matter before the court).

14 *Vavilov, supra* note 2 at para 36.

15 *South Yukon Forest Corp v R*, 2012 FCA 165 at para 46, cited with approval by the Supreme Court in *Benhaim v St-Germain*, 2016 SCC 48 [*Benhaim*]. See also Morissette JA's formulation in *JG v Nadeau*, 2016 QCCA 167 at para 77: "une erreur manifeste et dominante tient, non pas de l'aiguille dans une botte de foin, mais de la poutre dans l'œil. Et il est impossible de confondre ces deux dernières notions." The question arises here as to whether palpable and overriding error is more or less deferential than reasonableness review. Even on questions of fact, I think palpable and overriding error is more deferential than reasonableness review. Reasonableness review under *Vavilov* is more open-ended, certainly in terms of "factual and legal constraints," because it does not have the imposing twin requirements of palpable-ness and overriding-ness. I can imagine situations where an error of fact that touches on the governing statutory scheme, the harshness of the consequences for the individual concerned, or consistency with a previous tribunal decision could cause the court to lose confidence in the reasonableness of the decision (*Vavilov, supra* note 2 at para 106). I suppose any such factual error would have to be based on a "fundamental misapprehension" (*ibid* at para 126), but even that seems to be a lower barrier than palpable and overriding error. The other type of fundamental flaw described in *Vavilov* – a lack of internally coherent reasoning – could also conceivably rest on an error of fact. The Ontario Divisional Court has warned against conflating *Vavilovian* reasonableness review and the palpable and overriding error standard. I appreciate the conceptual distinction between the two, but I fear that these judges are rather like the Dutch youngster holding a finger in the dyke, as comparisons are inevitable given that the statutory appeal and judicial review streams run so close together: *Miller v College of Optometrists of Ontario*, 2020 ONSC 2573 at para 79; *Houghton v Association of Ontario Land Surveyors*, 2020 ONSC 863 at para 15. In particular, if the palpable and overriding error standard on appeal is less generous to appellants than reasonableness review would be, there will inevitably be pressure to expand the scope of the palpable and overriding error standard. I certainly expect comparison to continue, with conflation a distinct possibility.

16 See the discussion in *Nova Scotia (Attorney General) v S&D Smith Central Supplies Limited*, 2019 NSCA 22.

17 *Vavilov, supra* note 2 at para 199.

18 *Broadcasting Act*, SC 1991, c 11, s 31; *Telecommunications Act*, SC 1993, c 38, s 64.

19 See, e.g., *Securities Act*, RSBC 1996, c 418, s 167; *Securities Act*, RSA 2000, c S-4, s 38.

20 See, e.g., *Regulated Health Professions Act*, 1991, SO 1991, c 18, s 70; *Law Society Act*, SNL 1999, c L-9.1, s 55.2(1); *Veterinarians Act*, SBC 2010, c 15, s 64.

21 See, e.g., *Canada (Commissioner of Competition) v Superior Propane Inc,* 2001 FCA 104.

22 The discussion in *Canada (Director of Investigation and Research) v Southam Inc,* [1997] 1 SCR 748, 144 DLR (4th), 1 remains compelling, in my view.

23 *Vavilov, supra* note 2 at para 45.

24 *Ibid* at paras 38–46.

25 *Amici Factum* at para 109, online: <https://www.scc-csc.ca/WebDocuments -DocumentsWeb/37748/FM260_Amici-Curiae_Daniel-Jutras-Audrey-Boctor. pdf>.

26 *Vavilov, supra* note 2 at para 50. See also the comments at para 52.

27 2019 SCC 66.

28 *Broadcasting Act, supra* note 18, s 31(1).

29 See, e.g., *Dayco (Canada) Ltd v CAW-Canada,* [1993] 2 SCR 230, 102 DLR (4th) 609; *Pasiechnyk v Saskatchewan (Workers' Compensation Board),* [1997] 2 SCR 890, 149 DLR (4th) 577.

30 *Vavilov, supra* note 2 at para 52.

31 See, e.g., *Benhaim, supra* note 15 at para 37:

> Deference to factual findings limits the number, length and cost of appeals, which in turn promotes the autonomy and integrity of trial proceedings. Moreover, the law presumes that trial judges and appellate judges are equally capable of justly resolving disputes. Allowing appellate courts free rein to overturn trial courts' factual findings would duplicate judicial proceedings at great expense, without any concomitant guarantee of more just results.

32 It also creates something of a procedural morass, as a party may decide to appeal matters that are within the scope of a limited appeal clause, and also to judicially review matters that fall outside the appeal clause. See further Paul Daly, "Roadtesting the Vavilov Framework: Bell Canada v. Canada (Attorney General), 2019 SCC 66 and Canada Post Corp. v. Canadian Union of Postal Workers, 2019 SCC 67" (12 January 2020), *Administrative Law Matters* (blog), online: <https:// www.administrativelawmatters.com/blog/2020/01/13/roadtesting-the-vavilov -framework-bell-canada-v-canada-attorney-general-2019-scc-66-and-canada-post -corp-v-canadian-union-of-postal-workers-2019-scc-67/>.

33 *Vavilov, supra* note 2 at para 52.

34 Whether *Vavilovian* reasonableness review is, in fact, more or less deferential than the palpable and overriding error standard is impossible to tell at this point. Detailed empirical analysis is necessary before any firm conclusions can be drawn. My initial view is that applicants arguing *Vavilov* will have more strings to their bow than appellants arguing *Housen,* as explained in note 15 *supra.*

35 2008 SCC 9 [*Dunsmuir*]. See Chapter 3.

36 *Vavilov, supra* note 2 at para 53.

37 *Ibid.* Compare the rich discussion of the rule of law and constitutionalism in *Reference re Secession of Quebec,* [1998] 2 SCR 217 at paras 70–78, 161 DLR (4th) 385.

38 In *Dunsmuir,* this was "a question of law that is of central importance to the legal system as a whole and outside the specialized area of expertise of the administrative decision maker." *Dunsmuir, supra* note 35 at para 60.

39 *Vavilov, supra* note 2 at para 244.

40 *Peter v Public Health Appeal Board of Alberta,* 2019 ABQB 989 at para 12.

41 *Vavilov, supra* note 2 at para 61.

42 According to the majority in *Vavilov, supra* note 2 at para 114, sometimes international law will be "an important constraint" on administrative decision makers: "[I]nternational treaties and conventions, even where they have not been implemented domestically by statute, can help to inform whether a decision was a reasonable exercise of administrative power." For divergent views on whether questions of international law should attract correctness review (an issue never resolved by the Supreme Court), see *Hernandez Febles v Canada (Citizenship and Immigration),* 2012 FCA 324.

43 The most expansive view to date has been that of the Alberta Court of Appeal in *United Nurses of Alberta v Alberta Health Services,* 2021 ABCA 194, but it has not received an enthusiastic reception from other courts, at least so far.

44 *Vavilov, supra* note 2 at para 67.

45 *Ibid* at para 68 [emphasis added].

46 *Ibid* at para 70.

47 2011 SCC 61 [*Alberta Teachers*].

48 2018 SCC 31.

49 *Vavilov, supra* note 2 at para 70.

50 I will come back to this point in the Conclusion.

51 *Vavilov, supra* note 2 at para 71. See generally *Wilson v Atomic Energy of Canada Limited,* 2015 FCA 17, rev'd 2016 SCC 29.

52 *Ibid* at para 200.

53 *Ibid* at para 201.

54 See, e.g., Adrian Vermeule, *Law's Abnegation: From Law's Empire to the Administrative State* (Cambridge, MA: Harvard University Press, 2016); Pablo Ibañez Colomo, *The Shaping of EU Competition Law* (Cambridge: Cambridge University Press, 2018).

55 Diana Ginn and William Lahey, "How the Lower Courts Are 'Doing *Dunsmuir*'" in Daly and Sirota, *supra* note 6, 205.

56 See, e.g., *Delios v Canada (Attorney General),* 2015 FCA 117.

57 Paul Daly, "Waiting for Godot: Canadian Administrative Law in 2019" (2020) 33:1 Can J Admin L & Prac 1.

58 *Vavilov, supra* note 2 at para 11.

59 *Ibid* at para 73.

60 See, e.g., the remarkable episode described in *Olineck v Alberta (Environmental Appeals Board)*, 2017 ABQB 311 at paras 15–33, where the parties were sent away by the judge to read academic literature on reasonableness review before making further submissions on the application of the standard to the decision at issue.

61 *Vavilov, supra* note 2 at para 199.

62 *Ibid* at para 75.

63 *Ibid* at para 92.

64 *Ibid* at para 13. See the concurring reasons at para 294.

65 *Ibid* at para 81. See the concurring reasons at paras 291, 296.

66 *Ibid* at para 100. See the concurring reasons at para 312.

67 *Ibid* at paras 83–84. See the concurring reasons at paras 306, 313.

68 *Ibid* at para 90. See the concurring reasons at paras 292–93.

69 *Ibid* at para 93. See the concurring reasons at paras 297–99.

70 *Ibid* at para 96.

71 *Ibid* at paras 302–5.

72 *Ibid* at para 98, discussing *Alberta Teachers,' supra* note 47.

73 2018 SCC 2 [*Delta Air Lines*].

74 *Vavilov, supra* note 2 at para 96.

75 See generally *Catalyst Paper Corp v North Cowichan (District)*, 2012 SCC 2 [*Catalyst Paper*].

76 *Vavilov, supra* note 2 at paras 136–38.

77 See especially *Portnov v Canada (Attorney General)*, 2021 FCA 171.

78 *Vavilov, supra* note 2 at para 101.

79 *Ibid* at para 100.

80 *Ibid* at para 102.

81 *Ibid* at para 103.

82 *Ibid* at para 104.

83 I suspect that government lawyers will regularly cite paras 82–98 and their opponents paras 99–138.

84 *Vavilov, supra* note 2 at para 105.

85 *Ibid* at para 106.

86 *Ibid.*

87 *Ibid* at para 110.

88 *Ibid* at para 126.

89 *Ibid* at paras 111–13.

90 *Ibid* at paras 127, 128, 133. See also Lorne Sossin, "*Dunsmuir* – Plus ça change Redux" in Daly and Sirota, *supra* note 6, 225 at 227.

91 This point is brilliantly explained by Geneviève Cartier, "La perspective

de l'individu dans les décisions des pouvoirs publics" (2022) 101 Sup Ct L Rev (2d) 449.

92 *Vavilov, supra* note 2 at para 72.

93 *Ibid.*

94 *Ibid* at para 129.

95 *Ibid* at para 131 [emphasis in original].

96 *Ibid.*

97 *Catalyst Paper, supra* note 75 at para 15.

98 *Vavilov, supra* note 2 at para 110. See, e.g., *Garcia Balarezo v Canada (Citizenship and Immigration)*, 2020 FC 841 at para 47 (failure to have regard to the purposes of the discretion to grant humanitarian and compassionate relief for noncompliance with immigration law).

99 *Vavilov, supra* note 2 at para 108. See, e.g., *Immigration Consultants of Canada Regulatory Council v Rahman*, 2020 FC 832 at paras 22–24.

100 *Vavilov, supra* note 2 at para 109 [emphasis added].

101 *Dr Q v College of Physicians and Surgeons of British Columbia*, 2003 SCC 19 at para 24.

102 *Ibid* at para 22.

103 See, e.g., *Kane v Canada (Attorney General)*, 2011 FCA 19; *Canadian Association of Refugee Lawyers v Canada (Citizenship and Immigration)*, 2019 FC 1126 at para 57. Compare *Alberta (Director of Assured Income for the Severely Handicapped) v Januario*, 2013 ABQB 677 at paras 35–37; *Canada (National Revenue) v JP Morgan Asset Management (Canada) Inc*, 2013 FCA 250 at para 73.

104 As Professor Aileen McHarg observes, there is no "general presumption either for or against the legitimacy of administrative rule-making," but the no-fettering principle operates instead "as a means of judicial control over the *degree of structuring* of discretion that is appropriate in particular contexts": "Administrative Discretion, Administrative Rule-Making, and Judicial Review" (2017) 70:1 Curr Legal Probs 267 at 273. See further Daly, "Waiting for Godot," *supra* note 57 at 49–50. See also *Procureur général du Québec c Lamontagne*, 2020 QCCA 1137 at paras 41–52.

105 See, e.g., *Procureur général du Québec c PF*, 2020 QCCA 1220 at para 76, holding that, in the context of a statute providing for compensation for victims of criminal acts, it was reasonable to have a policy of not taking into account money earned on the black market when calculating an applicant's salary.

106 *Vavilov, supra* note 2 at para 124.

107 *Ibid* at para 119.

108 *Ibid* at para 121.

109 *Ibid* at para 122.

110 *Ibid* at para 143.

111 *Ibid.*

112 *Ibid.*
113 *Ibid.*
114 *Ibid.*
115 *Ibid.*
116 *Ibid* at para 144.
117 *Ibid* at para 142.
118 *Ibid* at para 139.
119 *Ibid* at para 140.
120 *Ibid.*
121 *Ibid.*
122 *Ibid* at para 142.
123 *Ibid.*
124 *Ibid* at para 140.
125 2014 FCA 95.
126 *Cf* the comment in *Vavilov, supra* note 2 at para 138: "[I]t is perhaps inevitable that without reasons, the analysis will then focus on the outcome rather than on the decision maker's reasoning process." But this comment is directed at a scenario in which reasons have not been provided at all (sometimes understandably so: at para 137) and would not warrant supplementation and/or refusal to remit in a case where reasons (however sparse) had been provided.
127 Thanks to Brendan van Niejenhuis for making this point.
128 *Housen, supra* note 13.
129 *Vavilov, supra* note 2 at para 200, Abella and Karakatsanis JJ.
130 *Ibid* at para 92.
131 Paul Daly, "One Year of Vavilov" (30 November 2020) Ottawa Faculty of Law Working Paper No 2020-34, online: SSRN, <https://ssrn.com/abstract=3722312>.
132 See generally Paul Daly, "A Week of Arguments about Deference" (18 June 2018), *Administrative Law Matters* (blog), online: <https://www.administrativelaw-matters.com/blog/2018/06/18/a-week-of-arguments-about-deference/>.

CHAPTER 5: *VAVILOV* HITS THE ROAD

Acknowledgment: This chapter draws substantially on my essay "Big Bang Theory: Vavilov's New Framework for Administrative Law" in Paul Daly and Colleen Flood, eds, *Administrative Law in Context*, 4th ed (Toronto: Emond Montgomery, 2021) 327.

1 *Radzevicius v Workplace Safety and Insurance Appeals Tribunal,* 2020 ONSC 319 at para 57 [*Radzevicius*], Swinton J. See also *Hildebrand v Penticton (City)*, 2020 BCSC 353 at para 26; *Teamsters Canada Rail Conference c Canadian Pacific Railway Company,* 2020 QCCA 729 at para 13.

2 2021 QCCA 177 at para 66.

3 *Alexion Pharmaceuticals Inc v Canada (Attorney General)*, 2021 FCA 157 at paras 12–18 [*Alexion*].

4 *Canada (Citizenship and Immigration) v Mason*, 2021 FCA 156 at para 37 [*Mason*], Stratas JA. See also *Canada (Attorney General) v Association of Justice Counsel*, 2021 FCA 37 at para 10; *Manitoba Government and General Employees' Union v The Minister of Finance for the Government*, 2021 MBCA 36 at para 59; *Trentway-Wagar inc c Cormier*, 2021 QCCA 983 at para 35.

5 2019 SCC 67 [*Canada Post*].

6 RSC 1985, c L-2.

7 *Canada Post, supra* note 5 at para 30.

8 *Ibid* at para 60.

9 *Ibid* at para 43.

10 *Ibid* at para 52.

11 *Ibid* at para 78 [emphasis in original].

12 See generally Paul Daly, "One Year of Vavilov" (30 November 2020) Ottawa Faculty of Law Working Paper No 2020-34, online: SSRN, <https://ssrn.com/abstract=3722312>.

13 See Paul Daly, "*Vavilov* and the Culture of Justification in Contemporary Administrative Law" (2021) 100 Sup Ct L Rev (2d) 279.

14 2020 FC 188 at para 22.

15 2020 SKQB 144 at para 55 [emphasis in original]. See similarly *Senadheerage v Canada (Citizenship and Immigration)*, 2020 FC 968 at para 10, Grammond J: "The decision itself must be justified, not only justifiable."

16 See Chapter 3 and, especially, *Edmonton (City) v Edmonton East (Capilano) Shopping Centres Ltd*, 2016 SCC 47.

17 2020 ONCA 216 [*Boros*].

18 *Ibid* at para 29.

19 2012 SCC 70.

20 *Boros, supra* note 17 at para 26.

21 *Ibid* at para 30. For a similar breach in the process-substance divide, see *AP v Canada (Citizenship and Immigration)*, 2020 FC 906 at para 27, quashing an Immigration Appeal Division decision because it disregarded the possibility that a homosexual man and a heterosexual woman could form a conjugal partnership: the decision "was based on a closed mind or bias resulting in an unreasonable assessment of the evidence regarding the possibility of a mixed-orientation couple meeting the criteria for a conjugal partnership." As Levesque JA put it in *Procureur général du Québec c PF*, 2020 QCCA 1220 at para 53 [*PF*], "Le droit d'être entendu se répercute ... dans la révision du mérite d'une décision administrative."

22 *Canada (Minister of Citizenship and Immigration) v Vavilov*, 2019 SCC 65 at para 135 [*Vavilov*].

23 2020 QCCA 134 at paras 39–44 [*Langlais*]. See also the cases mentioned in "One Year of Vavilov," *supra* note 12.

24 2020 FC 77 at para 17.

25 2020 FC 157 at para 22.

26 2020 FC 279 at para 13.

27 2020 FC 718 at paras 20, 26.

28 2020 FC 355 at para 25. Presumably, it is obvious enough that this means "Quality Assessment," but quite what the term denoted was obscure: an affidavit would have gone a long way here.

29 2020 FC 293 at para 13 [*Rodriguez*].

30 *Ibid* at paras 15–17.

31 2020 FC 295 at para 26. See also *Harrison v Canada (National Revenue)*, 2020 FC 772 at para 67 (conclusionary statement did not meet the *Vavilov* standard); *Party A v The Law Society of British Columbia*, 2021 BCCA 130 at para 30 (application of an unwritten, secret policy without explaining or justifying the policy).

32 *Alsaloussi v Canada (Attorney General)*, 2020 FC 364 at para 79. See also *Simelane v Canada (Immigration, Refugees and Citizenship)*, 2022 FC 1374 at para 64. Compare *Elangovan v Canada (Attorney General)*, 2020 FC 882 at para 26, where the consequences were taken into account and explained in a transparent manner to the individual, and the decision was thus upheld.

33 2020 NSSC 201 at para 37.

34 See also *Valiquette c Tribunal administratif du travail*, 2020 QCCS 11 at paras 69–70; *Mohammad v Canada (Citizenship and Immigration)*, 2020 FC 473 at para 42; *Ravandi v Canada (Citizenship and Immigration)*, 2020 FC 761 at para 36; *Randhawa v Canada (Public Safety and Emergency Preparedness)*, 2020 FC 905 at para 38. But see *Jean-Baptiste v Canada (Citizenship and Immigration)*, 2021 FC 1362 at para 31, imposing a "heightened" standard of justification when concluding that an individual is excluded from refugee protection. Compare *Sticky Nuggz Inc v Alcohol and Gaming Commission of Ontario*, 2020 ONSC 5916, where the applicant's application for a Retail Sales Authorization (RSA) to operate a cannabis store ran afoul of the commission's policy not to permit stores close to schools. As to harsh consequences, the Ontario Divisional Court responded at para 68:

> While the Applicant has perhaps suffered an adverse financial impact from the Decision at issue, this impact is the consequence of having made a financial commitment without appropriate due diligence. RSAs are not guaranteed by the Registrar and the statute provides no right or entitlement to a RSA. A RSA is granted to those that meet the eligibility and application requirements. The burden of ensuring those requirements

are met, and the risk of not meeting them, are both borne by the Applicant.

35 *Mao v Canada (Citizenship and Immigration)*, 2020 FC 542 at para 49 [*Mao*]; *Qasim v Canada (Citizenship and Immigration)*, 2020 FC 465 at para 42 [*Qasim*]; *Adeleye v Canada (Citizenship and Immigration)*, 2020 FC 640 [*Adeleye*] at para 16; and *Singh v Canada (Citizenship and Immigration)*, 2020 FC 687 at para 59 [*Singh*].

36 *Mao, supra* note 35 at para 49.

37 *Vavilov, supra* note 22 at para 128. See also *Qasim, supra* note 35 at para 42 (no need to "catalogue" the applicant's case); *Adeleye, supra* note 35 at para 16, commenting that this part of *Vavilov* "does not set a different standard for judicial review"; and *Singh, supra* note 35 at para 59.

38 *Edmonton (City of) v Edmonton Police Association*, 2020 ABCA 182 at para 27.

39 See the discussion in Chapter 4.

40 *Vavilov supra* note 22 at para 96.

41 *Canada v Kabul Farms Inc*, 2016 FCA 143 at para 47, Stratas JA.

42 *Mattar v The National Dental Examining Board of Canada*, 2020 ONSC 403 at paras 51–52.

43 See *Hasani v Canada (Citizenship and Immigration)*, 2020 FC 125 at paras 67–68; and see generally Gleason JA's even-handed analysis in *Canada (Attorney General) v Zalys*, 2020 FCA 81.

44 See text accompanying note 3 in the Introduction.

45 2020 FCA 25 [*Farrier*].

46 *Ibid* at para 12. See similarly *Walker v Canada (Attorney General)*, 2020 FCA 44 at para 10.

47 *Vavilov, supra* note 22 at para 94; *Haddad Pour v The National Dental Examining Board of Canada*, 2020 ONSC 555 at paras 37–40.

48 Compare *Centre intégré de santé et de services sociaux de la Montérégie-Ouest c Syndicat canadien de la fonction publique, section locale 3247*, 2020 QCCS 1603 at para 12, where it had been documented that the point at issue was raised at the oral hearing.

49 *Mason, supra* note 4 at para 37, Stratas JA. Stratas also suggests, *ibid* at paras 32 and 41, that there may be "implied" reasons that are not expressly found in the reasons of the decision maker. See similarly *Alexion, supra* note 3 at paras 16 and 18. For my part, the term "implied" or "implicit" reasons is too strongly associated with the darkest days of the *Dunsmuir* decade, so I prefer to simply say that administrative decisions should be read fairly, in their whole context. The point is well explained at paras 93–94 of *Vavilov, supra* note 22, without mention of the words "implied" or "implicit":

An administrative decision maker may demonstrate through its reasons that a given decision was made by bringing [its] institutional expertise and experience to bear ... In conducting reasonableness review, judges should be attentive to the application by decision makers of specialized knowledge, as demonstrated by their reasons. Respectful attention to a decision maker's demonstrated expertise may reveal to a reviewing court that an outcome that might be puzzling or counterintuitive on its face nevertheless accords with the purposes and practical realities of the relevant administrative regime and represents a reasonable approach given the consequences and the operational impact of the decision. This demonstrated experience and expertise may also explain why a given issue is treated in less detail. The reviewing court must also read the decision maker's reasons in light of the history and context of the proceedings in which they were rendered. For example, the reviewing court might consider the evidence before the decision maker, the submissions of the parties, publicly available policies or guidelines that informed the decision maker's work, and past decisions of the relevant administrative body. This may explain an aspect of the decision maker's reasoning process that is not apparent from the reasons themselves, or may reveal that an apparent shortcoming in the reasons is not, in fact, a failure of justification, intelligibility or transparency. Opposing parties may have made concessions that had obviated the need for the decision maker to adjudicate on a particular issue; the decision maker may have followed a well-established line of administrative case law that no party had challenged during the proceedings; or an individual decision maker may have adopted an interpretation set out in a public interpretive policy of the administrative body of which he or she is a member.

I would say that the best way to summarize this passage is that a decision is not unreasonable because of a failure to expressly mention a particular point, where it is obvious why the decision maker did not consider it. If a test is needed, it should be a test of obviousness.

50 2020 FCA 20 [*CNRC*].

51 *Ibid* at para 46.

52 *Ibid* at para 48.

53 *Ibid* at para 49.

54 *Ibid* at para 54.

55 2020 NLSC 34 at para 74.

56 2020 FC 397 at paras 34–35. See similarly *ViiV Healthcare ULC v Canada (Health)*, 2020 FC 756 at para 28. See also *Oxford v Newfoundland and Labrador (Municipal Affairs and Environment)*, 2020 NLSC 102 at paras 40–42.

57 *Canada (Health) v Glaxosmithkline Biologicals SA*, 2021 FCA 71.

58 2020 FC 788 at paras 55–60.

59 See *David Suzuki Foundation v Canada-Newfoundland and Labrador Offshore Petroleum Board*, 2020 NLSC 94 at para 245; *Alexion, supra* note 3.

60 2020 NSSC 60 at para 32.

61 2020 NSSC 175 at para 27. See generally *Weldemariam v Canada (Public Safety and Emergency Preparedness)*, 2020 FC 631 at paras 35–38.

62 *Vavilov, supra* note 22 at paras 136–38.

63 2020 BCCA 101 at para 88 [*Whistler*]. See also *O'Shea/Oceanmount Community Association v Town of Gibsons*, 2020 BCSC 698 at para 156, commenting that "significant deference" was due to the municipality on the compatibility of a bylaw with an official community plan; *Ville de Québec c Galy*, 2020 QCCA 1130; *Restaurants Canada c Ville de Montréal*, 2021 QCCA 1639.

64 2021 BCSC 1735 at paras 40–47. See also *Canadian Natural Resources Limited v Elizabeth Métis Settlement*, 2020 ABQB 210.

65 See *Vavilov, supra* note 22 at paras 108–10.

66 See also *Champag inc c Municipalité de Saint-Roch-de-Richelieu*, 2020 QCCA 613 at para 30, not a case about the authority to promulgate a bylaw but nonetheless an example of a municipality's discretion being constrained by statutory language; and see generally *Innovative Medicines Canada v Canada (Attorney General)*, 2020 FC 725 at paras 65–73 [*Innovative Medicines*]. It will not invariably be the case that reasons or reasoning are entirely absent in cases involving municipal bylaws; if so, the judicial review will look quite conventional. See, e.g., *GSR Capital Group Inc v The City of White Rock*, 2020 BCSC 489 at paras 107–14, 139 [*GSR Capital*].

67 2020 ONSC 4577 [*Scarborough*]. This section draws on Paul Daly, "Canadian Labour Law after *Vavilov*" (2021) 23 Can J Lab & Emp Law 103.

68 *Scarborough, supra* note 67 at para 6.

69 *Ibid* at para 8.

70 *Ibid* at para 22.

71 *Ibid* at para 15.

72 *Ibid* at para 26.

73 See also *Bragg Communications Inc v Unifor*, 2021 FCA 59.

74 See, e.g., *Zhang v Canada (Public Safety and Emergency Preparedness)*, 2021 FC 746.

75 See, e.g., *Manitoba Government and General Employees' Union v The Minister of Finance for the Government*, 2021 MBCA 36; *Northern Harvest Smolt Ltd v Salmonid Association of Eastern Newfoundland*, 2021 NLCA 26.

76 See, e.g., *Byun v Alberta Dental Association and College*, 2021 ABCA 272.

77 See, e.g., *Partridge v Nova Scotia (Attorney General)*, 2021 NSCA 60 at para 69 (misapplication of the test for causation by the Utility and Review Board

was an extricable error); *Quadra Properties Ltd v Gamble*, 2021 SKQB 16 (tenancy agreement).

78 See, e.g., *1085372 Ontario Limited v City of Toronto*, 2020 ONSC 1136; *Donaldson c Autorité des marchés financiers*, 2020 QCCA 401; and, in relation to costs awards, *Dell v Zeifman Partners Inc*, 2020 ONSC 3881 at para 42.

79 2020 ABCA 148 at para 32.

80 See Chapter 4.

81 2020 ABCA 98 at para 30.

82 Although in *Yee* the appeal was allowed! See also *Dr Jonathan Mitelman v College of Veterinarians of Ontario*, 2020 ONSC 3039 at para 18; *Olivier c Cayer*, 2020 QCCQ 2060 at para 45; *Commissaire à la déontologie policière c Lavallée*, 2020 QCCQ 1923 at para 24; *Shah v College of Physiotherapists of Ontario*, 2020 ONSC 6240 at para 17.

83 2020 NBCA 45 at para 18. The flip side could be glimpsed in *Thibeault v Saskatchewan (Apprenticeship and Trade Certification Commission)*, 2020 SKQB 192 at paras 49–52, considering the inadequacy of reasons to be an error of law on a statutory appeal on questions of law or jurisdiction. See also *Dr Rashidan v The National Dental Examining Board of Canada*, 2020 ONSC 4174 at para 41.

84 *Law Society of New Brunswick v Ryan*, 2003 SCC 20, Iacobucci J.

85 *Hughes v Law Society of New Brunswick*, 2020 NBCA 68 at para 41. See also *Mitelman v College of Veterinarians of Ontario*, 2020 ONSC 6171 at para 41: "penalty orders engage the heart of the expertise of self-governing tribunals"; *College of Registered Nurses of Manitoba v Hancock*, 2022 MBCA 70.

86 *Planet Energy (Ontario) Corp v Ontario Energy Board*, 2020 ONSC 598 at para 31. See also *Edmonton (City of) v Ten 201 Jasper Avenue Ltd*, 2020 ABCA 60, and *Borgel v Paintearth (Subdivision and Development Appeal Board)*, 2020 ABCA 192 at paras 21–22 (taking tribunal and lower court jurisprudence into account in applying the correctness standard to an extricable question of law).

87 See, e.g., *East Hants (Municipality) v Nova Scotia (Utility and Review Board)*, 2020 NSCA 41.

88 2019 SCC 66 [*Bell Canada*].

89 *Ibid* at para 35. The same majority from *Vavilov* concluded that the authority under the statutory provision the CRTC invoked "is limited to issuing orders that require television service providers to carry specific channels as part of their service offerings, and attaching [general] terms and conditions" (at para 44). In dissent, Abella and Karakatsanis JJ refused to follow the *Vavilov* framework. Applying reasonableness review to what they described as "an archetype of an expert administrative body" (at para 83), they found nothing to exclude the possibility that CRTC orders "could relate to a single program in this context" (at para 93). See further Mary Liston, "Bell Is the Tell I'm Thinking Of" (29 April 2020), *Admin-*

istrative Law Matters (blog), online: <https://www.administrativelawmatters.com/blog/2020/04/29/bell-is-the-tell-im-thinking-of-mary-liston/>.

90 See, e.g., *Canadian National Railway Company v Emerson Milling Inc,* 2017 FCA 79, especially at paras 20–28.

91 See, e.g., *Bell Canada v British Columbia Broadband Association,* 2020 FCA 140.

92 2020 MBCA 60 [*Manitoba*].

93 CCSM, c H190.

94 *Manitoba, supra* note 92 at paras 53–54.

95 *Ibid* at paras 55, 91.

96 *Ibid* at para 81.

97 *Ibid* at paras 85–86.

98 (2008) 293 DLR (4th) 684.

99 See, e.g., *ATCO Gas & Pipelines Ltd v Alberta (Energy & Utilities Board),* 2006 SCC 4.

100 *Ibid.* Compare the rich discussion of the rule of law and constitutionalism in *Reference re Secession of Quebec,* [1998] 2 SCR 217 at paras 70–78, 161 DLR (4th) 385.

101 2012 SCC 12 [*Doré*].

102 *Vavilov, supra* note 22 at para 53.

103 2019 ABQB 989.

104 2020 QCCS 95 at paras 17–19.

105 See also *Coldwater First Nation v Canada (Attorney General),* 2020 FCA 34 at para 27 [*Coldwater*]; *Borradaile v British Columbia (Superintendent of Motor Vehicles),* 2020 BCSC 363 at para 34; *Redmond v British Columbia (Forests, Lands, Natural Resource Operations and Rural Development),* 2020 BCSC 561 at paras 28–31; *Sagkeeng v Government of Manitoba et al,* 2020 MBQB 83 at para 101; *RB v British Columbia (Superintendent of Motor Vehicles),* 2020 BCSC 1496 at para 50.

106 See *Canada (Union of Correctionnel Officers) v Canada (Attorney General),* 2019 FCA 212 at para 21; *Organisation de la jeunesse Chabad Loubavitch c Ville de Mont-Tremblant,* 2022 QCCA 1331 at para 27.

107 *Canada (Attorney General) v Northern Inter-Tribal Health Authority Inc,* 2020 FCA 63 at paras 12–13.

108 *Canadian Broadcasting Corporation v Ferrier,* 2019 ONCA 1025 at para 37 [*Ferrier*]; *Coldwater, supra* note 105 at para 27.

109 *Vavilov, supra* note 22 at para 63.

110 2000 SCC 14.

111 2004 SCC 39.

112 *Vavilov, supra* note 22 at para 64.

113 2021 SCC 42 [*Horrocks*].

114 *Ibid* at para 7.

115 *Ibid* at para 9.

116 *Ibid* at para 12. See also para 31.

117 2020 BCSC 1972 at paras 66–67.

118 2020 FCA 22.

119 *Ibid* at para 28. See also *Beach Place Ventures Ltd v British Columbia (Employment Standards Tribunal)*, 2020 BCSC 327 at paras 32–34; *Brockville (City) v Information and Privacy Commissioner, Ontario*, 2020 ONSC 4413 at paras 24–25; *Syndicat canadien de la fonction publique, section locale 1108 v CHU de Québec – Université Laval*, 2020 QCCA 857 at paras 26–35; *Procureur général du Québec c Lamontagne*, 2020 QCCA 1137 at paras 23–28.

120 2021 ABCA 194. I was counsel for Alberta Health Services in its unsuccessful application for leave to appeal this decision to the Supreme Court of Canada.

121 *Ibid* at para 55.

122 Does the quasi-constitutional status of human rights law make much of a difference? The two hallmarks of quasi-constitutional legislation are that it is protected from implied repeal and to be given a "large and liberal interpretation." But all legislation is now to be given a "large and liberal interpretation" consistent with legislative intent: quasi-constitutional legislation is no different in this regard. And to the extent that it is protected from implied repeal, this indicates simply that its subject matter is of great public importance – but *per Vavilov*, great public importance does not make a general question of law one of central importance to the legal system. Rather, a "constitutional dimension" is required. Human rights laws, while of great public importance, are nonetheless statutory creations. There is no constitutional dimension that requires correctness review in all circumstances.

123 Contrast, e.g., *Gaudreau c Régie des marchés agricoles et alimentaires du Québec*, 2021 QCCA 330 at paras 31–32. But see *Langford Sharp c Autorité des marchés financiers*, 2021 QCCA 1364 at paras 42–48, where correctness review applied given that the constitutional applicability of a provincial law extraterritorially was in play.

124 *Vavilov, supra* note 22 at para 70. See also Paul Daly, "Exceptional Circumstances? O.K. Industries Ltd. v. District of Highlands, 2022 BCCA 12" (14 January 2022), *Administrative Law Matters* (blog), online: <https://www.administrativelawmatters.com/blog/2022/01/14/exceptional-circumstances-o-k-industries-ltd-v-district-of-highlands-2022-bcca-12/>.

125 2022 SCC 30 [*Entertainment Software Association*].

126 *Ibid* at para 28.

127 See further Paul Daly, "Future Directions in Standard of Review in Canadian Administrative Law: Substantive Review and Procedural Fairness," Can J Admin L & Prac (forthcoming).

128 2020 ONSC 8046 at para 37.

129 2013 SCC 64.

130 See also *Bricka c Procureur général du Québec*, 2022 QCCA 85 at para 18.

131 *Whistler, supra* note 63 at para 39; *GSR Capital, supra* note 66 at para 71; *Innovative Medicines, supra* note 66 at paras 65–73; *TransAlta Generation Partnership v Regina*, 2021 ABQB 37 at para 46.

132 2020 ABQB 137 at para 40.

133 *Ibid* at para 45.

134 See, e.g., para 108 on the governing statutory scheme and para 111 on other statutory or common law limitations.

135 *Vavilov, supra* note 22 at paras 136–38.

136 *GSR Capital, supra* note 66 at paras 107–14 and 139.

137 *Vavilov, supra* note 22 at para 88.

138 2021 FCA 171 [*Portnov*]. See also *Restaurants Canada c Ville de Montréal*, 2021 QCCA 1639 at para 25.

139 *Ibid* at para 20.

140 *Ibid* at para 21.

141 *Ibid* at para 23.

142 *Ibid* at para 25.

143 *Ibid* at para 26.

144 *Ibid* at para 27.

145 *Ibid* at para 17.

146 *Hudson's Bay Company ULC v Ontario (Attorney General)*, 2020 ONSC 8046 at para 39.

147 *Ibid* at para 71.

148 2012 SCC 2.

149 2021 ABQB 41 at para 62.

150 *Vavilov, supra* note 22 at para 108.

151 *Ibid* at para 111.

152 *Ibid.*

153 *Ferrier, supra* note 108.

154 *Ibid* at para 37.

155 *Ibid* at para 58. See *Langenfeld v Toronto Police Services Board*, 2019 ONCA 716 [*Langenfeld*].

156 *Ferrier, supra* note 108 at para 79.

157 *Ibid* at para 80. See *Langenfeld, supra* note 155.

158 *Canada (Attorney General) v Impex Solutions Inc*, 2020 FCA 171 at para 90.

159 *Downey v Nova Scotia (Attorney General)*, 2020 NSSC 201 at paras 40–41.

160 2020 ABCA 188.

161 *Ibid* at paras 188–92.
162 2020 ONSC 4239 at paras 111–18.
163 2020 ONSC 2984.
164 *Ibid* at para 91.
165 *Ibid* at para 159.
166 *Ibid* at para 161.
167 *Ibid* at para 160.
168 *Ibid* at para 163.
169 2020 SKQB 96.
170 2021 SKCA 28 at para 141.
171 *Chief Constable of the North Wales Police v Evans*, [1982] 1 WLR 1155.
172 John M. Evans, "Reflections on *Dunsmuir* of a Recovering Judge" in Paul Daly and Leonid Sirota, ed, *A Decade of Dunsmuir/Les 10 ans de Dunsmuir* (Toronto: Carswell, 2018) 175 at 175.

CHAPTER 6:
UNRESOLVED ISSUES AFTER *VAVILOV*

Acknowledgment: This chapter reproduces with minor alterations and additions Paul Daly, "Unresolved Issues after *Vavilov*" (2022) 85 Sask L Rev 89.

1 *Canada (Minister of Citizenship and Immigration) v Vavilov*, 2019 SCC 65 [*Vavilov*]. In their concurring reasons, Abella and Karakatsanis JJ accepted that it was important to "steady the ship" (at para 199) but rejected the course set by the majority.
2 *Bancroft v Nova Scotia (Lands and Forests)*, 2020 NSSC 175 at para 27, Brothers J. The point was about statutory interpretation but it has broad application.
3 See also Paul Daly, "Canada's Bipolar Administrative Law: Time for Fusion" (2014) 40:1 Queen's LJ 213.
4 See especially Joseph T. Robertson, QC, "The Merits of *Dunsmuir*: Rightly or Wrongly Decided (Then and Today)?" in Paul Daly and Leonid Sirota, ed, *A Decade of Dunsmuir/Les 10 ans de Dunsmuir* (Toronto: Carswell, 2018) 167.
5 See Paul Daly, "Deference on Questions of Procedural Fairness" (9 May 2013), *Administrative Law Matters* (blog), online: <https://www.administrativelaw-matters.com/blog/2013/05/09/deference-on-questions-of-procedural-fairness/>, discussing *Syndicat des travailleuses et travailleurs de ADF–CSN c Syndicat des employés de Au Dragon forgé Inc*, 2013 QCCA 793 [*Syndicat*]; and Paul Daly, "Deference, Weight and Procedural Fairness" (5 March 2014), *Administrative Law Matters* (blog), online: <https://www.administrativelawmatters.com/blog/2014/03/05/deference-weight-and-procedural-fairness/>.
6 *Mission Institution v Khela*, 2014 SCC 24 at para 89 [*Khela*].

7 See, e.g., *JD Irving, Limited v North Shore Forest Products Marketing Board*, 2014 NBCA 42 at para 6.

8 See, e.g., *Re:Sound v Fitness Industry Council of Canada*, 2014 FCA 48 at para 42.

9 See, e.g., *Syndicat, supra* note 5; *Forest Ethics Advocacy Association v Canada (National Energy Board)*, 2014 FCA 245 [*Forest Ethics*].

10 See, e.g., *Ontario Provincial Police v MacDonald*, 2009 ONCA 805 at para 37.

11 [1999] 2 SCR 817, 174 DLR (4th) 193 [*Baker*].

12 2017 FCA 132 at para 11.

13 Paul Daly, "Confusion and Contestation: Canada's Standard of Review" (23 April 2019), *Administrative Law Matters* (blog), online: <https://www.administrativelawmatters.com/blog/2019/04/23/confusion-and-contestation/>.

14 *Cf* Levi Graham, "The Persistent Jurisprudential Muddle: Determining the Standard of Review for Procedural Fairness in Saskatchewan" (31 March 2021), online: Law Society of Saskatchewan <https://www.lawsociety.sk.ca/saskatchewan-law-review-articles/sk-law-review-the-persistent-jurisprudential-muddle-determining-the-standard-of-review-for-procedural-fairness-in-saskatchewan/>, describing a "persistent jurisprudential muddle"; and David Stratas, "The Canadian Law of Judicial Review: Some Doctrine and Cases" (18 October 2022) at 89, online: SSRN: <https://papers.ssrn.com/sol3/papers.cfm?abstract_id=2924049>: "*Vavilov* does not address the issue [of the standard of review of procedural fairness]."

15 *Vavilov, supra* note 1 at para 23 [emphasis added].

16 *Ibid* at para 77.

17 *Baker, supra* note 11 at paras 23–27.

18 See especially Derek McKee, "The Standard of Review for Questions of Procedural Fairness" (2016) 41:2 Queen's LJ 382, who convincingly explains the inaptness of correctness review in the procedural fairness context.

19 See especially *Kelly v Nova Scotia Police Commission*, 2006 NSCA 27 at para 21.

20 *Bergeron v Canada (Attorney General)*, 2015 FCA 160 at para 70, Stratas JA. See also Paul Daly, "Investigating Process, Substance and Procedural Fairness" (2 October 2014), *Administrative Law Matters* (blog), online: <https://www.administrativelawmatters.com/blog/2014/10/02/investigating-process-substance-and-procedural-fairness/>, discussing *Robertson v British Columbia (Teachers Act, Commissioner)*, 2014 BCCA 331; and Paul Daly, "Process, Substance and the Influence of Judicial Review on Public Administration: Ofsted v Secretary of State for Education [2018] EWCA Civ 2813" (10 September 2019), *Administrative Law Matters* (blog), online: <https://www.administrativelawmatters.com/blog/2019/09/10/process-substance-and-the-influence-of-judicial-review

-on-public-administration-ofsted-v-secretary-of-state-for-education-2018-ewca
-civ-2813/>.

21 2020 BCSC 353 at paras 29–30.

22 *Vavilov, supra* note 1 at paras 136–38.

23 See the thoughtful engagement by McHaffie J in *Abiodun v Canada (Citizenship and Immigration)*, 2021 FC 642 at paras 6–10.

24 *Council of Canadians with Disabilities v VIA Rail Canada Inc*, 2007 SCC 15 at para 231. See also *Forest Ethics, supra* note 9 at para 72.

25 *Khela, supra* note 6 at para 89. In the particular context of undue delay, see *Sazant v College of Physicians and Surgeons of Ontario*, 2012 ONCA 727 at para 237, application for leave to appeal dismissed, 2013 CanLII 22324; *Nova Scotia Construction Safety Association v Nova Scotia Human Rights Commission*, 2006 NSCA 63 at para 62; *ADM v Canadian Institute of Actuaries*, 2008 ABQB 522 at para 27 [*ADM*]; *Hennig v Institute of Chartered Accountants of Alberta (Complaints Inquiry Committee)*, 2008 ABCA 241 at paras 12, 31.

26 [1984] 1 SCR 176, 7 DLR (4th) 1.

27 David J. Mullan, "Developments in Administrative Law: The 1983–84 Term" (1985) 7 Sup Ct L Rev (2d) 1 at 19.

28 This issue has been addressed to some extent by the Supreme Court of Canada in *Law Society of Saskatchewan v Abrametz*, 2022 SCC 29, an appeal on procedural fairness grounds from a disciplinary committee to the courts. The importance of this decision remains to be determined, but in my view, "the fairest reading of [the] reasons on standard of review, read in the context of the decision as a whole, is that the courts retain the last word on the ultimate issue in a procedural fairness case (i.e., was it "correct" to find (un)fairness?) but that an administrative decision maker's reasoned analysis is subject to deference." See Paul Daly, "Deference on Questions of Procedural Fairness after Law Society of Saskatchewan v. Abrametz, 2022 SCC 29, the Implications" (26 August 2022), *Administrative Law Matters* (blog), online: <https://www.administrativelawmatters.com/blog/2022/08/26/deference-on-questions-of-procedural-fairness-after-law -society-of-saskatchewan-v-abrametz-2022-scc-29-the-implications/>.

29 2012 SCC 12 [*Doré*].

30 [1986] 1 SCR 103, 26 DLR (4th) 200.

31 *Vavilov, supra* note 1 at para 57.

32 Paul Daly, "The Charter and Administrative Adjudication" (15 May 2012), *Administrative Law Matters* (blog), online: <https://www.administrativelawmatters. com/blog/2012/05/15/the-charter-and-administrative-adjudication/>, discussing *Doré*.

33 Paul Daly, "The Inevitability of Discretion and Judgement in Front-Line Decision-Making in the Administrative State" (2020) 2:1 J Commonwealth L 99.

34 Paul Daly, "Prescribing Greater Protection for Rights: Administrative Law and Section 1 of the Canadian Charter of Rights and Freedoms" (2014) 65 Sup Ct L Rev (2d) 247.

35 See, e.g., *Loyola High School v Quebec (Attorney General)*, 2015 SCC 12 [*Loyola*]; *Law Society of British Columbia v Trinity Western University*, 2018 SCC 32 [*Trinity Western University*].

36 See, e.g., Paul Daly, "The Court and Administrative Law: Models of Rights Protection" in Matthew Harrington, ed, *The Court and the Constitution: A 150-Year Retrospective* (Toronto: LexisNexis, 2017) 57; Peter Lauwers, "What Could Go Wrong with Charter Values?" (2019) 91 Sup Ct L Rev (2d) 1; Audrey Macklin, "*Charter* Right or *Charter*-Lite? Administrative Discretion and the *Charter*" (2014) 67 Sup Ct L Rev (2d) 561.

37 Mark Mancini, "The Conceptual Gap between Doré and Vavilov" (2020) 43:2 Dal LJ 793.

38 *Vavilov, supra* note 1 at para 23.

39 *Ibid.*

40 *Ibid.*

41 *Ibid* at para 32.

42 *Ibid* at para 53.

43 *Alberta (Information and Privacy Commissioner) v University of Calgary*, 2016 SCC 53 at para 20.

44 *Doré, supra* note 29 at para 38.

45 2010 SCC 43 at para 67.

46 2017 SCC 54 at paras 68–75. See also *Canadian Broadcasting Corporation v Ferrier*, 2019 ONCA 1025 at para 25; *Elementary Teachers Federation of Ontario v York Region District School Board*, 2022 ONCA 476 at para 37.

47 *Doré, supra* note 29 at paras 54, 56.

48 Lord Kerr explained this point very well in *Keyu v Foreign Secretary*, [2015] UKSC 69 at para 272:

> [I]t is important to start any debate on the subject with the clear understanding that a review based on proportionality is not one in which the reviewer substitutes his or her opinion for that of the decision maker. At its heart, proportionality review requires of the person or agency that seeks to defend a decision that they show that it was proportionate to meet the aim that it professes to achieve. It does not demand that the decision maker bring the reviewer to the point of conviction that theirs was the right decision in any absolute sense.

49 See Chapter 6.

50 *Vavilov, supra* note 1 at para 93. See also paras 14, 81.

51 Paul Daly, "The *Vavilov* Framework and the Future of Canadian Administrative Law" (2020) 33 Can J Admin Law & Practice 111 at 128–32.

52 *Vavilov, supra* note 1 at paras 81, 83–84, 108–10.

53 *Ibid* at para 118.

54 *Ibid* at para 119.

55 Paul Daly, "Unreasonable Interpretations of Law" (2014) 66 Sup Ct L Rev (2d) 233.

56 *Vavilov, supra* note 1 at para 121.

57 *Doré, supra* note 29 at para 57.

58 *Ibid* at para 58.

59 *Vavilov, supra* note 1 at paras 126–28, 133–35.

60 See, e.g., *Loyola, supra* note 35; *Trinity Western University, supra* note 35.

61 This section owes a great deal to David Mullan, who prompted this idea in his "Judicial Scrutiny of Administrative Decision Making: Principled Simplification or Continuing Angst?" (2020) 50:4 Adv Q 423 and has discussed the point further with me. See also Nigel Bankes, "Statutory Appeal Rights in Relation to Administrative Decision Maker Now Attract an Appellate Standard of Review: A Possible Legislative Response" (3 January 2020), *ABlawg* (blog), online: <https://ablawg.ca/2020/01/03/statutory-appeal-rights-in-relation-to-administrative-decision-maker-now-attract-an-appellate-standard-of-review-a-possible-legislative-response/>.

62 *Dunsmuir v New Brunswick,* 2008 SCC 9 at para 27 [*Dunsmuir*].

63 *Ibid* at para 29.

64 *Ibid* at para 30.

65 *Ibid* at para 27.

66 *Ibid* at para 31.

67 *Vavilov, supra* note 1 at para 9.

68 [1981] 2 SCR 220, 127 DLR (3d) 1 [*Crevier* cited to SCR].

69 *Ibid* at 238.

70 *Alberta (Information and Privacy Commissioner) v Alberta Teachers' Association,* 2011 SCC 61 at para 103.

71 *Vavilov, supra* note 1 at paras 65–67.

72 2019 FCA 41 [*Public Service Alliance*].

73 SC 2013, c 40, s 365.

74 *Public Service Alliance, supra* note 72 at para 30.

75 *Ibid* at para 31.

76 *Ibid* at para 34.

77 *Vavilov, supra* note 1 at para 35.

78 RSA 2000, c M-26.

79 *Traffic Safety Act,* RSA 2000, c T-6, s 47.1(3); *Environmental Assessment Act,* RSO 1990, c E-18, s 23.1; *Labour Relations Act,* SO 1995, c 1, Sch A, s 163.3(39); *Health Professions Act,* SY 2003, c 24, s 29.

80 *Administrative Tribunals Act*, SBC 2004, c 45, ss 58–59. See further Paul Daly, "Patent Unreasonableness after *Vavilov*" (2021) 34 Can J Admin L & Prac 167.

81 See, e.g., *Bell Canada v British Columbia Broadband Association*, 2020 FCA 140 [*Bell Canada*].

82 William Shakespeare, *Hamlet*, Act 3, Scene 1, Line 155.

83 *Vavilov, supra* note 1 at para 67 [emphasis added].

84 *Ibid* at para 14, citing Beverley McLachlin, "The Roles of Administrative Tribunals and Courts in Maintaining the Rule of Law" (1998) 12 Can J Admin L & Prac 171 at 174 [emphasis deleted].

85 Julius Grey, "Sections 96–100: A Defense" (1985) 1 Admin LJ 3 at 11 [emphasis in original].

86 *Bank of Montreal v Li*, 2020 FCA 22 at para 28.

87 There is disagreement between appellate courts about the extent to which judicial review is constitutionally entrenched. In *Canada (Attorney General) v Best Buy Canada Ltd*, 2021 FCA 161 [*Best Buy*], the majority of the Federal Court of Appeal endorsed my analysis. But in *Yatar v TD Insurance Meloche Monnex*, 2022 ONCA 446 at para 40 [*Yatar*], the Ontario Court of Appeal suggested that as long as a decision maker is not immunized from judicial review, there is no constitutional objection.

88 *Vavilov, supra* note 1 at para 52.

89 *Ibid* at para 110.

90 See, e.g., *Koebisch v Rocky View (County)*, 2021 ABCA 265 at para 24, accepting this argument. Equally, one could do as the Ontario courts have done and simply assimilate patent unreasonableness to reasonableness: *Ontario (Health) v Association of Ontario Midwives*, 2022 ONCA 458. I do not think this is a viable strategy in British Columbia, however, where patent unreasonableness has long been considered to have content that is distinct from the Supreme Court's reasonableness standard. See, e.g., *Speckling v British Columbia (Workers' Compensation Board)*, 2005 BCCA 80 at para 33; *West Fraser Mills Ltd v British Columbia (Workers' Compensation Appeal Tribunal)*, 2018 SCC 22 at para 28; *The College of Physicians and Surgeons of British Columbia v The Health Professions Review Board*, 2022 BCCA 10 at para 129.

91 See, e.g., *Residential Tenancies Act, 2006*, SO 2006, c 17, ss 30(1) and 32.

92 See, e.g., *Bell Canada, supra* note 81.

93 *Ortiz v Canada (Citizenship and Immigration)*, 2020 FC 188 at para 22.

94 As held by the majority of the Federal Court of Appeal in *Best Buy, supra* note 87. See also *BCE Inc v Québecor Média Inc*, 2022 FCA 152 at para 58. In *Yatar, supra* note 87, the Ontario Court of Appeal came to a different conclusion, in the context of a statutory scheme for the award of benefits to victims of motor vehicle accidents. The statute provided for an extensive administrative process,

including a right to ask for reconsideration of a negative decision, with a limited right of appeal to the courts on questions of law. The Court of Appeal held that judicial review of a reconsideration decision would be available only in "rare" cases, as the courts could exercise their residual discretion not to hear the judicial review (at para 47). In my view, this analysis is of dubious authority. As long as we have had judicial review, it has been the case that courts can judicially review any final administrative decision, whether or not there was an elaborate internal process leading up to that decision. To give courts a discretion not to hear judicial review applications because of their perception of the quality and quantity of internal reconsiderations would allow judicial discretion to trump constitutional principle. The quality and quantity of internal reconsiderations might have a bearing on how much deference is due to the decision maker, but it should not have a bearing on whether individuals challenging a decision are entitled to their day in court.

95 See generally *Milner Power Inc v Alberta (Energy and Utilities Board)*, 2007 ABCA 265.

96 There has been a good deal of interesting discussion of the constitutional foundations of *Vavilov*, which I summarize in "*Vavilov* on the Road" (2022) 35 Can J Admin L & Prac 1.

97 Paul Daly, "One Year of Vavilov" (30 November 2020) Ottawa Faculty of Law Working Paper No 2020-34, online: SSRN <https://ssrn.com/abstract=3722312> at 19–20, n 144.

CONCLUSION

1 *Citizenship Act*, RSC 1985, c C-29.

2 I use convoluted language here because the procedure involved revocation of Vavilov's citizenship certificate, not his citizenship as such. Is there a meaningful difference between the two types of revocation? The Supreme Court left this question for another day, noting that here the revocation of the certificate had the "same effect" as a revocation of citizenship: *Canada (Minister of Citizenship and Immigration) v Vavilov*, 2019 SCC 65 at para 193 [*Vavilov*].

3 *Ibid* at para 176.

4 *Ibid* at para 182.

5 *Ibid* at para 183.

6 *Ibid* at para 192.

7 *Ibid* at para 192.

8 *Canada (Public Safety and Emergency Preparedness) v Tran*, 2015 FCA 237.

9 2019 SCC 66 [*Bell Canada*].

10 *Ibid* at para 35.

11 *Ibid* at para 44.

12 *Ibid* at para 45 [emphasis in original].

13 *Ibid* at para 47.

14 *Ibid* at para 48 [emphasis in original].

15 *Ibid* at para 49.

16 *Ibid* at paras 52–55.

17 See also Mary Liston, "Bell Is the Tell I'm Thinking Of" (29 April 2020), *Administrative Law Matters* (blog), online: https://www.administrativelawmatters.com/blog/2020/04/29/bell-is-the-tell-im-thinking-of-mary-liston/.

18 [1979] 1 SCR 311, 88 DLR (3d) 671.

19 *Knight v Indian Head School Division No 19,* [1990] 1 SCR 653, 69 DLR (4th) 489.

20 *Canada (Attorney General) v Mavi,* 2011 SCC 30 at para 42.

21 As urged by Colleen Flood and Lorne Sossin, "The Contextual Turn: Iacobucci's Legacy and the Standard of Review in Administrative Law" (2007) 57:2 UTLJ 581.

22 See generally Martin Loughlin, "Procedural Fairness: A Study of the Crisis in Administrative Law Theory" (1978) 28:2 UTLJ 215.

23 Discussed in detail in Paul Daly, "Future Directions in Standard of Review in Canadian Administrative Law: Substantive Review and Procedural Fairness," Can J Admin L & Prac (forthcoming).

24 One of the authors of *Dunsmuir* so suggested, as it happens. Louis LeBel, "L'ordre et le rêve – Le contrôle judiciaire après *Dunsmuir*" in Paul Daly and Leonid Sirota, eds, *A Decade of Dunsmuir/Les 10 ans de Dunsmuir* (Toronto: Carswell, 2018) 257.

25 *Vavilov, supra* note 1 at para 14, quoting Beverley McLachlin, "The Roles of Administrative Tribunals and Courts in Maintaining the Rule of Law" (1998) 12 Can J Admin L & Prac 171 at 174 [emphasis deleted].

26 Cristie Ford, "Vavilov, Rule of Law Pluralism, and What Really Matters" (27 April 2020), *Administrative Law Matters* (blog), online: <https://www.administrativelawmatters.com/blog/2020/04/27/vavilov-rule-of-law-pluralism-and-what-really-matters-cristie-ford/>.

Selected Bibliography

JURISPRUDENCE

1085372 Ontario Limited v City of Toronto, 2020 ONSC 1136

1120732 B.C. Ltd. v Whistler (Resort Municipality), 2020 BCCA 101

Abiodun v Canada (Citizenship and Immigration), 2021 FC 642

Adams Fruit Co Inc v Barrett, 494 US 638 (1990)

Adeleye v Canada (Citizenship and Immigration), 2020 FC 640

ADM v Canadian Institute of Actuaries, 2008 ABQB 522

Advocacy Centre For Tenants-Ontario v Ontario Energy Board, (2008) 293 DLR
   (4th) 684

Air Canada v Toronto Port Authority, 2011 FCA 347

Alberta (Director of Assured Income for the Severely Handicapped) v Januario, 2013
   ABQB 677

Alberta (Information and Privacy Commissioner) v Alberta Teachers' Association, 2011
   SCC 61

Alberta (Information and Privacy Commissioner) v University of Calgary, 2016
   SCC 53

*Alberta Union of Provincial Employees, Branch 63 v Board of Governors of Olds
   College,* [1982] 1 SCR 923, 136 DLR (3d) 1

Albrifcani v Canada (Citizenship and Immigration), 2020 FC 355

Alexion Pharmaceuticals Inc v Canada (Attorney General), 2021 FCA 157

Alexis v Alberta (Environment and Parks), 2020 ABCA 188

Anisminic v Foreign Compensation Commission, [1969] 2 AC 147

AP v Canada (Citizenship and Immigration), 2020 FC 906

Apotex Inc v Canada (Attorney General), [2000] 4 FC 264, 188 DLR (4th) 145

ATCO Gas & Pipelines Ltd v Alberta (Energy & Utilities Board), 2006 SCC 4

Atlantic Mining NS Corp (DDV Gold Limited) v Oakley, 2019 NSCA 22

Attorney General of Quebec v Labrecque and al, [1980] 2 SCR 1057, 125 DLR
   (3d) 545

Bagge's Case, [1615] 11 Co Rep 93b

Baker v Canada (Minister of Citizenship and Immigration), [1999] 2 SCR 817, 174 DLR (4th) 193

Bancroft v Nova Scotia (Lands and Forests), 2020 NSSC 175

Bank of Montreal v Li, 2020 FCA 22

Barreau du Québec v Quebec (Attorney General), 2017 SCC 56

BCE Inc. v Québecor Média Inc., 2022 FCA 152

Beach Place Ventures Ltd v British Columbia (Employment Standards Tribunal), 2020 BCSC 327

Beals v Nova Scotia (Attorney General), 2020 NSSC 60

Bell Canada v British Columbia Broadband Association, 2020 FCA 140

Bell Canada v Canada (Attorney General), 2017 FCA 249

Bell Canada v Canada (Attorney General), 2019 SCC 66

Bell Canada v Canada (Environment and Climate Change), 2021 EPTC 3

Bell v Ontario Human Rights Commission, [1971] SCR 756, 18 DLR (3d) 1

Benhaim v St-Germain, 2016 SCC 48

Bergeron v Canada (Attorney General), 2015 FCA 160

Bernard v Canada (Attorney General), 2012 FCA 92

Bernard v Canada (Attorney General), 2014 SCC 13

Bibeault v McCaffrey, [1984] 1 SCR 176, 7 DLR (4th) 1

Borgel v Paintearth (Subdivision and Development Appeal Board), 2020 ABCA 192

Borradaile v British Columbia (Superintendent of Motor Vehicles), 2020 BCSC 363

Bragg Communications Inc v Unifor, 2021 FCA 59

Bricka c Procureur général du Québec, 2022 QCCA 85

British Columbia Telephone Co v Shaw Cable Systems (BC) Ltd, [1995] 2 SCR 739, 125 DLR (4th) 443

Brockville (City) v Information and Privacy Commissioner, Ontario, 2020 ONSC 4413

Byun v Alberta Dental Association and College, 2021 ABCA 272

Calgary Power Ltd and Halmrast v Copithorne, [1959] SCR 24, 16 DLR (2d) 241

Canada (Attorney General) v Association of Justice Counsel, 2021 FCA 37

Canada (Attorney General) v Best Buy Canada Ltd., 2021 FCA 161

Canada (Attorney General) v Downtown Eastside Sex Workers United Against Violence Society, 2012 SCC 45

Canada (Attorney General) v Igloo Vikski Inc, 2016 SCC 38

Canada (Attorney General) v Impex Solutions Inc., 2020 FCA 171

Canada (Attorney General) v Mavi, 2011 SCC 30

Canada (Attorney General) v Mossop, [1993] 1 SCR 554, 100 DLR (4th) 658

Canada (Attorney General) v Mowat, 2009 FCA 309

Canada (Attorney General) v Northern Inter-Tribal Health Authority Inc, 2020 FCA 63

Canada (Attorney General) v Public Service Alliance of Canada, [1993] 1 SCR 941, 101 DLR (4th) 673

Canada (Attorney General) v Public Service Alliance of Canada, 2011 FCA 257

Canada (Attorney General) v Public Service Alliance of Canada, 2019 FCA 41

Canada (Attorney General) v Tipple, 2011 FC 762

Canada (Attorney General) v Zalys, 2020 FCA 81

Canada (Canadian Human Rights Commission) v Canada (Attorney General), 2018 SCC 31

Canada (Canadian Human Rights Commission) v Canada (Attorney General), 2011 SCC 53

Canada (Citizenship and Immigration) v Khosa, 2009 SCC 12

Canada (Citizenship and Immigration) v Mason, 2021 FCA 156

Canada (Commissioner of Competition) v Superior Propane Inc, 2001 FCA 104

Canada (Director of Investigation and Research) v Southam Inc, [1997] 1 SCR 748, 144 DLR (4th) 1

Canada (Health) v Glaxosmithkline Biologicals SA, 2021 FCA 71

Canada (Minister of Citizenship and Immigration) v Vavilov, 2019 SCC 65

Canada (National Revenue) v JP Morgan Asset Management (Canada) Inc, 2013 FCA 250

Canada (Public Safety and Emergency Preparedness) v Tran, 2015 FCA 237

Canada (Union of Correctionnel Officers) v Canada (Attorney General), 2019 FCA 212

Canada v Kabul Farms Inc, 2016 FCA 143

Canada Post Corp. v Canadian Union of Postal Workers, 2019 SCC 67

Canada Post Corp. v Public Service Alliance of Canada, 2011 SCC 57

Canadian Association of Industrial, Mechanical and Allied Workers, Local 14 v Paccar of Canada Ltd, [1989] 2 SCR 983, 62 DLR (4th) 437

Canadian Association of Refugee Lawyers v Canada (Citizenship and Immigration), 2019 FC 1126

Canadian Broadcasting Corporation v Ferrier, 2019 ONCA 1025

Canadian National Railway Company v Canada (Transportation Agency), 2021 FCA 173

Canadian National Railway Company v Emerson Milling Inc, 2017 FCA 79

Canadian National Railway Company v Richardson International Limited, 2020 FCA 20

Canadian Natural Resources Limited v Elizabeth Métis Settlement, 2020 ABCA 148

Canadian Natural Resources Limited v Elizabeth Métis Settlement, 2020 ABQB 210

Canadian Pacific v Canadian Transport Commission, [1985] 2 FC 136

Canadian Union of Public Employees Local 963 v New Brunswick Liquor Corporation, [1979] 2 SCR 227, 97 DLR (3d) 417

Cardinal v Director of Kent Institution, [1985] 2 SCR 643, 24 DLR (4th) 44

Catalyst Paper Corp. v North Cowichan (District), 2012 SCC 2

Centre intégré de santé et de services sociaux de la Montérégie-Ouest c Syndicat canadien de la fonction publique, section locale 3247, 2020 QCCS 1603

Chagnon v Syndicat de la fonction publique et parapublique du Québec, 2018 SCC 39

Champag inc c Municipalité de Saint-Roch-de-Richelieu, 2020 QCCA 613

Chief Constable of the North Wales Police v Evans, [1982] 1 WLR 1155

Chieu v Canada (Minister of Citizenship and Immigration), 2002 SCC 3

Chippewas of the Thames First Nation v Enbridge Pipelines Inc, 2017 SCC 41

City of Arlington v Federal Communications Commission, 569 US 290 (2013)

Clyde River (Hamlet) v Petroleum GeoServices Inc, 2017 SCC 40

Coldwater First Nation v Canada (Attorney General), 2020 FCA 34

College of Registered Nurses of Manitoba v Hancock, 2022 MBCA 70

Commissaire à la déontologie policière c Lavallée, 2020 QCCQ 1923

Commission des relations ouvrières du Québec v Burlington Mills Hosiery Co. of Canada, [1964] SCR 342, 45 DLR (2d) 730

Commission scolaire de Laval v Syndicat de l'enseignement de la région de Laval, 2016 SCC 8

Communications Energy and Paperworkers Union of Canada, Local 30 v Irving Pulp & Paper, Limited, 2011 NBCA 58

Communications Energy and Paperworkers Union of Canada, Local 30 v Irving Pulp & Paper Ltd, 2013 SCC 34

Council of Canadians with Disabilities v VIA Rail Canada Inc., 2007 SCC 15

Council of Civil Service Unions v Minister for the Civil Service, [1985] AC 374

Crevier v Attorney General of Quebec, [1981] 2 SCR 220, 127 DLR (3d) 1

D'Errico v Canada (Attorney General), 2014 FCA 95

David Suzuki Foundation v Canada-Newfoundland and Labrador Offshore Petroleum Board, 2020 NLSC 94

Dayco (Canada) Ltd v CAW-Canada, [1993] 2 SCR 230, 102 DLR (4th) 609

Delios v Canada (Attorney General), 2015 FCA 117

Dell v Zeifman Partners Inc, 2020 ONSC 3881

Delta Air Lines Inc. v Lukács, 2018 SCC 2

Domtar Inc v Quebec (Commission d'appel en matière de lésions professionnelles), [1993] 2 SCR 756, 105 DLR (4th) 385

Donaldson c Autorité des marchés financiers, 2020 QCCA 401

Doré v Barreau du Québec, 2012 SCC 12

Douglas Aircraft Co of Canada v McConnell, [1980] 1 SCR 245, 99 DLR (3d) 385

Downey v Nova Scotia (Attorney General), 2020 NSSC 201

Dr Jonathan Mitelman v College of Veterinarians of Ontario, 2020 ONSC 3039

Dr Q v College of Physicians and Surgeons of British Columbia, 2003 SCC 19

Dr Rashidan v The National Dental Examining Board of Canada, 2020 ONSC 4174

Dunsmuir v New Brunswick, 2008 SCC 9

East Hants (Municipality) v Nova Scotia (Utility and Review Board), 2020 NSCA 41

Edmonton (City) v Edmonton East (Capilano) Shopping Centres Ltd, 2016 SCC 47

Edmonton (City of) v Edmonton Police Association, 2020 ABCA 182

Edmonton (City of) v Ten 201 Jasper Avenue Ltd, 2020 ABCA 60

Edmonton East (Capilano) Shopping Centres Limited v Edmonton (City), 2015 ABCA 85

Elangovan v Canada (Attorney General), 2020 FC 882

Elementary Teachers Federation of Ontario v York Region District School Board, 2022 ONCA 476

Farrier v Canada (Attorney General), 2020 FCA 25

Febles v Canada (Citizenship and Immigration), 2014 SCC 68

Forest Ethics Advocacy Association v Canada (National Energy Board), 2014 FCA 245

Garcia Balarezo v Canada (Citizenship and Immigration), 2020 FC 841

Gaudreau c Régie des marchés agricoles et alimentaires du Québec, 2021 QCCA 330

Glaxosmithkline Biologicals S.A. v Canada (Health), 2020 FC 397

Gould v Yukon Order of Pioneers, [1996] 1 SCR 571, 133 DLR (4th) 449

Groenvelt v Burwell, (1700) 91 ER 179, (1700) 1 Salkeld 200

Groia v Law Society of Upper Canada, 2018 SCC 27

GSR Capital Group Inc v The City of White Rock, 2020 BCSC 489

Haddad Pour v The National Dental Examining Board of Canada, 2020 ONSC 555

Harrison v Canada (National Revenue), 2020 FC 772

Hasani v Canada (Citizenship and Immigration), 2020 FC 125

Health Authority Inc. v Manitoba Association of Health Care Professionals, 2011 SCC 59

Hennig v Institute of Chartered Accountants of Alberta (Complaints Inquiry Committee), 2008 ABCA 241

Hernandez Febles v Canada (Citizenship and Immigration), 2012 FCA 324

Highwood Congregation of Jehovah's Witnesses (Judicial Committee) v Wall, 2018 SCC 26, [2018] 1 SCR 750

Hildebrand v Penticton (City), 2020 BCSC 353

Houghton v Association of Ontario Land Surveyors, 2020 ONSC 863

Housen v Nikolaisen, 2002 SCC 33

Hudson's Bay Company ULC v Ontario (Attorney General), 2020 ONSC 8046

Hughes v Law Society of New Brunswick, 2020 NBCA 68

Hupacasath First Nation v Canada (Foreign Affairs and International Trade Canada), 2015 FCA 4

Immigration Consultants of Canada Regulatory Council v Rahman, 2020 FC 832

Imperial Oil Ltd v Quebec (Minister of the Environment), 2003 SCC 58

Innovative Medicines Canada v Canada (Attorney General), 2020 FC 725

Irvine v Canada (Restrictive Trade Practices Commission), [1987] 1 SCR 181, 41 DLR (4th) 429

Irving Pulp & Paper, Limited v Communications, Energy and Paperworkers Union of Canada, Local 30, 2010 NBQB 294

Jarvis v Associated Medical Services Inc, [1964] SCR 497, 44 DLR (2d) 407

JD Irving, Limited v North Shore Forest Products Marketing Board, 2014 NBCA 42

JE and KE v Children's Aid Society of the Niagara Region, 2020 ONSC 4239

Jean-Baptiste v Canada (Citizenship and Immigration), 2021 FC 1362

JG v Nadeau, 2016 QCCA 167

Kane v Canada (Attorney General), 2011 FCA 19

Kanthasamy v Canada (Citizenship and Immigration), 2015 SCC 61

Katz Group Canada Inc. v Ontario (Health and Long-Term Care), 2013 SCC 64

Kelly v Alberta (Energy Resources Conservation Board), 2012 ABCA 19

Kelly v Nova Scotia Police Commission, 2006 NSCA 27

Keyu v Foreign Secretary, [2015] UKSC 69

Knight v Indian Head School Division No 19, [1990] 1 SCR 653, 69 DLR (4th) 489

Koebisch v Rocky View (County), 2021 ABCA 265

Komolafe v Canada (Citizenship and Immigration), 2013 FC 431

Ktunaxa Nation v British Columbia (Forests, Lands and Natural Resource Operations), 2017 SCC 54

Labour Relations Board v Canada Safeway Ltd, [1953] 2 SCR 46, [1953] 3 DLR 641

Langenfeld v Toronto Police Services Board, 2019 ONCA 716

Langford Sharp c Autorité des marchés financiers, 2021 QCCA 1364

Langlais c Collège des médecins du Québec, 2020 QCCA 134

Law Society of British Columbia v Trinity Western University, 2018 SCC 32

Law Society of New Brunswick v Ryan, 2003 SCC 20

Law Society of Saskatchewan v Abrametz, 2022 SCC 29

Leahy v Canada (Citizenship and Immigration), 2012 FCA 227

Lemus v Canada (Citizenship and Immigration), 2014 FCA 114

Li v Canada (Citizenship and Immigration), 2020 FC 279

Longphee v Workplace Health, Safety and Compensation Commission, 2020 NBCA 45

Loyola High School v Quebec (Attorney General), 2015 SCC 12

M.O. c Société de l'assurance automobile du Québec, 2021 QCCA 177

Manitoba (Hydro-Electric Board) v Manitoba (Public Utilities Board) et al., 2020
MBCA 60

*Manitoba Government and General Employees' Union v The Minister of Finance for
the Government*, 2021 MBCA 36

Mao v Canada (Citizenship and Immigration), 2020 FC 542

Martin v Alberta (Workers' Compensation Board), 2014 SCC 25

Martineau v Matsqui Institution Disciplinary Board (No. 2), [1980] 1 SCR 602,
106 DLR (3d) 385.

Mattar v The National Dental Examining Board of Canada, 2020 ONSC 403

McCarthy v Guest, 2020 NBQB 150

McLean (Re), 2010 BCSECCOM 262

McLean v British Columbia (Securities Commission), 2011 BCCA 455

McLean v British Columbia (Securities Commission), 2013 SCC 67

McLeod v Egan, [1975] 1 SCR 517, 46 DLR (3d) 150

Metropolitan Life Insurance v International Union of Operating Engineers, [1970]
SCR 425, 11 DLR (3d) 336

Miller v College of Optometrists of Ontario, 2020 ONSC 2573

Miller v Workers' Compensation Commission (Newfoundland), (1997) 154 Nfld &
PEIR 52, 2 Admin LR (3d) 178, LD Barry J (SC)

Milner Power Inc v Alberta (Energy and Utilities Board), 2007 ABCA 265

Mission Institution v Khela, 2014 SCC 24

Mitelman v College of Veterinarians of Ontario, 2020 ONSC 6171

Mohammad v Canada (Citizenship and Immigration), 2020 FC 473

Moore v Minister of Manpower and Immigration, [1968] SCR 839, 69 DLR
(2d) 273

Morris v Law Society of Alberta (Trust Safety Committee), 2020 ABQB 137

Mountain Parks Watershed Assn. v Chateau Lake Louise Corp, 2004 FC 1222

Mouvement laïque québécois v Saguenay (City), 2015 SCC 16

Nanaimo (City) v Rascal Trucking Ltd, 2000 SCC 13

Natco Pharma (Canada) Inc. v Canada (Health), 2020 FC 788

*Nation Rise Wind Farm Limited Partnership v Minister of the Environment,
Conservation and Parks*, 2020 ONSC 2984

National Corn Growers Association v Canada (Import Tribunal), [1990] 2 SCR
1324, 74 DLR (4th) 449.

National Football League v Canada (Attorney General), 2019 SCC 66

*New Brunswick Liquor Corporation v Canadian Union of Public Employees, Local
963*, (1978) 21 NBR (2d) 441, 1978 CanLII 2696 (NB CA)

*Newfoundland and Labrador Nurses' Union v Newfoundland and Labrador (Treasury
Board)*, 2011 SCC 62

Nicholson v Haldimand-Norfolk Regional Police Commissioners, [1979] 1 SCR 311,
88 DLR (3d) 671

Nolan v Kerry (Canada) Inc, 2009 SCC 39

Nor-Man Regional Health Authority Inc v Manitoba Association of Health Care Professionals, 2011 SCC 59

Northern Harvest Smolt Ltd v Salmonid Association of Eastern Newfoundland, 2021 NLCA 26

Northern Regional Health Authority v Horrocks, 2021 SCC 42

Northrop Grumman Overseas Services Corp v Canada (Attorney General), 2009 SCC 50

Nova Scotia (Attorney General) v S&D Smith Central Supplies Limited, 2019 NSCA 22

Nova Scotia Construction Safety Association v Nova Scotia Human Rights Commission, 2006 NSCA 63

O'Shea/Oceanmount Community Association v Town of Gibsons, 2020 BCSC 698

Oberg v Saskatchewan (Board of Education of the South East Cornerstone School Division No. 209), 2020 SKQB 96

Ofsted v Secretary of State for Education, [2018] EWCA Civ 2813

Olineck v Alberta (Environmental Appeals Board), 2017 ABQB 311

Olivier c Cayer, 2020 QCCQ 2060

Ontario (Community Safety and Correctional Services) v Ontario (Information and Privacy Commissioner), 2014 SCC 31

Ontario (Health) v Association of Ontario Midwives, 2022 ONCA 458

Ontario Provincial Police v MacDonald, 2009 ONCA 805

Operation Dismantle v The Queen, [1985] 1 SCR 441, 18 DLR (4th) 481

Organisation de la jeunesse Chabad Loubavitch c Ville de Mont-Tremblant, 2022 QCCA 1331

Ortiz v Canada (Citizenship and Immigration), 2020 FC 188

Osun v Canada (Citizenship and Immigration), 2020 FC 295

Oxford v Newfoundland and Labrador (Municipal Affairs and Environment), 2020 NLSC 102

Pacific Newspaper Group Inc v Communications, Energy and Paperworkers Union of Canada, Local 2000, 2014 BCCA 496

Padfield v Minister of Agriculture, [1968] AC 997

Partridge v Nova Scotia (Attorney General), 2021 NSCA 60

Party A v The Law Society of British Columbia, 2021 BCCA 130

Pasiechnyk v Saskatchewan (Workers' Compensation Board), [1997] 2 SCR 890, 149 DLR (4th) 577

Patchett & Sons Ltd v Pacific Great Eastern Railway Co., [1959] SCR 271, 17 DLR (2d) 449

Patel v Canada (Citizenship and Immigration), 2020 FC 77

Peter v Public Health Appeal Board of Alberta, 2019 ABQB 989

Pierson v Estevan Board of Police Commissioners, 2020 SKQB 144

Planet Energy (Ontario) Corp v Ontario Energy Board, 2020 ONSC 598

Portnov v Canada (Attorney General), 2021 FCA 171

Procureur général du Québec c Lamontagne, 2020 QCCA 1137

Procureur général du Québec c PF, 2020 QCCA 1220

Public Service Alliance of Canada v Canada Post Corporation, 2010 FCA 56

Public Service Alliance of Canada v Canada Post Corporation, 2011 SCC 57

Public Service Alliance of Canada v Canadian Federal Pilots Association, 2009 FCA 223

Pushpanathan v Canada (Minister of Citizenship and Immigration), [1998] 1 SCR 982, 160 DLR (4th) 193

Qasim v Canada (Citizenship and Immigration), 2020 FC 465

Quadra Properties Ltd v Gamble, 2021 SKQB 16

Quebec (Attorney General) v Guérin, 2017 SCC 42

Quebec (Commission des droits de la personne et des droits de la jeunesse) v Bombardier Inc (Bombardier Aerospace Training Center), 2015 SCC 39

Quebec (Commission des droits de la personne et des droits de la jeunesse) v Quebec (Attorney General), 2004 SCC 39

Quebec (Commission des normes, de l'équité, de la santé et de la sécurité du travail) v Caron, 2018 SCC 3

R (Agyarko) v Secretary of State for the Home Department, (2017) 1 WLR 823

R v Criminal Injuries Compensation Board, ex parte Lain, [1967] 2 QB 864 (HL)

R v Electricity Commissioners, ex parte London Electricity Joint Committee Co (1920) Ltd, [1924] 1 KB 171 (CA), [1923] 7 WLUK 128 (Atkin LJ)

R v Inland Revenue Commissioners, ex parte National Federation of Self-Employed and Small Businesses Ltd, [1982] AC 617

R v London Rent Tribunal, ex parte Honig, [1951] 1 KB 641

R v Nat Bell Liquors, [1922] 2 AC 128

R v Northumberland Compensation Appeal Tribunal, ex parte Shaw, [1952] 1 KB 338 (CA)

R v Oakes, [1986] 1 SCR 103, 26 DLR (4th) 200

R v Titchmarsh (1914), 22 DLR 272, 24 CCC 38 (Ont CA)

R(A) v London Borough of Croydon, [2009] UKSC 8

Radzevicius v Workplace Safety and Insurance Appeals Tribunal, 2020 ONSC 319

Randhawa v Canada (Public Safety and Emergency Preparedness), 2020 FC 905

Ravandi v Canada (Citizenship and Immigration), 2020 FC 761

RB v British Columbia (Superintendent of Motor Vehicles), 2020 BCSC 1496

Re Downing and Graydon (1978), 92 DLR (3d) 355, 21 OR (2d) 292

Re: Sound v Fitness Industry Council of Canada, 2014 FCA 48

Red Chris Development Co v United Steel, Paper and Forestry, Rubber, Manufacturing, Energy, Allied Industrial and Service Workers International Union, Local 1-1937, 2021 BCCA 152

Redmond v British Columbia (Forests, Lands, Natural Resource Operations and Rural Development), 2020 BCSC 561

Reference re Code of Civil Procedure (Que), art 35, 2021 SCC 27

Reference re Secession of Quebec, [1998] 2 SCR 217, 161 DLR (4th) 385

Regina Police Assn Inc v Regina (City) Board of Police Commissioners, 2000 SCC 14

Restaurants Canada c Ville de Montréal, 2021 QCCA 1639

Ridge v Baldwin, [1964] AC 40

Rio Tinto Alcan Inc. v Carrier Sekani Tribal Council, 2010 SCC 43

Robertson v British Columbia (Teachers Act, Commissioner), 2014 BCCA 331

Rodriguez Martinez v Canada (Citizenship and Immigration), 2020 FC 293

Rogers Communications Inc v Society of Composers, Authors and Music Publishers of Canada, 2012 SCC 35

Romania v Boros, 2020 ONCA 216

Sagkeeng v Government of Manitoba et al, 2020 MBQB 83

Samra v Canada (Citizenship and Immigration), 2020 FC 157

Saskatchewan (Board of Education of the South East Cornerstone School Division No. 209) v Oberg, 2021 SKCA 28

Saskatchewan (Energy and Resources) v Areva Resources Canada Inc., 2013 SKCA 79

Saskatchewan (Human Rights Commission) v Whatcott, 2013 SCC 11

Sazant v College of Physicians and Surgeons of Ontario, 2012 ONCA 727

Scarborough Health Network v Canadian Union of Public Employees, Local 5852, 2020 ONSC 4577

Senadheerage v Canada (Citizenship and Immigration), 2020 FC 968

Service Employees' International Union, Local No. 333 v Nipawin District Staff Nurses Association et al., [1975] 1 SCR 382, 41 DLR (3d) 6

Shah v College of Physiotherapists of Ontario, 2020 ONSC 6240

Simelane v Canada (Immigration, Refugees and Citizenship), 2022 FC 1374

Singh v Canada (Citizenship and Immigration), 2020 FC 687

Slemko v Canada (Public Safety and Emergency Preparedness), 2020 FC 718

Smith v Alliance Pipeline Ltd, 2011 SCC 7

Smith and Rhuland Ltd v The Queen, [1953] 2 SCR 95, [1953] 3 DLR 690

Society of Composers, Authors and Music Publishers of Canada v Entertainment Software Association, 2022 SCC 30

South Yukon Forest Corp v R, 2012 FCA 165

Speckling v British Columbia (Workers' Compensation Board), 2005 BCCA 80

Sriskandarajah v United States of America, 2012 SCC 70

Sticky Nuggz Inc v Alcohol and Gaming Commission of Ontario, 2020 ONSC 5916

Syndicat canadien des communications, de l'énergie et du papier, section locale 30 c Les Pâtes et Papier Irving, Limitée, 2011 NBCA 58

Syndicat des employé(e)s de l'école Vanguard ltée (CSN) c Mercier, 2020 QCCS 95

Syndicat des employés de production du Québec et de l'Acadie v Canada (Canadian Human Rights Commission), [1989] 2 SCR 879, 62 DLR (4th) 385

Syndicat des employés de production du Québec et de l'Acadie v Canada Labour Relations Board, [1984] 2 SCR 412, 14 DLR (4th) 457

Syndicat des travailleuses et travailleurs de ADF – CSN c Syndicat des employés de Au Dragon forgé Inc, 2013 QCCA 793

Teamsters Canada Rail Conference c Canadian Pacific Railway Company, 2020 QCCA 729

Terrigno v Calgary (City), 2021 ABQB 41

The College of Physicians and Surgeons of British Columbia v The Health Professions Review Board, 2022 BCCA 10

The Owners, Strata Plan BCS 435 v Wong, 2020 BCSC 1972

The Queen v Leong Ba Chai, [1954] SCR 10, [1954] 1 DLR 401

Thibeault v Saskatchewan (Apprenticeship and Trade Certification Commission), 2020 SKQB 192

Toronto (City) v Canadian Union of Public Employees, Local 79, 2003 SCC 63

Toronto Newspaper Guild v Globe Printing, [1953] 2 SCR 18, [1953] 3 DLR 561

Toronto Star v AG Ontario, 2018 ONSC 2586

Tran v Canada (Public Safety and Emergency Preparedness), 2017 SCC 50

TransAlta Generation Partnership v Regina, 2021 ABQB 37

Trentway-Wagar inc c Cormier, 2021 QCCA 983

Union des employés de service, local 298 v Bibeault, [1988] 2 SCR 1048, 95 NR 161

United Australia Ltd v Barclay's Bank Ltd, [1941] AC 1 (Lord Atkin)

United Brotherhood of Carpenters and Joiners of America, Local 579 v Bradco Construction, [1993] 2 SCR 316, 102 DLR (4th) 402

United Nurses of Alberta v Alberta Health Services, 2021 ABCA 194

United Taxi Drivers' Fellowship of Southern Alberta v Calgary (City), 2004 SCC 19

Valiquette c Tribunal administratif du travail, 2020 QCCS 11

Vavilov v Canada (Citizenship and Immigration), 2017 FCA 132

ViiV Healthcare ULC v Canada (Health), 2020 FC 756

Ville de Québec c Galy, 2020 QCCA 1130

Voice Construction Ltd. v Construction & General Workers' Union, Local 92, 2004 SCC 23

Volvo Canada Ltd v UAW, Local 720, [1980] 1 SCR 178, 99 DLR (3d) 193

Walker v Canada (Attorney General), 2020 FCA 44

Wall v Independent Police Review Director, 2013 ONSC 3312

Weldemariam v Canada (Public Safety and Emergency Preparedness), 2020 FC 631

West Fraser Mills Ltd v British Columbia (Workers' Compensation Appeal Tribunal), 2018 SCC 22

Westcoast Energy Inc v Canada (National Energy Board), [1998] 1 SCR 322, 156 DLR (4th) 456

Wilson v Atomic Energy of Canada, 2016 SCC 29
Wilson v Atomic Energy of Canada Limited, 2015 FCA 17
Wilson v Cowichan Valley (Regional District), 2021 BCSC 1735
Yatar v TD Insurance Meloche Monnex, 2022 ONCA 446
Yee v Chartered Professional Accountants of Alberta, 2020 ABCA 98
Zhang v Canada (Public Safety and Emergency Preparedness), 2021 FC 746

OTHER SOURCES

Arthurs, Harry W. "Rethinking Judicial Review: A Slightly Dicey Business" (1979) 17:1 Osgoode Hall LJ 1.

Bankes, Nigel. "Statutory Appeal Rights in Relation to Administrative Decision-Maker Now Attract an Appellate Standard of Review: A Possible Legislative Response" (3 January 2020), online (blog): *ABlawg* <https://ablawg.ca/2020/01/03/statutory-appeal-rights-in-relation-to-administrative-decision-maker-now-attract-an-appellate-standard-of-review-a-possible-legislative-response/>.

Bryden, Philip. "Justice Wilson's Administrative Law Legacy: The National Corn Growers Decision and Judicial Review of Administrative Decision-Making" (2008) 41 SCLR (2d) 225.

Craig, Paul. "Jurisdiction, Judicial Control, and Agency Autonomy." In Ian Loveland, ed, *A Special Relationship? American Influences on Public Law in the United Kingdom* (Oxford: Clarendon, 1995) 173.

Daly, Paul. "The Autonomy of Administration" (2023) UTLJ (forthcoming).

—. "Canada's Bi-Polar Administrative Law: Time for Fusion" (2014) 40:1 Queen's LJ 213.

—. "Canadian Labour Law after *Vavilov*" (2021) 23 Can J Lab & Emp L 103.

—. "The Court and Administrative Law: Models of Rights Protection." In Matthew Harrington, ed, *The Court and the Constitution: A 150-Year Retrospective* (Toronto: LexisNexis, 2017) 57.

—. "Future Directions in Standard of Review in Canadian Administrative Law: Substantive Review and Procedural Fairness" (forthcoming, Can J Admin Law & Practice).

—. "Patent Unreasonableness after *Vavilov*" (2021) 34:2 Can J Admin L & Prac 167.

—. "Prescribing Greater Protection for Rights: Administrative Law and Section 1 of the *Canadian Charter of Rights and Freedoms*" (2014) 65 SCLR (2d) 247.

—. *A Theory of Deference in Administrative Law: Basis, Application and Scope* (Cambridge: Cambridge University Press, 2012).

—. "*Vavilov* and the Culture of Justification in Contemporary Administrative Law" (2020) 100 Sup Ct L Rev (2d) 279.

—. "*Vavilov* On the Road" (2022) 35 Can J Admin L & Prac 1.

Daly, Paul, and Léonid Sirota, eds, *The Dunsmuir Decade/Les 10 ans de Dunsmuir: Special Issue of Canadian Journal of Administrative Law and Practice* (Toronto: Carswell, 2018).

Dyzenhaus, David. "Constituting the Rule of Law: Fundamental Values in Administrative Law" (2002) 27:2 Queens LJ 445.

—. "The Politics of Deference: Judicial Review and Democracy" in Michael Taggart, ed, *The Province of Administrative Law* (Oxford: Hart, 1997) 279.

Ellis, Ron. *Unjust by Design: Canada's Administrative Justice System* (Vancouver: UBC Press, 2013)

Evans, John M. "Triumph of Reasonableness: But How Much Does It Really Matter?" (2014) 27:1 Can J Admin Law & Prac 101.

Evans, John M., and Trevor Knight. "Cory on Administrative Law." In Patrick J. Monahan and Sandra A. Forbes, eds, *Peter Cory at the Supreme Court of Canada: 1989–1999* (Winnipeg: Canadian Legal History Project, 2001) 71.

Flood, Colleen, and Lorne Sossin. "The Contextual Turn: Iacobucci's Legacy and the Standard of Review in Administrative Law" (2007) 57:2 UTLJ 581.

Ford, Cristie. "Vavilov, Rule of Law Pluralism, and What Really Matters" (27 April 2020), online (blog): *Administrative Law Matters* <https://www.administrative lawmatters.com/blog/2020/04/27/vavilov-rule-of-law-pluralism-and-what -really-matters-cristie-ford/>.

—. "What People Want, What They Get, and the Administrative State." In Colleen Flood and Paul Daly, eds, *Administrative Law in Context*, 4th ed. (Toronto: Emond Montgomery, 2021).

Fox Decent, Evan, and Alexander Pless. "The Charter and Administrative Law: Cross-Fertilization in Public Law." In Colleen Flood and Lorne Sossin, eds, *Administrative Law in Context*, 2nd ed. (Toronto: Emond Montgomery, 2012) 407.

Grey, Julius. "Sections 96-100: A Defense" (1985) 1 Admin LJ 3.

Hogg, Peter W. "The Supreme Court of Canada and Administrative Law, 1949–1971" (1973) 11:2 Osgoode Hall LJ 187.

Jaffe, Louis. "Judicial Review: Constitutional and Jurisdictional Fact" (1957) 70:6 Harv L Rev 953.

Janisch, Hudson N. "Towards a More General Theory of Judicial Review in Administrative Law" (1989) 53:2 Sask L Rev 327.

Knight, Dean. *Vigilance and Restraint in the Common Law of Judicial Review* (Cambridge: Cambridge University Press, 2018).

L'Heureux-Dubé, Claire. "L'arrêt *Bibeault* : une ancre dans une mer agitée" (1994) 28:2-3 RJT 731.

Langille, Brian A. "Judicial Review, Judicial Revisionism and Judicial Responsibility" (1986) 17:1-2 RGD 169.

Lauwers, Peter. "What Could Go Wrong with Charter Values?" (2019) 91 SCLR (2d) 1.

Lawson, Gary, and Guy Seidman. Deference: *The Legal Concept and the Legal Practice* (New York: Oxford University Press, 2020).

Le Dain, Gerald E. "The Twilight of Judicial Control in the Province of Quebec?" (1952) 1 McGill LJ 1.

LeBel, Louis. "Some Properly Deferential Thoughts on Deference" (2008) 21:1 Can J Admin Law & Prac 1.

Lewans, Matthew. "Deference and Reasonableness Since *Dunsmuir*" (2012) 38 Queen's LJ 59.

Liston, Mary. "Bell is the Tell I'm Thinking Of" (29 April 2020), online (blog): *Administrative Law Matters* <https://www.administrativelawmatters.com/blog/2020/04/29/bell-is-the-tell-im-thinking-of-mary-liston/>.

—. "Transubstantiation in Canadian Public Law: Processing Substance and Instantiating Process." In John Bell et al., ed, *Public Law Adjudication in Common Law Systems: Process and Substance* (Oxford: Hart, 2016) 213.

Loughlin, Martin. "Procedural Fairness: A Study of the Crisis in Administrative Law Theory" (1978) 28:2 UTLJ 215.

Macklin, Audrey. "*Charter* Right or *Charter*-Lite? Administrative Discretion and the *Charter*" (2014) 67 SCLR (2d) 561.

MacLauchlan, H Wade. "Judicial Review of Administrative Interpretations of Law: How Much Formalism Can We Reasonably Bear?" (1986) 36:4 UTLJ 343.

Mancini, Mark. "The Conceptual Gap Between Doré and Vavilov" (2020) 43:2 Dal LJ 793.

McKee, Derek. "The Standard of Review for Questions of Procedural Fairness" (2016) 41:2 Queen's LJ 382.

Mullan, David J. "2015 Developments in Administrative Law Relevant to Energy Law and Regulation" (2016) 4:1 Energy Regulation Quarterly.

—. "Developments in Administrative Law: The 1983-84 Term" (1985) 7 SCLR (2d) 1.

—. "*Dunsmuir v New Brunswick*: Standard of Review and Procedural Fairness for Public Servants: Let's Try Again!" (2008) 21:2 Can J Admin Law & Prac 117.

—. "Judicial Scrutiny of Administrative Decision Making: Principled Simplification or Continuing Angst?" (2020) 50:4 Adv Q 423.

Stratas, David. "The Canadian Law of Judicial Review: A Plea for Doctrinal Coherence and Consistency" (2016) 42:1 Queen's LJ 27.

—. "The Canadian Law of Judicial Review: Some Doctrine and Cases" (18 October 2022), online: SSRN: <https://papers.ssrn.com/sol3/papers.cfm?abstract_id=2924049>.

Tremblay, Luc. "La norme de retenue judiciaire et les "erreurs de droit" en droit administratif : une erreur de droit? Au-delà du fondationalisme et du scepticisme" (1996) 52 R du B 141.

Vermeule, Adrian. *Law's Abnegation: From Law's Empire to the Administrative State* (Cambridge: Harvard University Press, 2016).

Wade, HWR. "Crossroads in Administrative Law" (1968) 21:1 Curr Legal Probs 75.

Wade, William. "Constitutional and Administrative Aspects of the *Anisminic* Case" (1969) 85 LQR 198.

Walters, Mark D. "Jurisdiction, Functionalism, and Constitutionalism in Canadian Administrative Law." In Christopher Forsyth et al., eds, *Effective Judicial Review: a Cornerstone of Good Governance* (Oxford: Oxford University Press, 2010) 300.

Weiler, Paul. "The Slippery Slope of Judicial Intervention: The Supreme Court and Canadian Labour Relations 1950-1970" (1971) 9:1 Osgoode Hall LJ 1.

Wildeman, Sheila. "Pas de Deux: Deference and Non-Deference in Action." In Lorne Sossin and Colleen Flood, eds, *Administrative Law in Context*, 2nd ed. (Toronto: Emond Montgomery, 2013) 323.

Willis, John W. "Administrative Law and the British North America Act" (1939) 53:2 Harv L Rev 251 at 262.

Index of Cases

1120732 BC Ltd v Whistler (Resort Municipality), 2020 BCCA 101, 132

Advocacy Centre For Tenants-Ontario v Ontario Energy Board, 2020 ONSC 598, 139

Agraira v Canada (Public Safety and Emergency Preparedness), [2013] 2 SCR 559, 81–82

Alberta (Information and Privacy Commissioner) v Alberta Teachers' Association, 2011 SCC 61, 65, 69, 71, 78–81, 102, 107, 165, 195n98, 196n42

Alberta (Information and Privacy Commissioner) v University of Calgary, 2016 SCC 53, 202n152

Alberta Union of Provincial Employees, Branch 63 v Board of Governors of Olds College, [1982] 1 SCR 923, 191n32

Albrifcani v Canada (Citizenship and Immigration), 2020 FC 355, 128

Alexion Pharmaceuticals Inc v Canada (Attorney General), 2021 FCA 157, 213n49

Alsaloussi v Canada (Attorney General), 2020 FC 364, 127, 212n32

Anisminic v Foreign Compensation Commission, [1969] 2 AC 147, 22

AP v Canada (Citizenship and Immigration), 2020 FC 906, 211n21

Apotex Inc v Canada (Attorney General), [2000] 4 FC 264, 185n52

Atlantic Mining NS Corp (DDV Gold Limited) v Oakley, 2019 NSCA 22, 90

Bagge's Case, [1615] 11, 182n4

Baker v Canada (Citizenship and Immigration), [1999] 2 SCR 817, 156–59, 178

Bancroft v Nova Scotia (Lands and Forests), 2020 NSSC 175, 132, 220n2

Bank of Montreal v Li, 2020 FCA 22, 143–44

Barreau du Quebec v Quebec (Attorney General), 2017 SCC 56, 202n152

Beals v Nova Scotia (Attorney General), 2020 NSSC 60, 132

Bell Canada v Canada (Attorney General), 2019 SCC 66, 7, 8, 12, 87, 93–95, 99, 137, 176, 206n32, 216n89

Bell v Ontario Human Rights Commission, [1971] SCR 756, 45–46

Benhaim v St-Germain, 2016 SCC 48, 205n15, 206n31

Bibeault v McCaffrey, [1984] 1 SCR 176, 159

British Columbia Telephone Co v Shaw Cable Systems (BC) Ltd, [1995] 2 SCR 739, 192n50

Canada (Attorney General) v Igloo Vikski Inc, 2016 SCC 38, 202n152

Canada (Attorney General) v Mossop, [1993] 1 SCR 554, 53–54

Canada (Attorney General) v Mowat, 2009 FCA 309, 65–66

Canada (Attorney General) v Public Service Alliance of Canada, 2019 FCA 41, 166

Canada (Canadian Human Rights Commission) v Canada (Attorney General), 2018 SCC 31, 65–66, 67, 69, 102, 182n24

Canada (Citizenship and Immigration) v Mason, 2021 FCA 156, 213n49

Canada (Minister of Citizenship and Immigration) v Vavilov, 2019 SCC 65, 4, 7–8, 10–15, 93–120, 122–53, 154–72, 174–75, 179–80, 205n15, 206n34, 207n42, 210n126, 213n37, 213n49, 218n122, 220n1, 226n2. See also *Vavilov v Canada (Citizenship and Immigration),* 2017 FCA 132

Canada (Public Safety and Emergency Preparedness) v Tran, 2015 FCA 237, 5–7, 85, 129, 176

Canada Post Corp v Canadian Union of Postal Workers, 2019 SCC 67, 123–25

Canadian Association of Industrial, Mechanical and Allied Workers,

Local 14 v Paccar of Canada Ltd, [1989] 2 SCR 983, 191n49

Canadian Broadcasting Corporation v Ferrier, 2019 ONCA 1025, 149–50

Canadian National Railway Company v Richardson International Limited, 2020 FCA 20, 131

Canadian Natural Resources Limited v Elizabeth Métis Settlement, 2020 ABCA 148, 135

Canadian Union of Public Employees, Local 963 v New Brunswick Liquor Corporation, [1979] 2 SCR 227, 9, 38, 43, 47–50, 62, 64, 105, 173

Cardinal v Director of Kent Institution, [1985] 2 SCR 643, 184n31

Catalyst Paper Corp v North Cowichan (District), 2012 SCC 2, 149–50

Centre intégré de santé et de services sociaux de la Monteregie-Ouest: c Syndicat canadien de la fonction publique, section locale 3247, 2020 QCCS 1603, 213n48

Chagnon v Syndicat de la fonction publique et parapublique du Quebec, 2018 SCC 39, 202n152

Champag inc c Municipalite de Saint-Roch-de-Richelieu, 2020 QCCA 613, 215n66

Chieu v Canada (Minister of Citizenship and Immigration), 2002 SCC 3, 193n75

Commission des relations ouvrières du Québec v Burlington Mills Hosiery Co of Canada, [1964] SCR 342, 45

Commission scolaire de Laval v Syndicat de l'enseignement de la region de Laval, 2016 SCC 8, 202n152

*Communications, Energy and Paper-
workers Union of Canada, Local 30
v: Irving Pulp & Paper, Ltd,* 2013
SCC 34, 83–85, 195n98, 199n87
Crevier v Attorney General of Quebec,
[1981] 2 SCR 220, 165, 167–69

Delta Air Lines Inc v Lukács, 2018
SCC 2, 107
D'Errico v Canada (Attorney General),
2014 FCA 95, 117–18
*Domtar Inc v Quebec (Commission
d'appel en matiere de lesions profes-
sionnelles),* [1993] 2 SCR 756,
192n50
Doré v Barreau du Québec, 2012 SCC
12, 73, 140, 155–56, 159–64, 172
*Douglas Aircraft Co of Canada v
McConnell,* [1980] 1 SCR 245,
191n32
*Downey v Nova Scotia (Attorney Gen-
eral),* 2020 NSSC 201, 128, 150
*Dr Q v College of Physicians and
Surgeons of British Columbia,* 2003
SCC 19, 194n92
Dunsmuir v New Brunswick, 2008
SCC 9, 4, 9, 10, 13, 43–44, 54,
56–62, 63–92, 100–1, 156, 164,
167, 173–74, 181n12, 193n77,
207n38

*Edmonton (City) v Edmonton East
(Capilano) Shopping Centres Ltd.,*
2016 SCC 47, 74, 76, 89–90, 98,
182n20
*Elangovan v Canada (Attorney Gen-
eral),* 2020 FC 882, 212n32

Farrier v Canada (Attorney General),
2020 FCA 25, 129–30

*Febles v Canada (Citizenship and
Immigration),* 2014 SCC 68, 86

*Garcia Balarezo v Canada (Citizenship
and Immigration),* 2020 FC 841,
209n98
*Glaxosmithkline Biologicals SA v Can-
ada (Health),* 2020 FC 397, 131
Gould v Yukon Order of Pioneers,
[1996] 1 SCR 571, 192n60
Groenvelt v Burwell, (1700) 91 ER
179, 19
Groia v Law Society of Upper Canada,
2018 SCC 27, 202n152
*GSR Capital Group Inc v The City of
White Rock,* 2020 BCSC 489,
204n13, 215n66

Harrison v Canada (National Revenue),
2020 FC 772, 212n31
*Hernandez Febles v Canada (Citizen-
ship and Immigration),* 2012 FCA
324, 207n42
Hildebrand v Penticton (City), 2020
BCSC 353, 158
*Houghton v Association of Ontario
Land Surveyors,* 2020 ONSC 863,
205n15
Housen v Nikolaisen, 2002 SCC 33,
97, 99–100, 104, 119, 155, 171,
204n13, 206n34
*Hudson's Bay Company ULC v Ontario
(Attorney General),* 2020 ONSC
8046, 146, 148

*Imperial Oil Ltd v Quebec (Minister of
the Environment),* 2003 SCC 58, 26
*Innovative Medicines Canada v Canada
(Attorney General),* 2020 FC 725,
215n66

Irvine v Canada (Restrictive Trade Practices Commission), [1987] 1 SCR 181, 184n31

Jarvis v Associated Medical Services Inc, [1964] SCR 497, 44

JE and KE v Children's Aid Society of the Niagara Region, 2020 ONSC 4239, 150

Jean-Baptiste v Canada (Citizenship and Immigration), 2021 FC 1362, 212n34

JG v Nadeau, 2016 QCCA 167, 205n15

Kanthasamy v Canada (Citizenship and Immigration), 2015 SCC 61, 88–89

Katz Group Canada Inc v Ontario (Health and Long-Term Care), 2013 SCC 64, 146–49

Keyu v Foreign Secretary, [2015] UKSC 69, 223n48

Koebisch v Rocky View (County), 2021 ABCA 265, 225n90

Komolafe v Canada (Citizenship and Immigration), 2013 FC 431, 78

Ktunaxa Nation v British Columbia (Forests, Lands and Natural Resource Operations), 2017 SCC 54, 162

Labour Relations Board v Canada Safeway Ltd, [1953] 2 SCR 46, 189n5, 190n20

Langenfeld v Toronto Police Services Board, 2019 ONCA 716, 150

Langford Sharp c Autorite des marches financiers, 2021 QCCA 1364, 218n123

Langlais c Collège des médecins du Québec, 2020 QCCA 134, 127

Law Society of British Columbia v Trinity Western University, 2018 SCC 32, 89

Law Society of Saskatchewan v Abrametz, 2022 SCC 29, 222n28

Lemus v Canada (Citizenship and Immigration), 2014 FCA 114, 200n109

Li v Canada (Citizenship and Immigration), 2020 FC 279, 127

Longphee v Workplace Health, Safety and Compensation Commission, 2020 NBCA 45, 136

Manitoba (Hydro-Electric Board) v Manitoba (Public Utilities Board) et al., 2020 MBCA 60, 137–39

Mao v Canada (Citizenship and Immigration), 2020 FC 542, 129

Martin v Alberta (Workers' Compensation Board), 2014 SCC 25, 197n56

Martineau v Matsqui Institution Disciplinary Board (No. 2), [1980] 1 SCR 602, 184n31, 185n52

McCarthy v Guest, 2020 NBQB 150, 204n13

McLean v British Columbia (Securities Commission), 2011 BCCA 455, 2013 SCC 67, 79–80, 195n98, 196n42

McLeod v Egan, [1975] 1 SCR 517, 192n55

Metropolitan Life Insurance v International Union of Operating Engineers, [1970] SCR 4254, 45, 47, 66

Miller v College of Optometrists of Ontario, 2020 ONSC 2573, 205n15

Mitelman v College of Veterinarians of Ontario, 2020 ONSC 6171, 216n85

MO c Société de l'assurance automobile du Québec, 2021 QCCA 177, 123

Morris v Law Society of Alberta (Trust Safety Committee), 2020 ABQB 138, 146–47

Nanaimo (City) v Rascal Trucking Ltd, 2000 SCC 13, 193n75

Natco Pharma (Canada) Inc v Canada (Health), 2020 FC 788, 131

Nation Rise Wind Farm Limited Partnership v Minister of the Environment, Conservation and Parks, 2020 ONSC 2984, 151–52

National Corn Growers Association v Canada (Import Tribunal), [1990] 2 SCR 1324, 193n71

National Football League v Canada (Attorney General), 2017 FCA 249, 2019 SCC 66, 7–8, 12, 87, 93–95

Newfoundland and Labrador Nurses' Union v Newfoundland and Labrador (Treasury Board), 2011 SCC 62, 77–78

Nicholson v Haldimand-Norfolk Regional Police Commissioners, [1979] 1 SCR 311, 22, 178

Nolan v Kerry (Canada) Inc, 2009 SCC 39, 195n98

Nor-Man Regional Health Authority Inc v Manitoba Association of Health Care Professional, 2011 SCC 59, 87–88, 195n98

Northern Regional Health Authority v Horrocks, 2021 SCC 42, 142–43

Northrop Grumman Overseas Services Corp v Canada (Attorney General), 2009 SCC 50, 195n98

Nova Scotia (Attorney General) v S&D Smith Central Supplies Limited, 2019 NSCA 22, 90–91

Oberg v Saskatchewan (Board of Education of the South East Cornerstone School Division No 209), 2020 SKQB 96, 151

Olineck v Alberta (Environmental Appeals Board), 2017 ABQB 311, 208n60

Ontario (Health) v Association of Ontario Midwives, 2022 ONCA 458, 225n90

Operation Dismantle v The Queen, [1985] 1 SCR 441, 23–24

Ortiz v Canada (Citizenship and Immigration), 2020 FC 188, 125

O'Shea/Oceanmount Community Association v Town of Gibsons, 2020 BCSC 698, 204n13, 215n63

Osun v Canada (Citizenship and Immigration), 2020 FC 295, 128

Padfield v Minister of Agriculture, [1968] AC 997, 22

Partridge v Nova Scotia (Attorney General), 2021 NSCA 60, 215n77

Party A v The Law Society of British Columbia, 2021 BCCA 130, 212n31

Patchett & Sons Ltd v Pacific Great Eastern Railway Co, [1959] SCR 271, 28

Patel v Canada (Citizenship and Immigration), 2020 FC 77, 127

Peter v Public Health Appeal Board of Alberta, 2019 ABQB 989, 140

Pierson v Estevan Board of Police Commissioners, 2020 SKQB 144, 125–27

Portnov v Canada (Attorney General), 2021 FCA 171, 147

Procureur general du Quebec c PF, 2020 QCCA 1220, 209*n*105, 211*n*21

Public Service Alliance of Canada v Canada Post Corporation, 2010 FCA 56, 199*n*87

Public Service Alliance of Canada v Canadian Federal Pilots Association, 2009 FCA 223, 68

Pushpanathan v Canada (Minister of Citizenship and Immigration), [1998] 1 SCR 982, 52–53, 173, 192*n*50

Quadra Properties Ltd v Gamble, 2021 SKQB, 215*n*77

Quebec (Attorney General) v Guérin, 2017 SCC 42, 69–70, 203*n*153

Quebec (Commission des droits de la personne et des droits de la jeunesse) v Bombardier Inc (Bombardier Aerospace Training Center), 2015 SCC 39, 86–88

Quebec (Commission des droits de la personne et des droits de la jeunesse) v Montreal (City), 2000 SCC 27, 192*n*60

Quebec (Commission des droits de la personne et des droits de la jeunesse) v Quebec (Attorney General), 2004 SCC 39, 141

Quebec (Commission des normes, de l'equite, de la sante et de la securite du travail) v Caron, 2018 SCC 3, 203*n*153

R v Criminal Injuries Compensation Board, ex parte Lain, [1967] 2 QB 864, 183*n*7

R v Oakes, [1986] 1 SCR 103, 73, 159

Re Downing and Graydon (1978), 92 DLR (3d) 355, 199*n*100

Reference re Secession of Quebec, [1998] 2 SCR 217, 207*n*37, 217*n*100

Regina Police Assn Inc v Regina (City) Board of Police Commissioners, 2000 SCC 14, 141, 193*n*75

Ridge v Baldwin, [1964] AC 40, 22

Rio Tinto Alcan Inc v Carrier Sekani Tribal Council, 2010 SCC 43, 162

Rodriguez Martinez v Canada (Citizenship and Immigration), 2020 FC 293, 128

Romania v Boros, 2020 ONCA 216, 126–27

Salmonid Association of Eastern Newfoundland v Her Majesty the Queen in Right of Newfoundland and Labrador, 2020 NLSC 34, 131

Samra v Canada (Citizenship and Immigration), 2020 FC 157, 127

Saskatchewan (Energy and Resources) v Areva Resources Canada Inc, 2013 SKCA 79, 80, 199*n*98

Saskatchewan (Human Rights Commission) v Whatcott, 2013 SCC 11, 73

Sazant v College of Physicians and Surgeons of Ontario, 2012 ONCA 727, 222*n*25

Scarborough Health Network v Canadian Union of Public Employees, Local 5852, 2020 ONSC 4577, 133–34

Senadheerage v Canada (Citizenship and Immigration), 2020 FC 968, 211*n*15

Service Employees' International Union, Local No. 333 v Nipawin District

Staff Nurses Association et al, [1975]
1 SCR 382, 47
Slemko v Canada (Public Safety and
Emergency Preparedness), 2020 FC
718, 127–28
Smith v Alliance Pipeline Ltd, 2011
SCC 7, 68
Smith and Rhuland Ltd v The Queen,
[1953] 2 SCR 95, 189n5
Society of Composers, Authors and
Music Publishers of Canada v
Entertainment Software Associ-
ation, 2022 SCC 30, 145
South Yukon Forest Corp v R, 2012
FCA 165, 205n15
Sriskandarajah v United States of
America, 2012 SCC 70, 126
Sticky Nuggz Inc v Alcohol and
Gaming Commission of Ontario,
2020 ONSC 5916, 212n34
Syndicat des employé(e)s de l'école
Vanguard ltée (CSN) c Mercier,
2020 QCCS 95, 140
Syndicat des employes de production
du Quebec et de l'Acadie v Canada
(Canadian Human Rights Commis-
sion), [1989] 2 SCR 879, 199n100
Syndicat des employés de production
du Québec et de l'Acadie v Canada
Labour Relations Board, [1984] 2
SCR 412, 50

Terrigno v Calgary (City), 2021 ABQB
41, 149
The Owners, Strata Plan BCS 435 v
Wong, 2020 BCSC 1972, 143
The Queen v Leong Ba Chai, [1954]
SCR 10, 189n5
Thibeault v Saskatchewan (Apprentice-
ship and Trade Certification

Commission), 2020 SKQB 192,
216n83
Toronto (City) v Canadian Union of
Public Employees, Local 79, 2003
SCC 63, 55
Toronto Newspaper Guild v Globe
Printing, [1953] 2 SCR 18, 47,
189n5
Tran v Canada (Minister of Public
Safety and Emergency Preparedness),
2015: FCA 237, 5–7, 85, 129, 176
Tran v Canada (Public Safety and
Emergency Preparedness), 2017
SCC 50, 85

Union des employés de service, local 298
v Bibeault, [1988] 2 SCR 1048,
51, 173
United Nurses of Alberta v Alberta
Health Services, 2021 ABCA 194,
144, 207n43
United Taxi Drivers' Fellowship of
Southern Alberta v Calgary (City),
2004 SCC 19, 193n75

Vavilov v Canada (Citizenship and
Immigration), 2017 FCA 132, 8,
155, 173–74. See also Canada
(Minister of Citizenship and Immigration) v Vavilov, 2019 SCC 65
Volvo Canada Ltd v UAW, Local 720,
[1980] 1 SCR 178, 191n32

West Fraser Mills Ltd v British Columbia (Workers' Compensation Appeal
Tribunal), 2018 SCC 22,
202n152, 203n153
Westcoast Energy Inc v Canada
(National Energy Board), [1998]
1 SCR 322, 197n56

Wilson v Atomic Energy of Canada,
2015 FCA 17, 2016 SCC 29, 89,
102

*Wilson v Cowichan Valley (Regional
District),* 2021 BCSC 1735,
132

Yatar v TD Insurance Meloche Monnex,
2022 ONCA 446, 225*n*87,
225*n*94

*Yee v Chartered Professional Account-
ants of Alberta,* 2020 ABCA 98,
136, 216*n*82

Index

Abbott, Justice Douglas Charles, 45
Abella, Justice Rosalie: deference, 11,
98, 103, 151; dissent and concurring reasons, 95, 105, 124, 174–
75, 177, 204n3, 204n6, 216n89,
220n1; reasonableness standard,
12, 77–78, 83, 107, 216n89; standard of review proposal, 91; term
of office, 76
administrative decision makers: about,
4–5; after-the-fact rationalizations,
80–81; assessment review boards,
74–76; attitudes toward, 44, 46;
authority of, 37, 39, 80–82, 122,
176–77; boilerplate assessments,
128, 212n31; contemporaneity,
129–30, 170, 213nn48–49; crown
corporations, 26, 186n54; discord,
113; discretion, 36–37, 114,
187n75, 209n98, 209nn104–5;
expertise, 77, 126–27, 137, 160,
161, 163, 215n77, 216n86; foreign vs home statutes, 72; home
statutes, 66, 67–68, 70, 71–72,
78–79, 195n13; international law,
207n42; justification, 110–11, 125–
26, 133–34, 211n15; may vs must
statutory considerations, 113; privative clause protections, 39, 43,
48, 52, 99, 192n52; procedural

fairness, 9, 22–23, 24, 158–60,
184n31, 222n25, 222n28; quality
assessments, 128, 212n28; quasi-
judicial, 26, 186n56; rationality
and fairness, 168, 180; reasons and
records of, 30; responsiveness, 125,
127–29; securities commissions,
79–80, 98; social and economic
regulation, 26, 186n55; spectrum
of powers, 26, 185n53; statutory
interpretations, 52–54, 75–76, 113,
124–25, 130–32, 164, 192n50,
192n55, 209n98, 215n63, 215n66;
types and examples of, 5, 16, 25–
30. See also deference; jurisdiction;
labour relations boards
administrative law: attitudes toward,
9, 16, 36–39, 187n75; challenges,
20–22; concepts and principles, 17,
27–36, 40; contexts, 26; courts
structure (inferior vs superior
courts), 19–20; evolution, 20–25,
40; form vs substance, 37, 38–39,
53, 63–64, 97, 114, 179, 188n84;
framework reformulation analysis,
10, 13–15; future, 179–80; history,
17–25; as "Jesuitical," 20; reason
vs authority, 37, 39, 62, 104, 113,
115, 174, 179; regulations, 29,
146–49; remedial discretion, 9,

117–19, 122, 149–51, 210*n*126; as a spectrum, 26–27, 185*nn*52–53, 186*nn*54–56; statutory appeal provisions, 97–100, 119–20, 204*nn*12–13, 206*n*32; writs, 17–19, 182*n*4, 183*n*7. *See also* deference; judicial review; jurisdiction; legislative intent; standards of review

Administrative Law Matters blog, 15
Administrative Tribunals Act, 204*n*12
adoption case, 150
Agraira, Muhsen Ahmed Ramadan, 81–82, 199*n*104, 200*n*105, 200*n*107
Alberta Court of Appeal, 74–76, 129, 135–36, 144, 150, 207*n*43
Alberta Court of Queen's Bench, 140, 146–47, 148–49
appeals. *See* statutory appeals
Arthurs, Harry, 22
Assessment Review Board, 74–76

Barnes, Justice Robert, 131
Bastarache, Justice Michel, 52, 57, 77, 164
Beetz, Justice Jean, 50–52, 191*n*37
Bennett, Clarence, 56
bereavement leave case, 53–54
Beveridge, Justice Duncan, 91
Binnie, Justice Ian, 58
Boctor, Audrey, 11, 94
Bodurtha, Justice John, 132
Boone, Justice Daniel, 131
British Columbia Court of Appeal, 79–80, 105, 132, 215*n*63
British Columbia Securities Commission, 79–80
British Columbia Supreme Court, 143, 158

Broadcasting Act, 99, 100, 176
Brothers, Justice Christa, 132, 220*n*2
Brown, Justice Russell: appointment, 89; correctness standard, 75, 202*n*152, 203*n*153; dissent and compromise, 102; jurisdictional questions, 69, 70, 203*n*153, 203*n*166; majority reasons, 95
Bryson, Justice Peter, 90, 91

Canada (Public Safety and Emergency Preparedness) v Tran, 2015 FCA 237, 5, 201*n*122, 226*n*8
Canada Border Services Agency (CBSA), 5, 81–82, 199*n*104, 200*n*105, 200*n*107
Canada Labour Code, 123, 124
Canada Transportation Act, 28
Canada-Europe Trade Agreement, 131
Canadian Charter of Rights and Freedoms, 6, 24, 73, 140–41, 159–64
Canadian Human Rights Tribunal, 53–54, 66, 67–68
Canadian Radio-television and Telecommunications Commission: (CRTC), 5 (*see also Bell Canada v Canada (Attorney General),* 2019 SCC 66 *in Index of Cases; National Football League v Canada (Attorney General),* 2017 FCA 249, 2019 SCC 66 *in Index of Cases*)
Canadian Transportation Agency, 28, 131
cannabis, 5, 212*n*34
Charron, Justice Louise, 57
citizenship, 8, 81–82, 174–75, 199*n*104, 200*n*105, 200*n*107, 226*n*2
Citizenship Act, 12, 174–75

Civil Code of Quebec, 20, 36
Constitution Act, 1867, 19, 165–66
Copyright Board of Canada, 146
copyright law, 145
correctness standard of review: constitutional issues, 140–41, 162, 168–69, 217*n*100; discord, 113; international law, 101, 207*n*42; jurisdictional questions, 101–2, 141–43, 146–47, 166; new categories, 145–49, 162; open court principle, 149; procedural fairness, 156, 157, 221*n*18; vs proportionality, 162, 223*n*48; questions of central importance, 143–45, 161, 218*n*122; vs reasonableness, 11–12, 57–58, 61, 65, 123, 194*n*92, 195*n*98; regulations challenges, 146–49, 219*n*134; selection criteria, 96. *See also* rule of law
Côté, Justice Suzanne: appointment, 89; correctness standard, 11, 75, 89, 182*n*24, 202*n*152, 203*n*153; dissent, 69, 102; jurisdictional questions, 69; majority reasons, 95; on tribunal authority, 87–88
COVID-19 lockdown challenges, 148
Criminal Code, 36
Cromwell, Justice Thomas, 26, 65, 67–68, 165, 186*n*54
crown corporations, 26, 186*n*54

Daly, Paul, 93, 193*n*77
De Montigny, Justice Yves, 143–44
de Smith, Stanley, 22
deference: about, 32–34, 42; attitudes toward, 10–11, 41, 191*n*39; beginnings, 47–49, 190*n*20, 191*n*32; controversy, 10–11; correctness review, 11–12, 98; limits, 46, 100,

206*n*31; vs nondeference, 37–38, 62, 188*n*78, 188*n*80; palpable and overriding error, 97, 99, 103–4, 119, 171, 205*n*15, 206*n*34; privative clause, 38, 39, 43, 48–49, 62, 192*n*52; procedural fairness, 158–60, 179, 222*n*25, 222*n*28; reasonableness review, 9, 107–8, 109–11, 152; reasons for, 48, 51–52; as respect, 39, 58, 60, 78; respect vs submission, 39; substantive factors for, 43–44. *See also* reasonableness standard of review
Deschamps, Justice Marie, 68
Dicey, Albert Venn, 37
Dickson, Justice Brian, 9, 43, 47–49, 184*n*31
Diner, Justice Alan, 125, 127, 128
Diplock, Lord, 22, 44
discrimination, 45–46, 53–54, 73, 86–88, 192*n*60
Dunsmuir, David, 56, 193*n*77. *See also Dunsmuir v New Brunswick,* 2008 SCC 9 *in Index of Cases*
Dyzenhaus, David, 39, 60, 77

Elson, Justice Richard, 125
Entertainment Software Association, 145
Environmental Review Tribunal, 151–52
Evans, Justice John, 68, 185*n*52, 199*n*87
Expropriation Act (Nova Scotia), 90–91

Favel, Justice Paul, 127, 129
Federal Court of Appeal (FCA): boilerplate statements, 128, 212*n*31; constitutional foundations, 166–67,

225n87; correctness, 66, 145; direct vs indirect appeal limitations, 225n94; jurisdictional issues and questions, 68, 166–67; *obiter dicta* comments, 131, 132; procedural fairness, 156; quality assessments, 128, 212n28; questions of central importance, 143–45; reasonableness, 6–7, 65–66, 85, 147–48; regulations challenges, 147–48; remedial discretion, 118–19; responsive decisions, 127–29, 212n28, 212n34, 212nn31–32, 213n37; statutory interpretations, 105, 131, 132, 167
Federal Public Sector Labour Relations and Employment Board Act, 166
Fichaud, Justice Joel, 90–91
First Nations, 18, 24, 137–39
Fish, Justice Morris, 65, 87–88
formalism, 38, 39, 62, 64–65, 89, 97, 163, 204n11
France (administrative law), 36
Fuhrer, Justice Janet, 127

Gascon, Justice Clément, 11, 69, 94–95, 182n24
Gauthier, Justice Johanne, 6–7
Gleason, Justice Mary, 166–67
Globe and Mail newspaper, 9
Grey, Julius, 168
Guérin, Ronald, 69–70

Health Insurance Act (Quebec), 69
Hogg, Peter, 22, 44, 46
Holt, Lord Chief Justice, 19
Horrocks, Linda, 142
human rights: discrimination, 53–54, 73, 86–88, 192n60; law, 144–45, 192n60, 218n122; tribunals, 53–54, 86–88, 141–42

hydroelectricity rates, 137–39

immigration appeals, 126–29, 211n21, 212n32, 212n34
immigration law, 5–6, 81, 86, 111, 209n98
Immigration and Refugee Board, 28–29
Immigration and Refugee Protection Act, 5–6, 81
Indigenous peoples, 18, 24, 137–39
Information and Privacy Commissioner, 71, 78–79
institutional design: appeals on questions of law or jurisdiction, 137–39, 216n89; classification, 135–36, 216n85, 216nn82–83; expertise, 137, 161, 215n77, 216n86; legislative intent, 115–16; limitations, 96–100, 119–20, 204n11; standard of review selection, 96–100, 135–39

Jeffrey, Justice Paul, 148
Johnstone test, 144
judicial review: about, 4–5; analysis, 173–80; applicant consequences, 128, 212n34; approaches, 13, 23–25, 173–74; constitutional function, 165–72, 224n61, 225n87; evolution of, 25, 40–41; factors vs presumptions, 59, 194n92; future, 179–80; history, 17–25, 173–74; jurisdictional vs non-jurisdictional errors, 21, 23; paper proceedings and records of, 18–19, 30; political interference, 27, 186n57; pragmatic and functional analysis, 23, 43, 51–54, 62, 192n50, 192n53, 192n55, 193n75; reformulation, 54–61, 194n92; regulations challenges,

146–49, 219n134; rights vs privileges, 21; twilight of, 44; writs, 17–19, 182n4, 183n7. *See also* administrative law; standards of review

jurisdiction: about, 31–32, 42, 187n66; boundaries, 24, 141–43, 161–62; error, 44–46, 48, 49–54, 137–39, 189n5, 191n37, 191n39, 192n50, 192n53, 195n98, 200n109; may vs must considerations, 113; vs non-jurisdictional error, 21, 23, 38, 46; questions, 69–70, 71–72, 96, 101–2, 141–43, 146–47, 166, 193n75, 196n42, 203n153, 203n166. *See also* administrative decision makers

justices: administrative law attitudes, 9, 10–11, 17, 36–41, 187n75, 191n39; appointments, 89, 92; deference vs nondeference, 37–38, 188n78, 188n80; discord, 63–64. *See also* Federal Court of Appeal (FCA); Supreme Court of Canada (SCC); *individual names of justices*

Jutras, Daniel, 11, 94

Karakatsanis, Justice Andromache: correctness standard, 142; deference, 11, 98, 103, 152; dissent and concurring reasons, 95, 105, 142, 143, 174–75, 177, 204n3, 204n6, 216n89, 220n1; reasonableness standard, 12, 74–75, 76, 105, 107, 216n89

Kerr, Lord, 223n48

labour laws, 83, 123, 124, 166
labour relations boards: decision justification, 133–34; deference, 43, 47–51, 111, 190n20, 191n32,

192n55; expertise, 66–67; jurisdiction, 44–46, 47–49, 141–42, 189n5; privative clauses, 43, 48; responsive decisions, 129; statutory interpretations, 48–49, 123–25, 190n20, 192n55; trade unions, 40, 45, 66–67. *See also* administrative decision makers

LaForest, Justice Gérard, 53–54, 191n49

land titles legislation, 128, 150
Laskin, Chief Justice Bora, 165, 192n55

Latif, Javed, 86–88
law schools, 89
laws: *Administrative Tribunals Act*, 204n12; *Broadcasting Act*, 99, 100, 176; *Canada Labour Code*, 123, 124; *Canada Transportation Act*, 28; *Canadian Charter of Rights and Freedoms*, 6, 24, 73, 140–41, 159–64; *Citizenship Act*, 12, 174–75; *Civil Code of Quebec*, 20, 36; *Constitution Act, 1867*, 19, 164–65; copyright, 144; *Criminal Code*, 36; *Expropriation Act* (Nova Scotia), 90–91; *Federal Public Sector Labour Relations and Employment Board Act*, 166; *Health Insurance Act* (Quebec), 69; human rights, 73, 144–45, 192n60, 218n122; immigration law, 5–6, 81, 86, 111, 209n98; labour rights, 83, 123, 124, 166; land titles, 128, 150; *Manitoba Hydro Act*, 138–39; *Municipal Government Act* (Alberta), 167; reforms, 93; *Saskatchewan Human Rights Code*, 73

Lawson, Gary, 32
lawyers, 73, 93

LeBel, Justice Louis, 26, 55, 57, 67–
68, 77, 164
legislative intent: about, 35–36, 40,
42; deference, 35, 51, 91, 115–
16, 191n49; institutional design,
115–16, 204n11; jurisdiction, 51,
52, 56; privative clauses, 35, 42,
52, 192n52. *See also* administrative law
Libyan National Salvation Front
(LNSF), 81–82, 199n104, 200n105
Loparco, Justice Anna, 146–47
Lyster, Justice Lindsay, 143

Mancini, Mark, 160, 163
Manitoba Court of Appeal, 138–39
Manitoba Hydro, 138–39
Manitoba Hydro Act, 138–39
marijuana, 5, 212n34
Martin, Justice Sheilah, 95, 124
McCreary, Justice Meghan, 151
McHaffie, Justice Nicholas, 128
McHarg, Aileen, 209n104
McLachlin, Chief Justice Beverley,
76, 92
McLean, Patricia, 79–80
ministers and government departments: deference, 14, 16, 123, 125,
134; legislative intent, 35, 52; political considerations, 26, 185n53;
statutory interpretations, 5–7, 81–
82, 131, 199n104; unreasonableness, 150–51
Moldaver, Justice Michael, 83–84,
88–89, 94, 95, 102
Morissette, Justice Yves-Marie,
205n15
Mullan, David, 22, 159, 224n61
municipal bylaws, 107, 132, 147,
148, 167, 215n63, 215n66

Municipal Government Act (Alberta),
167

Nadon, Justice Marc, 131, 132
National Football League (NFL), 8,
12, 93–94
New Brunswick Court of Appeal, 83,
136
Newfoundland and Labrador Supreme
Court, 131
Nova Scotia Court of Appeal, 90–91
Nova Scotia Supreme Court, 132

Oakley, Wayne, 90
Occupational Health and Safety
Tribunal Canada, 124
Ontario Court of Appeal, 44, 126–
27, 149–50, 225n87, 225n94
Ontario Divisional Court, 133–34,
139, 146, 148, 150–51
Ontario Labour Relations Board, 44–
45, 189n5
Ontario Securities Commission, 79
Ontario Superior Court, 136

palpable and overriding error standard, 97, 99, 103–4, 120, 171,
205n15, 206n34
Parker, Lord Chief Justice, 19
passport revocation, 128, 212n32
patent unreasonableness standard of
review, 23, 48, 52, 54–55, 166,
169, 191n32, 204n12, 225n90
Pentelechuk, Justice Dawn, 150
Petrie, Gordon, 56–57
police boards, 141, 149–50
privative clauses: about, 23; deference,
38, 39, 43, 48–49, 62, 192n52;
forms of, 35; protections, 43,
48, 49

property tax appeals, 74–76
proportionality review, 73, 140, 162–63, 223*n*48
Public Utilities Board (Manitoba), 137–39

quasi-judicial legislation, 140, 144–45, 218*n*122
quasi-judicial review, 21, 26, 186*n*56
Quebec: courts structure, 19–20; labour relations board, 45; radiologists, 69–70
Quebec Court of Appeal, 123
Quebec Human Rights Tribunal, 86, 141
Quebec Superior Court, 140

racial discrimination, 45–46, 86
railway companies, 28, 131
Rand, Justice Ivan, 47, 190*n*20
reasonableness standard of review: analysis, 13, 115–16, 119–21, 151–53, 154–56; application, 123–34; categorical approach, 71–77; Charter compliance, 159–64; compromise and its limits, 114–15, 154, 171, 177–78, 220*nn*1–2; considerations, 109–11; constitutionality, 73–76, 166–72, 197*n*56, 225*n*90, 226*n*96; contemporaneity, 129–30, 170, 213*nn*48–49; contradictions, 85–89; vs correctness review, 11–12, 57–58, 61, 65, 123, 194*n*92, 195*n*98; direct vs indirect appeal limitations, 169–71, 225*n*94; discord, 63–64, 89, 113; expertise, 126–27, 161; flaws, 108–9, 208*n*83; formalist vs functional, 89, 163; guidance limitations, 77–85; justification, 121,

125–26; methodology, 105–7, 208*n*60; vs palpable and overriding error, 99, 171, 205*n*15, 206*n*34; patent unreasonableness, 23, 169–70, 193*n*71, 225*n*90; reasonableness *simpliciter*, 23, 53, 54–56, 194*n*92; responsive justification principle, 13, 95, 99–100, 110–11, 130; responsiveness, 127–29; restorative vs restrictive approach, 10, 84; rule of law principle, 95, 100–2, 207*nn*37–38, 207*nn*42–43; selection of, 54–61, 96, 104–15; statutory interpretations, 130–32; vs unreasonableness, 130, 176, 213*nn*48–49. *See also* deference
Refugee Protection Division, 28
Refugee Settlement Act (RSA), 212*n*34
refugees, 28–29, 81–82, 212*n*34
regulations, 29, 146–49
Reid, Lord, 22
remedial discretion, 118–20, 149–51, 151, 210*n*126
Rennie, Justice Donald, 78
Robertson, Justice Joseph, 83
Rothstein, Justice Marshall, 69, 71, 78, 81, 83–84, 196*n*42
Rowe, Justice Malcolm: appointment, 89; correctness standard, 11, 89, 145, 182*n*24, 202*n*152, 203*n*153; jurisdictional questions, 69, 70, 203*n*153; majority reasons, 95; statutory interpretation, 124, 145
Ruel, Justice Simon, 123
rule of law: consistency, 140–41; constitutional questions, 140–41, 162, 217*n*100, 218*nn*122–23; interpretations, 95, 100–2, 105, 119–20, 145–49; jurisdictional

boundaries, 141–43, 161–62; questions of central importance, 143–45, 161, 218nn122–23. *See also* correctness standard of review

Saskatchewan Court of Appeal, 80, 151
Saskatchewan Court of Queen's Bench, 125, 151
Saskatchewan Human Rights Code, 73
securities market misconduct, 79–80
Seidman, Guy, 32
Sharpe, Justice Robert, 149–50
Slatter, Justice Frans, 74, 135–36
standards of review: analysis, 151–53, 154–56, 173–80; categorical approach, 64–77, 195n13; deference vs nondeference, 37–38, 62, 188n78, 188n80; factors vs presumptions, 59, 194n92; form vs substance, 37, 39, 53, 63–64, 97, 114, 179; home statute category, 66, 67, 195n13; institutional design principle, 95, 96–100, 104, 119–20, 135–39, 168; over vs under-inclusive categories, 64–67; palpable and overriding error, 97, 99, 103–4, 119, 171, 205n15, 206n34; patent unreasonableness, 23, 48, 52, 54–55, 167, 169, 191n32, 204n12, 225n90; precedent, 115–16; principles, 95, 97; procedural fairness, 155, 156–60, 221n14, 222n25, 222n28; proportionality review, 73, 140, 162–63, 223n48; reason vs authority, 37, 39, 62, 104, 111, 115, 174, 179; reformulation, 54–61, 194n92; selection, 95–104, 134–49; simplification and clarification, 91,

154, 157–58, 172, 204n6, 220n1; substantive review, 9, 43, 174, 178–79, 182n21. *See also* correctness standard of review; judicial review; reasonableness standard of review
statutory appeals: deference, 14, 74, 121, 135, 152; vs judicial review, 100, 204n13, 205n15; law or jurisdiction questions, 10, 74, 76, 90, 98, 104, 137–39, 152, 167, 216n83; palpable and overriding error, 97–100, 103–4, 120, 171, 205n15, 206n34
St-Pierre, Justice Marc, 140
Stratas, Justice David, 104, 147, 156, 200n109
Strickland, Justice Cecily, 128, 212n28
substantive review, 9, 43, 174, 178–79, 182n21
Super Bowl advertising, 8, 12, 137, 176–77, 216n89
Supreme Court of Canada (SCC): about, 3; *amici curiae* appointments, 11, 94; appointments, 89, 92; contradictions and inconsistencies, 63–64, 77–82, 85–89; correctness standards, 11–12, 57–58, 61, 65, 74–75, 122–23, 194n92, 195n98; criticisms toward, 90–91; deference, 10–11, 43–44, 47–55, 182n20, 182n24, 190n20; discord, 63–64, 89, 91–92, 203n166; factors vs presumptions, 59, 194n92; framework analysis, 4–14; jurisdictional errors, 44–46, 48, 49–54, 189n5, 191n39, 192n50, 192n53, 195n98; jurisdictional questions, 69–70, 71–72,

196*n*42; nonjusticiability, 23–24; pragmatic and functional analysis, 23, 43, 51–54, 62, 192*n*50, 192*n*53, 192*n*55, 193*n*75; procedural protections, 22–23, 27, 184*n*31; reasonableness *simpliciter* vs patent unreasonableness, 23, 53, 54–56, 193*n*71, 194*n*92; reasonableness standard, 10, 12, 58–61, 65, 71–77, 83–91, 105–7; standard of review analysis, 56–61, 77–82, 194*n*92. *See also individual names of SCC justices*

Swinton, Justice Katherine, 136, 139

television service providers, 5, 8, 12, 94, 99, 137, 176–77, 216*n*89
terrorism, 81–82, 199*n*104, 200*n*105, 200*n*107
The Americans television series, 3, 4
Tran, Thanh Tam, 5–6. *See also Canada (Public Safety and Emergency Preparedness) v Tran,* 2015 FCA 237

Tysoe, Justice David, 132

United Nations *Convention Relating to the Status of Refugees,* 86
Utility and Review Board (Nova Scotia), 90, 215*n*77

Vavilov, Alexander, 3, 7–8. *See also Canada (Citizenship and Immigration) v Vavilov,* 2019 SCC 65 *in Index of Cases*

Wagner, Chief Justice Richard, 11, 87–88, 92, 94–95, 202*n*152
Walker, Justice Elizabeth, 127–28
Watson, Justice Jack, 135
Weatherill, Justice Gary, 158
Weiler, Paul, 22, 46
Whatcott, William, 73
Wilson, Justice Bertha, 47
wind farm project, 150–51

Printed and bound in Canada by Friesens

Set in Garamond by Artegraphica Design Co.

Copy editor: Frank Chow

Proofreader: Judith Earnshaw

Indexer: Margaret de Boer

Cover designer: Will Brown